THE EDUCATION
OF ENGLISH LANGUAGE LEARNERS

CHALLENGES IN LANGUAGE AND LITERACY

Elaine R. Silliman and C. Addison Stone, *Series Editors*

The Education of English Language Learners

Research to Practice

Edited by

Marilyn Shatz
Louise C. Wilkinson

Series Editors' Note by
Elaine R. Silliman and C. Addison Stone

THE GUILFORD PRESS
New York   London

KH

To two of our parents, who were ELLs—
Sylvia Polonsky Cherry (1917–2009)
and Morris Karpman (1906–1979)

© 2010 The Guilford Press
A Division of Guilford Publications, Inc.
72 Spring Street, New York, NY 10012
www.guilford.com

Printed in the United States of America

This book is printed on acid-free paper.

Last digit is print number: 9 8 7 6 5 4 3 2 1

Library of Congress Cataloging-in-Publication Data

The education of English language learners : research to practice / edited by
Marilyn Shatz, Louise C. Wilkinson.
    p. cm. — (Challenges in language and literacy)
  Includes bibliographical references and index.
  ISBN 978-1-60623-659-8 (hardcover)
  1. Second language acquisition—Study and teaching.   2. Language and
languages—Study and teaching.   3. Multilingualism in children.   4. Language
and culture.   5. Sociolinguistics.   I. Shatz, Marilyn.   II. Wilkinson, Louise
Cherry.
  P118.2.E36 2010
  428.2'4—dc22
                                                                    2009043289

7/25/11

About the Editors

Marilyn Shatz, PhD, is Professor Emerita of Psychology and Linguistics at the University of Michigan and Adjunct Professor of Psychology at the University of North Carolina, Wilmington. She is a fellow of the American Psychological Society and has been a Guggenheim Fellow; a Senior Research Fulbright Scholar; a recipient of a National Institute of Education fellowship; and a visiting scholar at Harvard University, the University of California, Berkeley, New York University, the University of Wisconsin, Cambridge University, and the Max Planck Institute for Psycholinguistics. An expert in language and the development of communication skills, Dr. Shatz has used both naturalistic and experimental methods to carry out research on the interrelations among social, cognitive, and language development in young children. Much of her work addresses cultural issues, examining whether and how particular languages influence cognitive processing or how particular cultural practices affect language use and even the language in children's books. Among the languages represented in her writings are Spanish, Italian, Korean, and Turkish. Dr. Shatz has written more than 70 chapters and articles and a book, *A Toddler's Life*; coedited the recent *Blackwell Handbook of Language Development*; and served as an editor and editorial board member of numerous journals, including *First Language* and *Mind and Language*. In her current research, she investigates how young children acquire abstract vocabulary.

Louise C. Wilkinson, EdD, is Distinguished Professor of Education, Psychology, and Communication Sciences at Syracuse University, where she teaches courses on literacy learning for first/second English language learners. An internationally recognized leader in education, she is best known for her extensive research on school-age children's language and literacy learning and has published 150 articles, chapters, and volumes, including *Communicating for Learning* (coauthor); *Communicating in the Classroom* (editor); and *The Social Context of Instruction, Gender Influences in Classroom Interaction, The Integrated Language Arts, Language and Literacy Learning in Schools*, and *Improving Literacy Achievement in Urban Schools* (coeditor). Dr. Wilkinson has served on the editorial boards of major research journals, including the *British Journal of Education Studies; American Education Research Journal; Linguistics and Education; Discourse Processes;* and *Language, Speech, and Hearing Services in Schools.* She has also served on the advisory/ governing boards of the National Reading Research Center, the National Association of Universities and Land-Grant Colleges' Commission for Human Resources and Social Change, and the U.S. Department of Education's Laboratory for Student Success. She is a fellow of the American Psychological Association, the Association for Psychological Science, the American Educational Research Association, and the American Association of Applied and Preventive Psychology; has chaired panels for the U.S. Department of Education and the National Science Foundation; has served as dean of the schools of education at both Syracuse University and Rutgers University; has held visiting professorships at East China Normal University, Brown University, and King's College London; and has taught at Harvard University, MIT, Boston University, the University of Wisconsin–Madison, City University of New York Graduate Center, Rutgers University, and Syracuse University. Dr. Wilkinson has been vice president and national program chair of the American Educational Research Association; Honorary Professor at Beijing Normal University; Education Advisor for the New Jersey Legislature; and Delegate to the Organisation for Economic Cooperation and Development and the Asia–Pacific Economic Cooperation Organization. She cochairs the Literacy Leadership for Urban Teacher Education Commission of the International Reading Association.

Contributors

Diane August, PhD, Center for Applied Linguistics, Bethesda, Maryland

Alison L. Bailey, EdD, Department of Education, University of California, Los Angeles, Los Angeles, California

Lisa M. Bedore, PhD, Department of Communication Sciences and Disorders, University of Texas at Austin, Austin, Texas

Ellen Bialystok, PhD, Department of Psychology, York University, Toronto, Ontario, Canada

Karin Boerger, MS, Graduate School, University of Texas at Austin, Austin, Texas

María Estela Brisk, PhD, Department of Teacher Education, Special Education, and Curriculum and Instruction, Lynch School of Education, Boston College, Boston, Massachusetts

Barbara T. Conboy, PhD, Department of Communicative Disorders, University of Redlands, Redlands, California

Cheryl Dressler, EdD, Center for Applied Linguistics, Bethesda, Maryland

Susan Ervin-Tripp, PhD, Department of Psychology, University of California, Berkeley, Berkeley, California

Claude Goldenberg, PhD, School of Education, Stanford University, Stanford, California

Deborah Hwa-Froelich, PhD, Department of Communication Sciences and Disorders, St. Louis University, St. Louis, Missouri

Kathryn Kohnert, PhD, CCC-SLP, Department of Speech–Language–
Hearing Sciences, University of Minnesota, Minneapolis,
Minnesota

Ellen H. Newman, PhD, School of Psychology, IE University, Segovia,
Spain

Kathleen F. Peets, EdD, Department of Psychology, York University,
Toronto, Ontario, Canada

Elizabeth D. Peña, PhD, Department of Communication Sciences and
Disorders, University of Texas at Austin, Austin, Texas

Giang Pham, MA, CCC-SLP, Department of Speech–Language–Hearing
Sciences, University of Minnesota, Minneapolis, Minnesota

Leslie Reese, PhD, Center for Language Minority Education and
Research, California State University, Long Beach, California

Iliana Reyes, PhD, Second Language Acquisition Program and
Department of Language, Reading, and Culture, College of
Education, University of Arizona, Tucson, Arizona

Betsy Rymes, PhD, Graduate School of Education, University of
Pennsylvania, Philadelphia, Pennsylvania

William M. Saunders, PhD, Center for Culture and Health, Semel
Institute, University of California, Los Angeles, Los Angeles,
California

Marilyn Shatz, PhD, Departments of Psychology and Linguistics,
University of Michigan, Ann Arbor, Michigan

Carol Westby, PhD, Bilingual Multicultural Services, Albuquerque,
New Mexico

Louise C. Wilkinson, EdD, Department of Reading and Language Arts,
School of Education, Syracuse University, Syracuse, New York

Series Editors' Note

This book is the first in the series Challenges in Language and Literacy to focus explicitly on the challenges faced by English language learners (ELLs) and by those professionals who seek to provide them with effective learning opportunities. We believe that Marilyn Shatz and Louise Wilkinson have assembled a set of chapters that bring much-needed conceptual and pragmatic clarity to an area often clouded by uncertainty about how best to teach ELLs. This uncertainty has long included two major questions that one of the book's contributors, Claude Goldenberg, reiterated in 2008: Is it possible to hasten the development of students' English language learning while preserving, if not enhancing, the home language? If so, what are the most effective ways to teach the academic language competence needed for successful educational outcomes? The chapters in this volume take us to the next steps in answering these vexing questions about instructional practices in second-language and literacy learning by bringing together a select group of interdisciplinary contributors whose expertise in this arena is well established.

As Shatz and Wilkinson note in their introductory chapter, content-area teachers in science, mathematics, and social studies are frequently unaware that their responsibilities extend to integrating language and literacy into instruction. An important purpose of the book, therefore, is to raise the awareness of educators that ELL students cannot learn subject-area content without having an underlying understanding of the discourse, syntax, and vocabulary that uniquely defines the various branches of academic learning in elementary and secondary school. An equally critical aim is to extend this increased awareness to the arena of preservice education and the subsequent implementation of more effective classroom practices through administrators' commitment to optimal

ELL programs. The chapters in this volume, while grounded solidly in current research, speak effectively to stakeholders in these various constituencies and offer pragmatic advice regarding both policy and practice. As such, the book contributes to the goal of improving the education of ELLs.

One source of our optimism regarding the potential impact of this volume comes from its strong organization and thematic continuity. Each chapter has a common structure: focus bullets that summarize the main topics covered, a clearly specified chapter purpose, a review of research and theory, a best-practices section, a summary of the main ideas, and, finally, implications for research, policy, and practice. These structural elements will prove beneficial for integrating similarities and differences among the 12 chapters. As a result, the book will be effective as a text for graduate courses and as a resource for practicing professionals who seek new ideas regarding best practices for both program development and day-to-day practice.

While the volume may seem primarily oriented to educators—both teachers and administrators—Shatz and Wilkinson, in assembling contributors, were mindful of the fact that the complexities of educating ELLs required an assembly of expertise if successful outcomes were to be maximized. To that end, the appeal of the book extends to professionals in both school and related settings who are concerned with ELL education, from speech–language pathologists, to special educators, to school psychologists. We are pleased that the book's purposes and the individual chapters reflect the coeditors' collaborative commitment to attaining educational excellence for all ELLs, a dual commitment that is consistent with the aims of the Challenges in Language and Literacy series.

ELAINE R. SILLIMAN
C. ADDISON STONE

REFERENCE

Goldenberg, C. (2008). Teaching English language learners: What the research does—and does not—say. *American Educator, 32*(1), 8–23, 42–44.

Preface

More than three decades ago, aware of our mutual interest in language and development, we sought each other out after a lecture at the University of Pennsylvania. Although one of us has focused on language development in preschoolers and the other on communication in the classroom, we have continued these many years to share an appreciation of the role of language in knowledge acquisition. Taken together, our research includes many books, book chapters, and journal articles attesting to the importance of conversational experience, at home and at school, for both social and cognitive development. This book is a joint product of our many years of experience as psychologists and educators; we contributed equally and the editorship is alphabetical. It fulfills our wish to bring our expertise to bear on a pressing issue currently facing our educational system, namely, how to best educate the growing number of dual-language learners in our schools.

In discussing what we could do to address the problem, we realized that educators, despite their dedication and professionalism, are often unschooled about the nature of the linguistic conundrum facing them. They know little about the myriad and varied languages and cultures now represented by our nation's students, and they often have to contend with demanding standards that ignore the problems they face as educators of dual-language learners. We decided that our expertise could be most usefully applied to the task of equipping future educators with the tools they need to face the challenges brought by the changing student populace. We considered several factors: We wanted state-of-the-art information about both the nature of language and the teaching methods that are effective. We wanted such information to be useful for both prospective teachers and for those who teach and administer daily in the classrooms around the country. Finally, we wanted to present the information in an accessible format to which readers could refer for a "refresher course," as needed. Importantly, we wanted our product to be free of theoretical cant and abstruse language.

Our solution was to seek out the most knowledgeable and thoughtful researchers on the topics we considered important for educators and to ask them to join us in the project. We then asked them to write their chapters in a consistent format, giving readers both a broad range of evidence for their claims and a series of practical suggestions for enhancing dual-language learners' educational experience and achievement. The responses were gratifying. As a group, our writers bent enthusiastically to their task, evaluating up-to-the-minute research, offering suggestions for teachers and administrators alike, and working with us to make the volume come together into a readable whole. We thank them for their willingness to take our advice, and we thank our series editors, Elaine Silliman and Addison Stone, for their support and assistance to us. We also thank our editors at The Guilford Press for their interest in seeing the project to fruition. Finally, we thank our spouses, Richard Feingold and Alex Wilkinson, for patiently waiting to join us for some fun after the long "work" visits we have had together over the last few years as we planned and executed this project.

Contents

Contents

Introduction

Marilyn Shatz
Louise C. Wilkinson

I teach math. I don't teach reading or ESL.
—HEAD OF MATH DEPARTMENT,
MAJOR URBAN HIGH SCHOOL

PURPOSE OF THIS VOLUME

This volume integrates findings on the sociocultural, cognitive, and communicative-linguistic systems central to a child's development and education, thus providing the basis of practical implications for both assessment and instruction of school-age learners of English within and outside of the classroom. Our purpose is to provide educators up-to-date, evidence-based information about how to educate children who have varied language backgrounds and limited experience with English. In doing so, we aim to help redress the achievement gap for students often referred to as English language learners (ELLs).

THE CHALLENGE

A crisis is brewing in U.S. schools. Rates of graduation from high school are poor, especially for minority students; the achievement gap between majority and minority students has not been closed; and the numbers of children of immigrant parents entering elementary and higher grades are increasing, not just in New York and Los Angeles, but across the country (Wilkinson, Morrow, & Chou, 2008a). Such children often have English language skills that are insufficient for attaining educational goals. Consider that the proportion of ELLs in U.S. schools is rapidly increasing: From 1990 to 2005 the number of students classified as ELLs by the U.S. Department of Education more than doubled (National Clearinghouse for English Language Acquisition, 2004–2005), amounting to 10.5% of the total school enrollment in 2005. Not only do many of these children reside in non-English-speaking homes, but many of their families are also low-income, and poverty is a strong predictor of ELL difficulties (Westby & Hwa-Froelich, Chapter 9, this volume). Although high numbers of ELL students are enrolled in urban schools, many attend schools in smaller cities and rural communities as well. Hence, this is a national challenge.

Some children of immigrants are native English speakers, yet they come from homes where other languages are spoken, and even these native English speakers too often underachieve at school (Garcia, 2008). As an example, consider the largest group of non-English speakers at home: More than 31 million U.S. residents 5 years of age and older report that they speak Spanish at home, and more than half of these also report that they speak English very well (U.S. Census Bureau, 2006). However, everyday, social, conversational proficiency does not predict academic school success (Wilkinson & Silliman, 2008). Thus, although many Spanish-speaking ELLs entering school may indeed have such conversational skills, they may not have the necessary oral language underpinnings for entering into academic discourse and for ultimately achieving academic success in school.

Of particular concern is the education of ELLs in content areas such as science, mathematics, and social studies, each of which involves using language in unique ways to think and communicate orally and in writing (Schleppergrell, 2007). As the quotation above from a math teacher shows, content-area specialists often do not recognize that their responsibilities include instruction in language or literacy. Yet, teaching about the language of one's discipline would allow educators to mutually exploit the language and the content for increased understanding in the student. From the students' perspective, they cannot succeed in learning the content of the disciplines without understanding the relevant academic language (Wilkinson & Silliman, 2008; Brisk, Chapter 7, and Rymes, Chapter 8, this volume). However, teachers receive little preparation in how to go about integrating language instruction into the disciplines. Not only content specialists, but even primary school teachers who teach across content areas are unschooled in how to embed language teaching into other content areas. To be able to do so, all teachers of ELLs, not just teachers of English, need to understand better the strengths as well as the unique challenges of ELLs, whatever content is being taught.

Despite the No Child Left Behind (2000) initiative and large investments in support services such as special education, teaching English as a second language, language pathology, and reading instruction, American children trail children from other countries in math and science achievement (see Program for International Student Assessment, 2006; Progress in International Reading Literacy Study, 2006; Trends in International Mathematics and Science Study, 2007). Thus, the challenge of educating successfully all American children persists—this, despite the fact that educational attainment in other countries such as Finland is growing. The deficiencies in American educational attainment are of concern for several reasons. One is that we must have an educated workforce to compete in a global economy. Another concern is that we have an ethical obligation to fulfill the promise of a better life that America offers to immigrants. We pride ourselves on that promise, and to fulfill it, we must offer adequate—even excellent—education to all children, not just monolingual, native English-speaking children of native English-speaking parents.

OUR RESPONSE: EDUCATING EDUCATORS

Addressing the educational crisis successfully will depend, in large part, on enhancing communication between ELLs and their teachers. To do so, educators need to know who these students are and how to reach them, and prospective teachers need to have such information readily accessible to them. Accordingly, we asked our authors to clearly organize their chapters using these sections: focus points, chapter purpose, research review, best practices, summary, and implications. All but the first and last chapters follow this format.

We use the term *ELL* broadly throughout the volume to include more than those students who enter the education system not speaking any, or very limited, English. In addition, we include students whose experience with English may be limited in register and range. Indeed, some children, as noted above, may be native English speakers but are bilingual, speaking a different language in the home. Or, they may have had little experience with what counts as academic English, a register appropriate to argumentation and scientific reasoning. Many authors in this volume show how all such children are different from monolingual native speakers in a variety of ways.

Also, for the purpose of this volume, we have taken a broad view of what constitutes evidence because our authors drew from not only scientifically designed, controlled studies but also from well-documented observations, case studies, expert reports, and clinical experiences. What struck us as we reviewed the chapters was that the sum total of the material submitted by our contributors coalesced into a coherent view, incorporating a wealth of various methods and consequent research findings. This richness encouraged us in the presentation of our resulting position (see also van Kleeck & Norlander, 2008).

In this first chapter we offer what we have learned from our authors and from many years of teaching about language and communication. Most importantly, we argue for a solid foundation in language and communication for quality education across the curriculum, and we emphasize that all educators need to understand language and language learning, as well as how both the first language (L1) and the second language (L2) impact learning in the classroom and more generally. Specifically, we offer an evidence-based view of child learners not as empty vessels to be filled with knowledge by their teachers, but as constructors of understandings who need the guidance of their teachers. The teachers, in turn, need to know how the students can best learn, given their past and present experiences, both cultural and linguistic. And teachers need the support of administrators and families to sustain their efforts.

Our introductory chapter is organized into four main sections as follows: In the next section we describe the important cross-cutting themes emerging from the other chapters, along with several chapter references for each point. In many cases, we could not cite all relevant chapters for each point, but we have tried to give some guidance to our readers, with apologies to our authors for any omissions. We relate these themes in the next two sections, first, to students and the abilities they bring to the educational process and, second, to our view of educators and the need to empower them to be better-prepared partners in that process. General comments in this latter section are followed by two important subsections: one on the emerging best practices, especially relevant for classroom teachers as facilitators of learning in ELLs, and one for administrators as supporters of the teaching and learning process. Our final section introduces the three-part organization of the book.

CROSS-CUTTING THEMES

L2 Learning Benefits from L1 Learning

ELLs arrive at school with a variety of language skills (or as Rymes, Chapter 8, this volume, says, "communicative repertoires"); some may have had some schooling or can read in their first language, some cannot. Many of our authors provide evidence showing that L1 can be a beneficial steppingstone for L2. That is, learning in L1 encourages learning in L2, *even when the languages are not formally related*. Although it is clear that the more advanced a child is in L1, the more likely it is that those skills will facilitate L2, it is also clear that language learning from a variety of sources and experiences goes on beyond the preschool years (see Hoff & Shatz, 2007; Westby & Hwa-Froelich, Chapter 9, this volume). It is wise, then, to encourage continued learning in L1 when introducing the child to L2. There are several ways in which L2 can benefit from L1: (1) mastery of L1 (e.g., reading in L1) can give children pride in accomplishment and a love of learning that positively affects their interest in other subjects; (2) encouraging L1 learning signals to children that their languages and cultures are respected; (3) explicit comparisons between L1 and L2 characteristics can help children see how L1 and L2 are alike or different; and (4) bilingualism offers some unique cognitive advantages to the speaker (see Conboy, Chapter 1; Kohnert & Pham, Chapter 2; Reyes & Ervin-Tripp, Chapter 3; Bialystok & Peets, Chapter 6; Brisk, Chapter 7; Rymes, Chapter 8, this volume; see also Silliman & Wilkinson, 2009).

Below we expand on some specific ways, especially relevant for education, in which L1 and L2 are related.

Phonological Awareness Is Important in All Languages

Much evidence shows that phonological awareness, the ability to recognize and manipulate the sounds of one's language, is an important skill for a beginning reader of English. The conventional wisdom has been that such awareness is important for alphabetic languages like English but not for nonalphabetic languages. However, this apparently is not so: Phonological knowledge is relevant to reading in *all* languages, but the way it manifests is different, depending on several factors. Hence, how phonological knowledge in L1 will mitigate L2 differs by language pairs (see Newman, Chapter 5, this volume, especially Appendix 5.1).

Translation "Equivalents" for Words May Not Index Conceptual Equivalents

Contrary to the belief that early bilingual vocabulary building is done by finding equivalents in one language for words in the other, there seem to be few translation equivalents in early bilingual lexicons (Bedore, Peña, & Boerger, Chapter 4, and August, Dressler, Goldenberg, & Saunders, Chapter 12, this volume). One reason for this may be that children are conservative learners: They cannot be certain that words in one language will map to precisely the same conceptual space that they do in another language (see, e.g., Bowerman & Choi, 2001, on differences in spatial concepts encoded by Korean and English). However, recent research shows that for bilingual toddlers, like adult bilinguals, the larger the proportion of one's vocabulary devoted to translation equivalents the more lexical access is facilitated (Poulin-Dubois, Bialystok, Blaye, Coutya, & Yott, 2009). Hence, encouraging discussion of translation equivalents and possible similarities and differences in conceptual underpinnings should facilitate both conceptual and lexical understanding.

The Foundation of Literacy Is Oral Language

Many of our authors stress the importance of oral language as a foundation for literacy (Conboy, Chapter 1; Kohnert & Pham, Chapter 2; August et al., Chapter 12, this volume). Noted as well is that conversational oral language proficiency is insufficient as a basis for academic success. Even native English speakers with everyday conversational competence need experience with oral academic language skills to achieve acceptable literacy skills. Thus, stopping ELLs' access to English language teaching once conversational competence is achieved is premature. Moreover, if students have had some opportunity to develop academic language in L1, they are likely to be able to transfer that knowledge to L2. (See Westby & Hwa-Froelich, Chapter 9, this volume).

Opportunities to Use L2 Need to Be Meaningful

We have noted above that L1 can serve as a base for L2, but for such relational experiences to be useful, they must be meaningful. Allowing L1 to serve as a base from which to launch L2 experiences can help ELLs see value in their own background and how it relates and compares to the language and culture of English-speaking students (Reyes & Ervin-Tripp, Chapter 3; Brisk, Chapter 7; Rymes, Chapter 8, this volume).

Importantly, isolating ELLs from English-speaking peers in the name of efficient education does nothing to facilitate the growth of their L2 use or the kind of understanding that is so crucial for assimilation into the larger culture.

English Language Development Needs to Be Explicit

Meaningful experiences with L1 and L2 are not enough, however. Explicit instruction in English language development (ELD) that supplements meaningful experiences is necessary for success with ELLs. Indeed, the integration of ELD with carefully planned, meaningful experiences is likely to produce the best results (Reese & Goldenberg, Chapter 11, and August et al., Chapter 12, this volume). That is, ELD is not mutually exclusive with using language in meaningful contexts.

Bilinguals Are Different from Monolinguals

Bilinguals are not just like monolinguals except that they know (or are learning) more than one language. Recent research has informed us that bilinguals differ in many ways from monolinguals. Because brain development is sensitive to environmental input, learning two languages has an impact on the young language-learning brain (Conboy, Chapter 1, this volume); ways of learning are affected by previous experiences with language (i.e., L1) (Newman, Chapter 5, and Brisk, Chapter 7, this volume); and cognitive and social skills differ from monolinguals. As Bialystok and Peets (Chapter 6, this volume) point out, differences from monolinguals can be positive or negative for standard educational practices, but all provide opportunities to exploit those differences for bilinguals' learning. For example, when code switching is seen as a sociocognitive skill instead of a deficit, it can be utilized by the teacher to help engage the bilingual speaker (Reyes & Ervin-Tripp, Chapter 3, this volume).

Low L2 proficiency does not necessarily indicate language disorder. Just as code switching need not be seen as a deficit, so many of the characteristics of low L2 proficiency do not necessarily indicate language disorder. Diagnosing language impairment in ELLs is notoriously difficult. Language impairment tests for monolinguals may not be appropriate for ELLs because of the many differences in brain development and in language typologies (Conboy, Chapter 1; Westby & Hwa-Froelich, Chapter 9; Bailey, Chapter 10, this volume). Assessments focusing on interaction allow the bilingual or ELL to demonstrate responsiveness and learning skills, not just static knowledge. Finding the appropriate services for ELLs without subjecting them to a diagnosis of language impairment may be the best path, given the current state of development in appropriate tests for language impairment in such children.

Families Are Important to the Educational Process

Among the best predictors of poor academic outcomes are low income and low language proficiency. Obviously, educators alone cannot counteract this important fact. However, they can enlist the help of their students' families and engage them in the task of educating their children. As several of our authors report, most parents, whether immigrants and/ or low-income, are interested in seeing their children succeed in school. Families need encouragement and understandable information about how to help their children (see Brisk, Chapter 7; Reese & Goldenberg, Chapter 11, this volume). From learning about their students' languages and cultures to finding translators to help with family communication, teachers and administrators alike need to facilitate interaction with ELL families.

Mutual Respect Guides Learning

In a recent film made by an education professor (Martinez, 2009), both teachers and administrators spoke about the importance of relationships between teachers and students, teachers and other teachers, and administrators with teachers and students. Underlying those comments was the belief that quality education can be attained only with mutual respect among all parties. Offering the students meaningful experiences, reaching out to families, allowing creativity among teachers, supporting the needs of students and teachers—all these require mutual respect. All the authors in this volume assume the need for that respect; without it, students cannot construct an educated view of the world for themselves, teachers cannot guide them in that enterprise, and administrators cannot offer the necessary support.

THE WHOLE CHILD AS LEARNER

Psychologists tend to consider children analytically. That is, they study aspects of children's language development, their cognitive development, or their social development. Educators too may lose sight of the whole child: Beyond primary schools, when content-area specialization is the model, all too often children are seen only as science learners, or math students, or test takers. However, just as analytic study is the province of researchers and not the domain of the developing child, so too are the content-area specializations the province of practitioners and not the domain of the student. That is, the whole child draws on his or her skills as needed or appropriate, regardless of the boundaries set by the specialists.

The case for bootstrapping, or helping one's own efforts in an area by using whatever skills one has in other areas, is strong. Even prelinguistic children use whatever skills they have to acquire more competence as members of a family and then a community. For example, Shatz (1994, 2007b) offers many examples of how toddlers use cognitive and social skills to bootstrap their language development, with language then becoming a powerful device for acquiring more advanced cognitive and social skills. A related behavior can be seen with older children as well, when, for example, they group together words that they have experienced in common discourse contexts, creating abstract lexical categories for color, time, and number, even before they know what the individual words mean (Shatz, Tare, Nguyen, & Young, 2010). The message from such research is that children are creative users of their knowledge: They will utilize their skills, whatever they are, to operate in their social worlds, be they home, the playground, or school. Perhaps no one understood this better than Vygotsky (1978), who argued that children needed to be met at their "zone of proximal development" if they were to be guided successfully by adults. That is, adults need to gauge what skills children currently possess in order to guide them in measured steps toward higher goals.

Two implications follow from this perspective. The first is that language skill affects every realm of social and cognitive life. It is the medium in which culture is carried and education is attained. Without adequate language skills, individuals are hampered in their ability to achieve their full potential as persons (Shatz, 1994.) The second is that children are not blank slates ready to be inscribed with a dominant culture's standard practices. Because from infancy they have been constructing their own reality based on their experiences, new realities and experiences must be explicitly compared to and integrated with the old if children are to make sense of them and make them their own. (See Rymes, Chapter 8, this volume, on utilizing ELLs' communicative repertoires.)

Related to these implications is the notion that children are prepared to learn language. This notion does not require one to believe that children are born with grammars in their heads. Rather, in this view, all human infants have brains that are designed to attend to language and to analyze and organize what they hear into a coherent, hierarchically structured system. Increasingly, regardless of their theoretical biases, researchers in language development both discover the remarkable capacities of infants to handle linguistic phenomena (Saffran & Thiessen, 2007) and recognize their abstract abilities (Lieven, 2009). Like any system, language has parts (like the phonological system) that have their own integrity but that influence, and are influenced by, other parts of the system, and that function in concert with the other parts to produce fluent performance.

The infant brain may be prepared to learn language, but that learning organization incorporates flexibility, and the brain develops as a function not only of maturation but of experience (Gathercole & Hoff, 2007; Conboy, Chapter 1, and Kohnert & Pham, Chapter 2, this volume). We do not yet fully understand all the ways in which the environment affects brain development (and language development), but researchers have begun to document disparities in learning as early as 9 months of age (Halle et al., 2009). However rich or poor the environment, language learning takes place in a social context (Shatz, 2007a). This is true for L2 as well as L1. The more educators can learn about the processes of language development, the better prepared they will be to deal with the disparate language backgrounds of ELLs (see Hoff & Shatz, 2007, for discussions on the development of different parts of language as well as bilingualism and literacy).

Students' language skills impact not only their test-taking abilities but every discipline they study. No matter how young, children come to school with a world of experience in home and community that frames their attitudes about learning and how they use language to learn. By the time they enter school, they are a social member of a language community. School represents a wider community with possibly different standards from home for behavior and for language use. It is a tenet of American education that all children come to school with brains adequate to learning, to constructing knowledge, and to expressing themselves. Less well recognized is that children's prior experiences have formed a framework into which the schools' standards and goals must be integrated. The time-honored role of teachers is to mediate students' creation of links between their earlier experience and the new school context (Bransford, Brown, & Cocking, 2000).

This perspective is even more compelling when we address the education of ELLs, who, regardless of their age, come to school with a different set of capacities and experiences from monolinguals. Educators need to appreciate those differences and to find ways to work within and beyond the constraints imposed by them. To help facilitate what may sometimes seem like a daunting task, we highlight below many of the best practices proposed in the chapters that follow.

THE TEACHER AS GUIDE FOR LEARNING AND THE ADMINISTRATOR AS FACILITATOR

U.S. legislation, No Child Left Behind (2000), requires that each classroom has a "highly qualified teacher." A major source of the persistent education gaps between ELLs and their counterparts is the disparity between what teachers know and what they need to know about ELLs and other at-risk students (Wilkinson & Silliman, 2008). This gap needs to be bridged to improve the academic preparation and professional development of all school-based practitioners. The existing knowledge base of many practitioners appears disconnected from what is necessary for promoting and maximizing successful educational outcomes for individual students, and even more so for ELLs (Silliman, Wilkinson, & Brea-Spahn, 2004.) The concern is that ELLs often enter school without the background experiences and literacy skills, including proficiency in academic language (Wilkinson & Silliman, 2008), that form the foundation for future literacy development. ELLs require "teachers who are capable of accelerating the learning of students who experience the greatest difficulty acquiring literacy" (Dozier, Johnston, & Rogers, 2006, p. 11). The quality of classroom instruction is, by far, the most significant element in formal education. To improve ELL learning, we must provide innovative ways to educate preservice teachers about the unique strengths and challenges of ELL students, as well as provide meaningful and comprehensive continuing professional development for teachers and other educational practitioners who encounter ELLs in school. Only those teachers who are prepared for cultural and linguistic diversity and who have developed a deep understanding of how to teach diverse students to acquire academic literacy will be prepared to make a difference in the lives of ELL students.

We argue that teachers of ELLs must, therefore, have explicit knowledge of contrastive linguistics in order to develop sensitivity to individual differences (Valdes, Bunch, Snow, & Lee, 2005; Wong Fillmore & Snow, 2000). Oller and Jarmulowicz (2007) accentuate how similarities in the linguistic features of two languages facilitate L2 learning. Of equal importance are the ways in which distinctive differences may interfere with L2 learning. The value of this knowledge is that teachers are then capable of recognizing cross-language comparisons that allow them to (1) discover the linguistic strengths of individual children for the support of language transfer strategies, and (2) discern sites of potential linguistic interference, which will vary for each ELL in his or her classroom.

The research literature on teachers' pedagogical knowledge about ELLs emphasizes the relevance of oral language experiences for L2 learning (e.g., August & Shanahan, 2008). The need for both regular and special education teachers to be explicitly schooled in cross-linguistic differences (and similarities) in the phonological, morphological, and syntactic systems of first languages versus English (e.g., Gersten et al., 2007) is paramount. These cross-linguistic contrasts may affect, in many ways, the ability of ELLs to decode and spell in English, thereby interfering with the achievement of academic language proficiency. Knowledge of language contrasts is not a natural consequence of being literate: A monolingual English-speaking teacher may not be able to access the explicit phonemic awareness necessary for the effective teaching of beginning reading (Silliman, Bahr, Beasman, & Wilkinson, 2000). Even a bilingual teacher who has the requisite cultural knowledge about Spanish-speaking communities and speaks Spanish and English "fluently" may not have sufficient metalinguistic knowledge of critical linguistic contrasts between the two languages. Additionally, all teachers of ELLs, and not just English as a second language (ESL) teachers, need to develop metalinguistic awareness about the social differences between the everyday language use of students from different backgrounds and the demands of language in the classroom (Rymes, Chapter 8, this volume.)

We are mindful of the real research-to-practice divide. Many practitioners believe that research findings lack utility relative to the experiences that constitute the exigencies of their classroom life. Educational practitioners want feasible and defined procedures that can be applied to their specific situations in order to meet the particular needs of their students. They do not want radically different methods. Often, teachers find that the actual mastery of new practices for instructional innovations takes much longer to incorporate into everyday use than did the original research-based intervention used by the researchers. One consequence is that teachers may either abandon the innovation or fail to maintain a high level of fidelity to the implementation because the magnitude of effort does not justify their time. The likelihood of sustaining new practices is significantly decreased when on-site mentoring by researchers, including the ongoing support afforded by professional networking, and administrative leadership are absent (Foorman & Nixon, 2006; Silliman et al., 2004).

Best practices, then, must be seen in the context of effective classrooms, one where all students learn and progress to meet the standards set. Such classrooms are informed by sociocultural theory. Student learning is dependent upon what a teacher knows, how students come to understand that knowledge, and the context in which the learning takes place (Vygotksy, 1978). Classrooms that are well organized are collaborative, with teachers guiding instruction and student participation. This context takes into consideration the relationship between teachers and students, the community of the classrooms, and the larger community of the school and how all these "parts" are organized and managed throughout every school day (Wilkinson, Morrow, & Chou, 2008b).

Emerging Best Practices for Teachers

- *Recognize that ELLs are different from monolinguals.*

Investigations of early brain development confirm that children who are developing two languages are different from those developing only one very early on (Conboy, Chapter 1, this volume). Since children's brains are developing throughout the school years, there is every reason to think that developmental differences occur as children are exposed to a second language. Some of these differences will facilitate learning, others will not (Bialystok & Peets, Chapter 6, this volume), but all will require a knowledgeable teacher to exploit them in the furtherance of ELLs' education.

- *Recognize or learn differences between English and children's L1, and exploit these for the children.*

Languages can be sorted into types according to their sound, grammar, and vocabulary characteristics. How close a child's L1 is to English (according to the characteristics of both) impacts how easily children can transfer their knowledge across languages. But, even when L1 is quite different from L2, teachers can help children to discover how the languages differ and to learn what they need to know about English. (See, e.g., Newman, Chapter 5, this volume.) To learn more about language similarities and differences, educators should avail themselves of courses in linguistic typology. For assistance with particular languages, teachers can seek help in the school community from bilingual speakers, such as other teachers or family members.

- *Encourage ELLs to use L1 and its learning strategies in learning L2, as appropriate.*

Several authors report that strong L1 skills predict better learning of L2. Thus, encouraging the continued development of L1 is likely to have positive effects on the acquisition of L2 (Kohnert & Pham, Chapter 2, this volume). Especially in the early stages of L2 vocabulary learning, ELLs are aware of the links between the two languages (Bedore et al., Chapter 4, this volume). Despite the finding cited above that they do not have many translation equivalents, early sequential bilinguals who continue to learn L1 link their lexicons and underlying semantic representations. Although there is little influence from this linkage to ELLS' production of vocabulary, nonetheless instruction in a student's primary language (L1) makes a positive contribution to literacy achievement in the student's second language when compared to students receiving instruction only in L2 (Reese & Goldenberg, Chapter 11, this volume). Therefore, the research points to cross-language transfer from L1 to L2 not necessarily just of vocabulary skills but also of skills such as phonological awareness and decoding and comprehension strategies. Again, teachers can use their creativity to bring L1 into the classroom in engaging and supportive ways that can guide such transfer of skills (Reyes & Ervin-Tripp, Chapter 3; Brisk, Chapter 7; Rymes, Chapter 8, this volume).

- *Create interactive activities that engage ELLs with more proficient speakers.*

Few productive interactions happen without creative forethought on the teacher's part. August and colleagues (Chapter 12, this volume) report that interactive activities effectively mixing ELLs and more English-proficient ELLs (or native English speakers) typically require the teacher to carefully structure the tasks. If classroom interactive activities are to benefit ELL language-learning efforts, careful consideration must be given to (1) the design of the tasks in which students engage, (2) training of the more proficient English speakers who interact with ELLs, and (3) the language proficiency of the ELLs themselves.

- *Designate ELLs to serve as "teachers" of their language and culture to other students, drawing upon ELLs' "funds of knowledge."*

Building upon the knowledge and experience that ELLs bring from home is a way to bridge the gaps between home and school—gaps that so often interfere with ELLs' successful learning and achieving in mainstream schools. The *funds-of-knowledge* term refers to the knowledge, skills, experiences, and competencies that exist in children's homes and communities, and that teachers can draw upon to develop classroom learning activities that help ELLs achieve academic learning goals. *Funds of knowledge* may include, for example, knowledge of ranching and farming, construction, herbal and folk medicine, and appliance repair, and are typically discovered by teachers through home visits. Reese and Goldenberg (Chapter 11, this volume) argue that aspects of the diverse knowledge bases can sometimes be incorporated effectively into classroom lessons. Teachers who have tried this methods report positive changes in ELLs' attitudes and increased communication and rapport with parents—which are critical to fostering ELLs' success in school (Kohnert & Pham, Chapter 2, and Brisk, Chapter 7, this volume).

• *Recognize that code switching indexes skills and use it to help the child see uses of L1 and L2.*

Understanding when and why ELLs code-switch is important to figuring out how best to facilitate their L2 learning. Sometimes what is best to do is counterintuitive. ELLs may make errors early in L2 learning that suggest that they are developing representations of the L1 sound system as they learn new L2 vocabulary. Bedore and colleagues (Chapter 4, this volume) give the following examples: A first grader called a rhinoceros a "rinocornio," and another called a boat a "bark" (noting that the Spanish word for *boat* is *barco*). Sometimes it may be difficult for ELLs to call up the correct phonological representation of a word. In cases of language loss (i.e., lack of access to low-frequency words or grammatical structures), Bedore and colleagues report that it may be facilitative to long-term vocabulary growth to continue to use L1 in speaking with an ELL, even if it is temporarily frustrating. The tendency to cease using L1 with ELLs may undermine their efforts in continuing to build vocabulary systematically. Reyes and Ervin-Tripp (Chapter 3, this volume) note that code switching does not necessarily indicate a deficit. Rather, it can be a sociolinguistic skill that is sanctioned in the family and community and can be used for a variety of communicative purposes. The teacher's task, then, is to recognize when it may be appropriate to use it versus when it may indicate only partial learning of English.

• *Use relevant opportunities to teach language even when teaching another content area.*

All teachers, not just ESL instructors or speech therapists, need to engage ELLs in learning the language relevant to their discipline. As an example, Brisk (Chapter 7, this volume) recounts how a second-grade history teacher taught characteristics of English (capitalization and past tense) relevant to her history topic as part of her history lesson. And an experimental program for engaging kindergartners in science activities includes relevant vocabulary exercises (Gelman, Brenneman, Macdonald, & Román, 2009). But embedding appropriate language within content instruction requires careful thought about the language aspects that can be most seamlessly interwoven with the content material.

• *Relate ELD classes to instructional goals and classroom work; proficiency in academic language is critical for school success.*

ELD instruction is an important component of education for ELLs that should incorporate meaningful content relating to other classroom learning activities that extend the content focus (August et al., Chapter 12, this volume). The use of instructional objectives is often considered a centerpiece of effective instruction, with the objectives working as starting points to keep the lesson and activities focused and aimed toward student learning. Both content-area and ESL teachers can work together in a teamwork approach to forge links between ESL lessons and content lessons. Students' mastery of academic language—the language of the text, the test, and teacher talk—is essential, and teachers in all content areas must explicitly teach elements such as grammar, vocabulary, and discourse structure of the disciplines (see Brisk, Chapter 7; Westby & Hwa-Froelich, Chapter 9; Bailey, Chapter 10, this volume).

• *Continual language assessment is essential for ELL education.*

Formative assessment of ELLs' language development should be conducted repeatedly by every teacher who teaches ELL students reading, mathematics, science, or U.S. history. Without continual up-to-date information on a student's language needs and abilities, teachers will not be able to teach either language or content material effectively.

• *Tailor lessons and interventions to students' levels of proficiency.*

Although there are similarities between the kinds of teaching that best support first- and second-language learners in literacy learning, there are significant differences (August et al., Chapter 12, this volume). Consequently, when designing lessons and other interventions, educators must keep in mind the roles of background knowledge and experience. Lessons should be tailored to the level of students' L2 proficiency—which may involve individualizing the task for different levels within the same classroom and lesson.

  • *Maintain interventions beyond the "conversational" stage.*

All too often, students receiving special language services are redesignated as not in need of services once they gain only conversational proficiency in English. However, success in school is related to proficiency in *academic* language. Moreover, greater academic language development in L1 forms the basis for higher levels of development in L2 (Reese & Goldenberg, Chapter 11, this volume). The bottom line: ELLs who receive special services will benefit from instruction in academic language before being redesignated as capable in English.

Our discussion of best practices for teachers highlights the importance of creative teamwork among all educational practitioners. Although we have focused primarily on the opportunities for classroom teachers of ELLs, the work of all educational practitioners—teachers of content areas, speech–language pathologists, school psychologists, school counselors, school librarians—is crucial for the success of all students and ELLs in particular. Recognizing the financial and political pressures under which administrators function, next we offer several suggestions for how they might support the best practices outlined above.

Suggested Best Practices for Educational Administrators

School leaders play a key role in ensuring that teachers are both inspired and supported in their efforts to provide optimal instruction for ELLs. Importantly, leaders should nurture school communities that identify ELLs' learning as a priority.

  • *Encourage teamwork and cross-disciplinary collaboration among staff.*

Interaction, cooperation, and assistance among specialists and classroom teachers are essential for the school success of all students (see Bailey, Chapter 10, this volume). Principals need to have the teaching and learning of ELLs as a priority within the school community: They need to nurture the school community with specific actions, such as scheduling time and opportunities for regular classroom teachers to collaborate with ESL teachers in comparing teaching strategies, in reviewing the progress of ELLs in their classes, and in identifying key resources that can be applied to the education of ELLs. Moreover, in their roles as instructional leaders, principals must identify instructional techniques to use when working with ELLs, such as scaffolded instruction, targeted vocabulary development, connections to student experiences, student-to-student interaction, and the use of supplementary culturally relevant materials. In short, principals need to support instruction that builds language lessons into content areas and integrates L1 and L2 in meaningful ways in the classroom.

  • *Encourage home–school relationships.*

It is essential to support ways that bridge the gap between language and literacy practices both inside and outside of school (e.g., in the home). Providing support for home visits and training teachers how to speak with parents respectfully and without using jargon are just two suggestions for encouraging more home–school communication. Utilizing community resources for translation and communication assistance for teachers and parents is another way to support ELL education efforts.

  • *Arrange for or support instruction in language typologies for teachers.*

Kohnert and Pham (Chapter 2, this volume) urge administrative support for the study of language development as part of teachers' required continued professional development. In addition to basic courses, an important topic for workshops that could be extremely helpful to teachers would be courses on language typologies relevant to the student population. Providing for or encouraging attendance at such workshops or classes would be an important step in preparing teachers to understand more about the language difficulties faced by ELLs. One possible source of such instruction might be language education and linguistics faculty in local colleges who would be willing to offer such preparation for teachers.

  • *Support and respect creative efforts of teachers to work with ELLs and their families.*

Finally, we note the main lesson emerging from all the research reports, examples, and implications in the chapters that follow: There is no substitute for creative, thoughtful, well-educated teachers dedicated to educating all their students to the best of their abilities. Effective teacher education must recognize the varied cultural and linguistic backgrounds of the students of today and tomorrow and must prepare the educators of the future accordingly. In this volume we have collected many suggestions for working with ELLs that teachers and/ or researchers have found promising or successful. We are sure, however, that creative and resourceful educators can and do add to them.

Such efforts, especially in the context of collaborative team activities, deserve our support.

THE ORGANIZATION OF THIS BOOK

The remainder of this book is divided into three parts. Part I, Early Language Experience and School Readiness, introduces the kind of children about whom we write. Conboy, in Chapter 1, explains how the brain develops in response to experience as well as maturation, particularly with regard to potential influences of early exposure to more than one language. Kohnert and Pham (Chapter 2) discuss a model of first- and second-language acquisition that is sensitive to a variety of factors, both internal and external. The final chapter in this section, by Reyes and Ervin-Tripp, presents the linguistic behavioral characteristics of bilinguals, revealing their unique social–linguistic experiences. Together, these chapters provide a multifaceted profile of ELLs for educators.

The next section, Language and Literacy Principles and Practices in School, concentrates on ELLs' school learning, particularly on learning to speak and write English. The first two chapters are particularly useful in seeing how a first language might relate to learning a second. The Bedore, Peña, and Boerger chapter focuses on vocabulary acquisition and the relations between L1 and L2. Newman (Chapter 5) addresses L1 and L2 differences and similarities with regard to phonology and its role in reading. The next two chapters consider how the status of ELL affects learning. In their chapter, Bialystok and Peets discuss the pluses and minuses of being bilingual for the cognitive task of learning to read. And Brisk (Chapter 7) offers many suggestions for using the status of ELL to engage the student in learning.

The final section, Assessment and Interaction: Working with Children and Families, includes chapters that stress the active role educators can play in working with ELLs. The first, by Rymes, encourages teachers to discover the communicative competencies of ELLs and to utilize these in the learning process. The next two chapters, one by Westby and Hwa-Froelich and one by Bailey, are concerned with the important issue of how to assess whether ELL children are normal learners or language disordered, and how this determination impacts instruction. Reese and Goldenberg (Chapter 11) provide support for the view, espoused in earlier chapters, that family involvement in the learning process is crucial for ELL success. The authors of the last chapter, August, Dressler, Goldenberg, and Saunders, draw on decades of research to support what we know: To accommodate their unique present-day status, ELLs need explicit and meaningful training in the use of language for academic purposes.

REFERENCES

August, D., & Shanahan, T. (2008). *Developing reading and writing in second language learners: Lessons from the Report of the National Literacy Panel on Language-Minority Children and Youth.* Mahwah, NJ: Erblaum/Taylor & Francis.

Bowerman, M., & Choi, S. (2001). Shaping meaning for language: Universal and language-specific in the acquisition of spatial semantic categories. In M. Bowerman & S. C. Levinson (Eds.), *Language acquisition and conceptual development* (pp. 475–511). New York: Cambridge University Press.

Bransford, J. D., Brown, A. L., & Cocking, R. R. (2000). Introduction. In J. D. Bransford, A. L. Brown, & R. R. Cocking, (Eds.), *How people learn: Brain, mind, experience, and school* (pp. 130–138). Washington, DC: National Academy Press.

Dozier, C., Johnston, P., & Rogers, R. (2006). *Critical literacy/critical teaching.* New York: Teachers College Press.

Foorman, B. R., & Nixon, S. M. (2006). The influence of public policy on reading research and practice. *Topics in Language Disorders, 26,* 157–171.

Garcia, O. (2008). *Bilingual education in the 21st century: A global perspective.* New York: Wiley–Blackwell.

Gathercole, V. C. M., & Hoff, E. (2007). Input and the acquisition of language: Three questions. In E. Hoff & M. Shatz (Eds.), *Blackwell handbook of language development* (pp. 107–127). Oxford, UK: Blackwell.

Gelman, R., Brenneman, K., Macdonald, G., & Román, M. (2009). *Preschool pathways to science: Facilitating scientific ways of knowing, thinking, talking, and doing.* Baltimore: Brookes.

Halle, T., Forry, N., Hair, E., Perper, K., Wandner, L., & Vick, J. (2009). *Disparities in early learning and development: Lessons from the Early Childhood Longitudinal Study—Birth Cohort (ECLS-B).* Executive Summary, Washington, DC: Child Trends.

Hoff, E., & Shatz, M. (Eds.). (2007). *Blackwell handbook of language development.* Oxford, UK: Blackwell.

Lieven, E . (2009, April). *Discussion. Using structural priming to reveal developing linguistic representations.* Symposium presented at the biennial meeting of the Society for Research in Child Development, Denver, CO.

Martinez, M. (2009). *No teacher left behind* [Film]. Wilmington: University of North Carolina.

No Child Left Behind Act of 2001, Public Law 107-110. Retrieved November 7, 2009, from *www.ed.gov/policy/elsec/leg/esea02/107-110.pdf.*

Office of English Language Acquisition, Language Enhancement and Academic Achievement for Limited English Proficient Students, National Clearinghouse for English Language Acquisition & Language Instruction Educational Programs. (2004–2005). *The growing numbers of limited English proficient students* (Consolidated State Performance Report, 6). Retrieved November 10, 2009, from *www.ncela.gwu.edu/files/uploads/4/Growing-LEP_0506.pdf.*

Oller, D. K., & Jarmulowicz, L. (2007). Language and literacy in bilingual children in the early years. In E. Hoff & M. Shatz (Eds.), *Blackwell handbook of language development* (pp. 368–386). Oxford, UK: Blackwell.

Poulin-Dubois, D., Bialystok, E., Blaye, A., Coutya, J., & Yott, J. (2009, April). *Vocabulary development and lexical access in 24-month-old bilinguals.* Poster presented at the biennial meeting of the Society for Research in Child Development, Denver, CO.

Program for International Student Assessment, U.S. Department of Education (PISA). (2006). Retrieved April 16, 2009, from *nces.ed.gov/Surveys/PISA/pisa2006highlights.asp*.

Progress in International Reading Literacy Study (PIRLS). (2006). Retrieved April 16, 2009, from *nces.ed.gov/pubs2004/pirlspub*.

Saffran, J. R., & Thiessen, E. D. (2007). Domain-general learning capacities. In E. Hoff & M. Shatz (Eds.), *Blackwell handbook of language development* (pp. 68–86). Oxford, UK: Blackwell.

Schleppergrell, M. (2007). The linguistic challenges of mathematics teaching and learning: A research review. *Reading and Writing Quarterly, 23*, 139–159.

Shatz, M. (1994). *A toddler's life: Becoming a person.* New York: Oxford University Press.

Shatz, M. (2007a). On the development of the field of language development. In E. Hoff & M. Shatz (Eds.), *Blackwell handbook of language development* (pp. 1–15). Oxford, UK: Blackwell.

Shatz, M. (2007b). Revisiting *A Toddler's Life* for the toddler years: Conversational participation as a tool for learning across knowledge domains. In C. A. Brownell & C. B. Kopp (Eds.), *Socioemotional development in the toddler years: Transitions and transformations* (pp. 241–260). New York: Guilford Press.

Shatz, M., Tare, M., Nguyen, S. P., & Young, T. (2010). Acquiring non-object terms: The case for time words. *Journal of Cognition and Development, 11*, 16–36.

Silliman, E., Bahr, R., Beasman, J., & Wilkinson, L. (2000). Scaffolds for learning to read in an inclusion classroom. *Language, Speech, and Hearing Services in Schools, 20*, 265–279.

Silliman, E., & Wilkinson, L. (2009). Literacy. In P. Hogan (Ed.), *The Cambridge encyclopedia of the language sciences* (pp. 121–142). Cambridge, UK: Cambridge University Press.

Silliman, E. R., Wilkinson, L. C., & Brea-Spahn, M. R. (2004). Policy and practice imperatives for language and literacy learning: Who shall be left behind? In C. A. Stone, E. R.Silliman, B. J. Ehren, & K. Apel (Eds.), *Handbook on language and literacy: Development and disorders* (pp. 97–129). New York: Guilford Press.

Trends in International Mathematics and Science Study (TIMSS). (2007). Retrieved April 16, 2009, from *nces.ed.gov/timss/index.asp*.

U.S. Census Bureau. (2006, September 5). Hispanic heritage month: Sept. 15–Oct. 15, 2006. Retrieved May 17, 2007, from *www.census.gov/Press-Release/www/releases/archives/facts_for_features_special_editions/007173.html*.

Valdes, G., Bunch, G., Snow, E., & Lee, C. (2005). Enhancing the development of
    students' language(s). In L. Darling-Hammond, J. Bransford, P. LePage, K.
    Hammerness, & H. Duffy (Eds.), *Preparing teachers for a changing world:
    What teachers should learn and be able to do* (pp. 126–168). San Francisco:
    Jossey-Bass.
van Kleeck, A., & Norlander, E. (2008). Fostering form and meaning in emerg-
    ing literacy using evidence-based practice. In M. Mody & E. R. Silliman
    (Eds.), *Brain, behavior, and learning in language and reading disorders* (pp.
    275–314). New York: Guilford Press.
Vygotsky, L. (1978). *Mind in society: Development of higher psychological pro-
    cesses* (M. Cole, V. John-Steiner, & S. Scribner, Trans.). Cambridge, MA:
    Harvard University Press.
Wilkinson, L., Morrow, L., & Chou, V. (2008a). *Improving literacy achievement
    in urban schools: Critical elements in teacher preparation*. Newark, DE:
    International Reading Association.
Wilkinson, L., Morrow, L., & Chou, V. (2008b). Policy, research, and socio-
    cultural issues affecting the preparation of teachers of reading for urban
    settings. In L. Wilkinson, L. Morrow, & V. Chou (Eds.), *Improving literacy
    achievement in urban schools: Critical elements in teacher preparation* (pp.
    1–11). Newark, DE: International Reading Association.
Wilkinson, L., & Silliman, E. (2008). Academic language proficiency and lit-
    eracy instruction in urban settings. In L.Wilkinson, L. Morrow, & V. Chou
    (Eds.), *Improving literacy achievement in urban schools: Critical elements
    in teacher preparedness* (pp. 121–142). Newark, DE: International Reading
    Association.
Wong Fillmore, L., & Snow, C. (2000, August). *What teachers need to know
    about language*. Retrieved February 26, 2009, from *faculty.tamu.commerce.
    edu/jthompson/Resources/FillmoreSnow2000.pdf*.

PART I

EARLY LANGUAGE EXPERIENCES AND SCHOOL READINESS

1

The Brain
and Language Acquisition

*Variation in Language Knowledge
and Readiness for Education*

Barbara T. Conboy

FOCUS POINTS

- Early brain development is characterized by a series of events that are influenced by experience and maturation; research has suggested that experience plays an important role in establishing brain organization for language functioning.

- Children raised in bilingual environments have varying experiences with each of their languages, and these variations are reflected in measures of brain activity. There is evidence that bilingual experience during early childhood affects brain structure and function.

- Professionals involved in developing language and literacy skills in young ELLs should consider that children might not be equally ready for learning to read in both languages, given different brain organization for each language that results from variations in experience.

CHAPTER PURPOSE

Educators are highly aware of individual differences across children in rates and styles of learning. Classroom walls display developmental milestone charts that reflect ranges in ages of skill acquisition, and teachers frequently advise parents to adjust their expectations to fit children's individual learning styles. But what do individual differences in behavior reflect about brain structure and function? Teachers and other educational professionals recognize that although brain structure is remarkably similar across humans, subtle variations in development can give rise to noticeable differences in behavior. And, they recognize that the brain continues to develop throughout childhood and across the lifespan. Yet many educators lack the background to interpret new findings in developmental cognitive neuroscience. This chapter aims to help bridge that gap, providing an overview of some recent research on brain development as it relates to language learning. By showing how maturation and experience mold the developing brain, research in developmental cognitive neuroscience can provide insights regarding individual differences in children's readiness to learn oral and written language skills. Such information is of particular relevance to the education of children raised with dual language experience, who have varying amounts and types of experience with each of their languages and may be at different levels of readiness to learn in each language.

REVIEW OF RESEARCH AND THEORY

Early in development, the brain undergoes rapid growth, with changes that pave the way for normal cognitive functioning and learning. Brain development has been described in terms of additive and regressive events that are hardwired and those that are subject to environmental influences (e.g., Gottlieb, 2007). A dynamic interplay between nature and nurture influences brain organization throughout childhood and, to some extent, the lifespan. Relationships between language learning and brain development may be best understood within a *neuroconstructivist* approach, according to which cognitive abilities emerge in response to bidirectional influences between neural and cognitive levels (Mareschal et al., 2007; Westermann et al., 2007). This section provides a summary of how brain development both constrains and is influenced by experience with language (for a more extensive review, see Bates, Thal, Finlay, & Clancy, 2003).

Prenatal Brain Development and Learning

The major additive events of brain development that occur prenatally are *neurogenesis* (the formation of neurons) and *synaptogenesis* (the formation of connections between neurons, or synapses). Connections between neurons consist of two types of processes that extend from the cell body: axons, which transmit electrochemical signals away from the cell body, and dendrites, which receive electrochemical signals from the axons of other neurons (Figure 1.1). A synapse is the gap between the axon of one neuron and the region of a connecting neuron where it receives information from that axon (that neuron's dendrites or cell body). During the first two trimesters of gestation, neurons form, differentiate into particular subtypes, express neurotransmitters and neuromodulators, migrate to particular destinations in the brain, and begin producing axons and dendrites. Almost adult-like patterns of connections between the cerebral cortex (the outer layers of the cerebrum, primarily involved in higher cognitive functions, Figure 1.2) and the thalamus (a region of the brain below the cortex that receives input from peripheral sensory systems, such as visual and auditory information) are laid down during the second trimester, whereas connections among areas of the cerebral cortex are formed more gradually. A regressive event called *apoptosis* (programmed cell death) begins in the second trimester and continues into

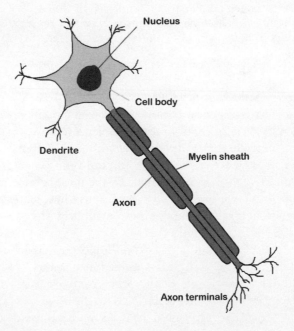

FIGURE 1.1. Schematic of a neuron. Based on *commons.wikimedia.org/wiki/File:Neuron1.jpg.*

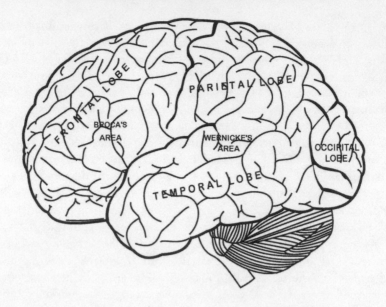

FIGURE 1.2. Schematic of the left cerebral cortex, depicting general locations of the frontal, temporal, parietal, and occipital lobes, as well as Broca's and Wernicke's areas. Based on *commons.wikimedia.org/wiki/File:Gray728. svg* and *commons.wikimedia.org/wiki/File:Brain_Surface_Gyri.SVG*.

the third, at the same time new neurons are formed. The overproduction and subsequent trimming away of neurons at this point in development takes place regardless of environmental influences. However, experience-dependent aspects of brain development do occur prenatally. During the second trimester, activity in the motor and visual systems establishes basic mechanisms for organizing input. By the third trimester, connectivity from higher to lower processing areas begins; thus, many foundations for learning are in place during the last few months of gestation (Clancy & Finlay, 2001).

Clancy and Finlay (2001) discuss an important distinction between "absolute functionality" and "task-specific functionality" of brain mechanisms: Although many areas of the brain are mature in structure and metabolic activity by the time of birth, immaturity in other brain areas prevents them from being recruited for tasks in the same way that mature adult brains use those areas for the same tasks. Moreover, learning is constrained by the physical environment. Examples of this latter point are found in studies that probe learning *in utero*. Fetal heart rate monitors show that by the third trimester, heart rates decrease in response to a familiar sound (habituation) and subsequently increase in response to a novel sound. For example, when women recited a nursery rhyme daily during the last few weeks of their pregnancies, their fetuses' heart rates showed habituation to the rhyme that was read but not to an unfamiliar rhyme (DeCasper, Lecanuet, Busnel, Granier-Deferre, & Maugeais, 1994). Given that acoustic frequencies above 500 hertz (Hz) are filtered out by the uterine environment, fetuses may tune into features of speech present in the low frequencies, such as pitch contours, rhythm, and stress patterns, but not higher-frequency information that cues distinctions between vowel and consonant sounds (for a review, see Moon & Fifer, 2000).

Evidence that language learning relying on low-frequency acoustic information occurs prior to birth has been provided by studies of newborn infants. One behavioral technique used with infants is high-amplitude sucking (HAS), in which a non-nutritive sucking response is registered using a pacifier connected to a transducer. Infants learn to time their sucking responses to activate delivery of a preferred auditory stimulus. HAS studies have shown that 2-day-old infants prefer their native language to an unfamiliar language that has a different rhythmic pattern (Nazzi, Bertoncini, & Mehler, 1998), and that newborn infants recognize stories their mothers read aloud during the last 6 weeks of pregnancy as opposed to similar stories not read, even when the stories are read in an unfamiliar voice (DeCasper & Spence, 1986). Therefore, although limited by physical aspects of the uterine environment, late-term fetal brains can process and encode important characteristics of speech and store this information in memory.

Studies of preterm infants conducted soon after birth also suggest that the auditory perceptual system is considerably advanced by the late gestational period. Cheour and colleagues (1998) used the event-related potential (ERP) technique in which electrodes placed on the scalp record postsynaptic electrical activity produced by cortical neurons in response to particular stimuli. In this research, an auditory "oddball" mismatch paradigm was used to test infants' discrimination of two vowels: one vowel served as a standard stimulus (repeated at constant intervals) and the other as a deviant stimulus (randomly presented 10% of the time within the stream of standards). Infants born preterm (30–35 weeks conceptual age at the time of testing) showed a discriminatory response to the deviant sounds in the form of larger amplitude voltage to deviants versus standards from 200 to 500 milliseconds (msec) after the onset of the vowel. This response was similar, though not identical, to that shown by full-term newborns, 3-month-old infants, and adults using the same stimuli. It is important to note that the acoustic difference between the vowels used in this research was in the high frequencies (above 1,700 Hz). Therefore, though 30- to 35-week-old fetuses cannot hear frequencies above 500 Hz *in utero*, their brains can process that information once exposed to a full range of speech sounds outside the uterus. Numerous studies have found that infants begin life able to perceive fine-grained distinctions between speech sounds and that perception is subsequently shaped by exposure to the language of the community. This work is discussed later in this chapter.

Postnatal Growth and Pruning

A sharp increase in the rate of synaptogenesis across cortical areas is seen around the time of birth and continues into the early postnatal months. During this burst, changes in the kinds of synaptic connections being created—a decline in the formation of synapses that tend to be excitatory along with stable production of synapses that tend to be inhibitory—result in a balance that may be related to the coordination of perception and action during infancy (Clancy & Finlay, 2001). Coordination between perception and action is thought to be important for social–cognitive and language development. For example, infants match vowel sounds to other speakers' mouth shapes and may use correspondences between audio and visual information to match their vocalizations to those of caregivers (Best & McRoberts, 2003; Kuhl, 2007).

The acceleration in synaptogenesis that occurs around birth slows several months later and is followed by a regressive event known as *synaptic pruning*. As the metaphor implies, pruning refers to the elimination of unnecessary synapses and is essential for proper brain function. The balance between synaptogenesis and pruning determines synaptic densities of different areas of the cortex, which exceed adult values within 6 months to several years of age, and subsequently decline (see Clancy & Finlay, 2001). Whereas acceleration in synaptogenesis around birth appears to happen independently of experience, later synaptogenesis, pruning, and neurogenesis are experience-dependent processes. Experience-dependent synaptogenesis was first reported in rodents reared in enriched versus austere cages; later studies showed that multiple synapses form in adult animals in response to learning situations, that neurogenesis occurs in adult brains, and that new neurons become functional in response to challenging situations (for review, see van Praag, Kempermann, & Gage, 2000). Studies of this type with humans are limited for methodological reasons, but results with rodents are believed to apply to humans.

At the same time unnecessary synapses are pruned away, regularly used pathways become surrounded by fatty sheaths (*myelin*) that assist in the transmission of impulses between neurons (Figure 1.1). The efficiency of language processing may rely on the myelination of axons that connect language areas (Aslin & Schlagger, 2006; Pujol et al., 2006). There are also changes throughout development in the amounts and types of neurotransmitters and neuromodulators available for synaptic functioning, and these variations may play a role in children's readiness to learn particular aspects of language at certain points (Clancy & Finlay, 2001).

The experience-dependent aspects of brain development suggest that differences across populations of children in brain structure and/ or function may result from previous learning as well as cause difficulties in future learning. This possibility has profound consequences for children with language-based learning disabilities and for children raised in diverse learning environments. In the first case, a genetically based predisposition that alters some aspect of early brain development could diminish an individual's readiness to learn from the environment—which in turn could affect subsequent experience-driven aspects of brain development, further diminishing learning and widening the gap between the affected individual and typically developing peers. In the second case, a normally developing brain could be altered in response to even small variations in experience. For children learning two languages, differences in experience with each language could lead to slightly different patterns of activity for the functioning of each language, affecting subsequent learning. This possibility is discussed in more detail below.

Functional Specializations for Language Processing

Insights from Studies of Adults

Language deficits in adults with focal brain injury and functional imaging studies with healthy adults have demonstrated that different regions of the brain play distinct roles in language functioning (for a review, see Hickok & Poeppel, 2004). Functional specializations for language are reflected in relative variations in the amounts of brain activity linked to different aspects of language processing, not to complete confinement of activity to one brain region. Studies of adults with acquired receptive and/or expressive language problems secondary to brain lesions (*aphasia*) have shown how damage to particular areas selectively disrupts specific aspects of language processing. Acquired language disorders characterized by halting speech, errors with grammatical conventions such as word order and verb forms, and word-finding problems are called "non-fluent" or "Broca's" aphasia, whereas those characterized by speech that is fluent and free of grammatical errors but full of misuses of words and comprehension deficits are known as "fluent" or "Wernicke's" aphasia. Lesions to the left inferior frontal area of the cortex ("Broca's area") typically result in Broca's aphasia, and those to the left superior temporal area ("Wernicke's area"), in Wernicke's aphasia (see Figure 1.2). However, because language processing relies on wide networks across the brain rather than discrete regions, symptoms do not always map onto lesion sites in a clear, one-to-one fashion (Dronkers, Wilkins, Van Valin, Redfern, & Jaeger, 2004). Moreover, left-hemisphere specialization for language is not observed in all adults, and right-hemisphere areas are also important for certain aspects of language processing.

Imaging studies have provided further information about which brain areas are involved in various aspects of language processing. Functional magnetic resonance imaging (fMRI) and ERPs are the techniques most widely used in language-processing research (see Dehaene-Lambertz, Hertz-Pannier, & Dubois, 2006). In fMRI, hemodynamic (blood flow) responses of brain regions that occur several seconds after the firing of neurons indirectly measure brain activity. Due to this lapse of several seconds, fMRI does not measure brain activity with precise temporal accuracy, but is remarkably good at localizing primary regions of activation (Heeger & Reiss, 2002). In contrast, because ERPs are obtained by averaging together numerous epochs of brain electrical activity that are time-locked to the onset of a stimulus, they provide direct records of neural responses to those stimuli and yield information about language processing on a millisecond-by-millisecond basis. Because electrical potentials spread through the skull before they are recorded at the scalp, ERPs do not offer precise information about where processing occurs, though the location of sources may be inferred using mathematical algorithms (see Luck, 2005, for discussion).

Several other functional brain-imaging techniques exist, but they are less frequently used for studying language processing. Magnetoencephalography (MEG), in which magnetic fields created by neural activity are measured at the scalp, is ideally suited for studying language processing because it has the same high temporal sensitivity as ERP but better spatial sensitivity, given that magnetic fields are not distorted before they reach the scalp (Hari, Levänen, & Raij, 2000). However, MEG has high operating costs. Other functional brain-imaging techniques include positron emission tomography (PET), single photon emission computed tomography (SPECT), and transcranial magnetic stimulation (TMS), but these are somewhat invasive and are not used with infants and children. Near infrared spectroscopy (NIRS), which noninvasively measures neural activity indirectly by assessing changes in hemoglobin levels using infrared light, is just beginning to be used in developmental studies (Aslin & Mehler, 2005).

Developmental Patterns

In children, adult patterns of functional specialization for language are not consistently observed. As with adults, insights about functional specializations for language in children come from cases of brain injury. Children who sustained focal brain lesions pre- or perinatally exhibit significant delays in early language development, regardless of whether the lesion was in the left or right hemisphere (Thal, Reilly, Seibert, Jeffries, & Fenson, 2004). By school age, these children tend to have language test scores in the normal range, although subtle deficits continue to be noted (Bates & Roe, 2001). Brain injury later in childhood is more likely to follow the adult pattern, in which more severe language deficits result from left- than from right-hemisphere lesions.

Evidence of developmental changes in functional specialization for language also comes from brain-imaging studies. Both ERP and fMRI studies of newborn infants have indicated that left-hemisphere temporal areas may be biased for processing auditory stimuli that have rapidly changing acoustic information, such as speech sounds (e.g., Dehaene-Lambertz et al., 2006). Over the first year, there are shifts in how speech sounds are processed. Early behavioral studies, in which infants were conditioned to turn their heads toward a reinforcing toy each time they detected a change from one speech sound to another, indicated that infants discriminated speech-sound contrasts from both their native and non-native languages at 6–8 months, but only native contrasts at 10–12 months (Werker & Tees, 1984). This pattern of developmental change linked to language experience was replicated in subsequent behavioral studies, and later in ERP studies (for reviews, see Cheour, Leppanen, & Kraus, 2000; Conboy, Rivera-Gaxiola, Silva-Pereyra, & Kuhl, 2008). As mentioned above, brain discriminatory responses can be measured using an ERP oddball paradigm in which a deviant syllable is inserted into a stream of repeated standard stimuli. The brain's detection of the change in stimulus is reflected in increases in the amplitude of the neural activity to the deviant versus standard stimuli. More recent work has shown that as infants' non-native sound perception declines, perception of native language sounds improves, in behavior (Kuhl et al., 2006) and in ERP responses (Rivera-Gaxiola, Silva-Pereyra, & Kuhl, 2005). MEG data also show that a coupling of activity between left superior-temporal (Wernicke's) and inferior-frontal (Broca's) areas in response to speech sounds emerges during the first year, possibly reflecting a functional link between brain areas underlying speech perception and production (Imada et al., 2006). Brain activity in response to different types of words also changes with experience. In a series of studies (reviewed in Mills & Conboy, 2009), Mills and colleagues recorded the brain activity of mono-lingual infants of different ages while they passively listened to words they understood and to unknown words. Infants as young as 9 months showed larger ERP amplitudes to known versus unknown words by 200 msec after the onset of the word. Younger infants (13- to 17-month-olds) showed the effects bilaterally, whereas older infants (20-month-olds) showed effects only at electrodes placed at left-hemisphere temporal and parietal sites. Moreover, infants with larger vocabularies showed more focal ERP responses, and when infants learned new words in meaningful contexts, a more focalized response to those words emerged (Mills, Plun-kett, Prat, & Schafer, 2005). Despite the poor spatial resolution of ERPs, such findings at least indicate a functional specialization.

Bilingual Development

Most research on how the young brain responds to language stimuli has been limited to monolingual developmental situations. Children raised with two languages provide a natural experiment in how brain development is linked to language experience because they typically learn each language from different speakers and in different situations. Conboy and Mills (2006) recorded ERPs to known and unknown Eng-lish and Spanish words from 19- to 22-month-old bilingual toddlers. All children were learning English and Spanish simultaneously, but in a variety of ways. Each child's dominant language was determined based on two sets of parent-report data. First, parents completed a question-naire in which they answered questions about their children's exposure to each language across a range of activities. Second, parents completed the vocabulary checklist of the MacArthur–Bates Communicative Devel-opment Inventories (CDI) in English (Fenson et al., 1993) and Spanish (Jackson-Maldonado et al., 2003). ERPs to known and unknown words were compared for each child's dominant and nondominant languages. For both languages, ERP amplitudes were significantly larger for the known versus unknown words, as reported for monolingual infants and toddlers. However, the patterns varied for the same children's dominant and nondominant languages; this can be explained only by experiential factors, not brain maturation. For children's dominant language, the ERP effects were evident by 200 msec after the onset of the word. For the nondominant language, only children with larger combined (English and Spanish) vocabulary sizes showed ERP effects by 200 msec after the onset of the word; children with smaller combined vocabulary sizes did not show effects until almost 400 msec later. In comparison, monolingual children show familiar–unfamiliar word effects by 200 msec, even as young as 11 months of age and regardless of vocabulary size (Mills, Coffey-Corina, & Neville, 1997; Thierry, Vihman, & Roberts, 2003). More rapid processing of words from bilingual children's dominant versus nondominant language may reflect word familiarity and ease of lexical access.

Unlike monolingual children of the same age, bilingual toddlers showed effects that were broadly distributed across the brain, rather than limited to left electrode sites. In this sense, the distribution of brain activity of bilingual 19- to 22-month-olds was more similar to that of 13- to 17-month-old monolingual infants, supporting the hypothesis that the organization of brain activity for language processing is influenced by infants' experience with particular words. Although there is no evidence that bilingualism hinders early language learning, the nature of bilingual lexical learning leads to initially smaller vocabularies in *each separate language* than for monolingual learners of those same languages (Pearson, Fernández, Lewedeg, & Oller, 1997). Bilingual children often learn words according to the language used in particular activities; thus children whose home language differs from the school language might know many different words in each of their two languages but few words with the same meaning in both. Therefore, the differences noted in brain activity across bilingual and monolingual 20-month-old toddlers should not be interpreted as evidence for a delay induced by bilingualism but rather a distinct developmental pattern linked to experience with each language.

Another possible reason why bilingual children's processing is different from that of monolingual peers is that they learn conflicting sets of cues for each language. For example, the ways in which speech sounds are produced in words vary across languages. Many English disyllabic words have a stress pattern in which the initial syllable is of longer duration and higher intensity (loudness) than the second syllable (e.g., "mommy"). Initial consonants in English words are thus perceptually salient and provide a fairly reliable cue to the beginnings of words in ongoing speech, which helps listeners recognize individual words. This emphasis on the initial parts of words is not as common in all languages. Research that used both behavioral and ERP methods to test infants' recognition of English and Welsh words showed that the stress patterns of each language accounted for distinct results across learners (Vihman, Thierry, Lum, Keren-Portnoy, & Martin, 2007). Monolingual Welsh-learning infants did not show recognition of consonant-initial words at any point between 9 and 12 months of age, but monolingual English-learning infants did so by 10 months, reflecting the stronger cues to word onset provided by initial consonants in English compared to Welsh. Bilin-gual English–Welsh infants recognized both English and Welsh words by 11 months, a pattern intermediate to those of the monolingual infants. These results suggest that bilingual infants learning English and another language with a different stress pattern (e.g., French, Spanish, Welsh) may temporarily reduce attention to initial consonants in words from both languages (see also Fennell, Byers-Heinlein, & Werker, 2007). How-ever, this finding does not reflect a delay induced by bilingualism, because bilingual infants outperformed monolingual Welsh infants.

Research on speech-sound discrimination in infants has also shown how behaviors and brain responses that are shaped by the characteris-tics of bilingual input masquerade as delays when compared to a mono-lingual standard. Bilingual infants raised in Barcelona (with input in Catalan and Spanish) showed behavioral evidence of discriminating two Catalan vowel sounds at 4 and 12 months but not at 8 months of age (Bosch & Sebastián-Galles, 2003). The vowels tested, /e/ and /ɛ/ (similar to the vowels in the English words "raid" and "red"), exist in Catalan, but in Spanish there is a single vowel, the acoustic values of which lie between those for the Catalan vowels (the Spanish /e/). The authors inter-preted the bilingual infants' behavior as reflecting a temporary perceptual merging of the Catalan vowels with the Spanish vowel that is acousti-cally between them. The research also showed that monolingual Catalan-learning infants, who hear the two Catalan vowels without perceptual interference from the Spanish vowel, discriminated the Catalan vowels at all ages tested. Separation of acoustic cues in language input has been shown to facilitate perceptual learning of vowel categories (Liu, Kuhl, & Tsao, 2003), thus the bilingual and monolingual infants responded in predictable ways given their input. Whether uniquely bilingual ways of perceiving speech continue throughout the lifespan is a topic of ongoing research (see Flege & MacKay, 2004; García-Sierra, Diehl, & Champlin, 2009). The fact that the oldest bilingual infants discriminated the Cata-lan vowel contrast suggests that continued experience with the language

allows infants to overcome a temporary lapse in discrimination performance.

Some studies show similar discrimination across bilingual and monolingual infant learners of the same languages at the same ages (Burns,
Yoshida, Hill, & Werker, 2007; Sundara, Polka, & Molnar, 2008). Conflicting results across studies of bilingual learners may be explained by
differences in the stimuli used, but they are also likely influenced by variations in the samples tested regarding relative amounts of experience with
each language (Conboy, Jackson-Maldonado, & Kuhl, 2009; García-
Sierra, Rivera-Gaxiola, Conboy, Romo, & Kuhl, 2008). For example,
García-Sierra and colleagues presented bilingual infants with English and
Spanish speech-sound contrasts in an ERP oddball paradigm. Infants
who heard more English in the home showed a larger neural discriminatory response for the English than for the Spanish contrast, whereas
infants who heard more Spanish at home showed the opposite pattern,
and infants with more balanced input across languages showed similar
discrimination for each language. Because that study was not designed
to directly compare bilingual and monolingual infants, it is not known
whether the brain activity of any of the three subgroups showed patterns
that were more closely related to that of monolingual infants the same
age.

The research reviewed above reminds us that regarding brain function and structure as well as behavior, "bilinguals are not two monolinguals in one" (Grosjean, 1989). The unique challenges faced by bilingual speakers lead them to develop abilities that are different from those
of monolinguals. In addition to sorting out conflicting cues to speech
sounds, word structure, and sentence structure, bilingual speakers frequently process language under mixed-language conditions. Translation
and code switching are uniquely bilingual behaviors and require skill
in both languages (see Reyes & Ervin-Tripp, Chapter 3, this volume).
Even at the earliest stages of acquiring a second language, learners must
inhibit one language's lexicon, or mental dictionary, in order to retrieve
words from the target language (Levy, McVeigh, Marful, & Anderson,
2006). Enhanced functioning on nonlinguistic tasks that require executive functions, such as working memory, inhibitory control, and the
ability to control attention to relevant versus irrelevant cues, is seen in
bilingual individuals as young as preschool and kindergarten age (e.g.,
Carlson & Meltzoff, 2008) and as old as later adulthood (Bialystok,
Craik, Klein, & Viswanathan, 2004). The attentional skills of infants are
also influenced by dual language experience (Kovács & Mehler, 2009).
Thus the cognitive demands of managing two languages, which may

result in slower access to words on receptive or expressive tasks, may also sharpen other abilities (Bialystok, 2009; Bialystok & Peets, Chapter 6, this volume).

The unique language behaviors and resultant cognitive abilities of individuals who are life-long bilinguals are reflected in brain structure and function. For example, bilingual adults showed increased density of gray matter (brain tissue consisting of nerve cells and fibers) in inferior parietal areas of the cerebral cortex when compared to monolingual adults (Mechelli et al., 2004). This enhancement was more pronounced in individuals who were bilingual from infancy, in those who were highly proficient in both languages, and in the left versus right hemisphere. Other research using fMRI with bilingual adults has shown that language-related brain activity is also influenced by how much individuals use each language on a daily basis (Perani et al., 2003). In the research on bilingual toddlers conducted by Conboy and Mills (2006), children showed more enhanced neural activity at right- versus left-hemisphere frontal electrode sites while processing words in their dominant language. This pattern was only observed in toddlers who were tested in a condition in which words randomly switched between English and Spanish. A group of bilingual toddlers tested in a condition in which words were presented separately for each language did not show the larger effect at right frontal sites, and there was evidence that they processed words more quickly. In other respects, their ERP patterns resembled those of the bilingual toddlers tested in the language-switching condition. Thus, the increased cognitive load imposed by switching between languages may have recruited additional neural tissue, as well as slowed processing. Most importantly, the results suggest that additional processing time and resources may be needed when both languages are activated. Current research is examining how bilingual children's brains process language under switched conditions, and how that relates to other cognitive skills (Conboy, Sommerville, Wicha, & Kuhl, 2010).

It is important to remember that although there are some differences between bilingual and monolingual language learning and processing, there are many similarities. In both cases, language learning requires experience with language and *takes time*. Even when two languages are acquired simultaneously, development in each proceeds in mostly language-specific ways, and children are often at different levels of readiness to learn in each (for a review, see De Houwer, 2009). This means that educators should not expect children to automatically transfer knowledge gained in one language to the other language. For example, Conboy and Thal (2006) examined changes in vocabulary composition and grammar in English–Spanish bilingual toddlers and found an association between vocabulary and grammatical development within each separate language, but not across languages (see also Marchman, Martínez-Sussman, & Dale, 2004). Gathercole (2007) reported that preschool children learning a second language did not simply apply grammatical rules to both languages, but showed separate patterns of learning for each language, resembling those seen in monolingual learners of each language.

BEST PRACTICES

As the fields of child development, cognitive neuroscience, and education increasingly work together to better understand the neural bases of language learning, practitioners benefit by being able to use that knowledge to provide optimal learning conditions for students. The foregoing research review on early brain development highlights the role of experience in shaping children's learning mechanisms, but also shows that we have only begun to understand the neural bases of learning. Caution must be taken to *not* overgeneralize and misinterpret findings in an effort to stimulate brain development at ages when plasticity is believed to be greatest.

Attempts to stimulate early brain development may result in activities that are not developmentally appropriate and are of questionable benefit. For example, prenatal stimulation should be approached with extreme caution, as the potential hazards are not yet completely understood (Moon & Fifer, 2000). Television programs and videos designed to enrich the learning environments of infants and toddlers should also be used cautiously. Although older children have been shown to learn vocabulary from educational programs (Evans Schmidt, Rich, Rifas-Shiman, Oken, & Taveras, 2009), viewing of educational videos before the age of 2 years has been linked to slower language development (Zimmerman, Christakis, & Meltzoff, 2007). There is evidence that infants do not learn about foreign-language speech sounds from videos but instead need live interaction with speakers of the language (Kuhl, Liu, & Tsao, 2003), and even then require high levels of engagement with those speakers (Conboy, Brooks, Taylor, Meltzoff, & Kuhl, 2008). Patterson (2002) reported that amounts of television viewing did not account for language learning in toddlers raised bilingually, but amounts of parent–child book-reading did. Educators and parents must be careful not to replace natural social-communicative activities with gimmicks that lack evidence of efficacy. Instead, adults can promote children's language learning by providing socially engaging interactions in which language is used (see Brisk, Chapter 7, this volume, for a similar point).

Misconceptions about sensitive or critical periods for language learning have also been used to support questionable educational practices and policies with young ELLs. It is widely believed that language learning is optimal during the early years of life and that a second language may best be learned within this optimal, or "critical," period. Although there is evidence that supports a critical or sensitive period for first-language acquisition (Mayberry & Lock, 2003; but see Bruer, 2008), the results are less clear with regard to second-language acquisition (Hakuta, 2001). Advocates of English-only educational approaches with minority language students in the United States have used ideas about critical periods and early brain plasticity to support their position, arguing that delaying children's learning of English will prevent optimal learning of English. One obvious problem with that argument is that it conflates the use of bilingual educational approaches with delays in the *onset* of English learning. Given that bilingualism is possible (and flourishes throughout the world), there is no logical reason to believe that maintenance of a first language and the initial learning of academic material in that language impedes acquisition of a second language. In fact, research has shown that ELL children benefit from transitional bilingual programs that allow them to gain the English skills needed for reading in English while learning the mechanics of reading in their dominant, primary language (Krashen & McField, 2005). Another problem with the idea of critical periods for second-language acquisition is the lack of evidence for a predetermined moment in time when the window of opportunity for learning is abruptly closed (Bialystok & Hakuta, 1994). There is no definitive evidence regarding an optimal age for introducing a second language.

Given the cognitive benefits of bilingualism reviewed in this chapter (and in Bialystok & Peets, Chapter 6, this volume), as well as the social benefits provided by the ability to communicate in another language, teachers of ELL children have good reason to encourage children's continued use of their primary language, and they have no scientifically based reason to discourage it. When the goal is the development of preliteracy skills, teachers can help children build on skills in their primary language. Several emergent literacy and metalinguistic skills have been shown to transfer from the first to the second language, including phonological awareness, print awareness, and word-learning skills (López & Greenfield, 2004; see also Newman, Chapter 5, this volume). At the same time, teachers should keep in mind that children's vocabulary, grammar, semantics, and speech-sound development may be at different levels for each language.

SUMMARY OF MAIN IDEAS

The research reviewed in the previous sections shows that language acquisition is influenced by developmental brain changes that are additive (neurogenesis and synaptogenesis) and regressive (apoptosis and synaptic pruning). Proper brain development is critical for language learning, which may start *in utero* during the third trimester when fetuses begin processing sounds. While some predetermined factors provide the basis for development, experience also shapes development. Exposure to a language determines which neural connections are strengthened, retained, or discarded and leads to further acquisition of that language. Language deficits in patients with brain injury and neural imaging studies with healthy individuals are showing that experience with language influences how the brain becomes organized for language processing and that such changes continue throughout the lifespan.

The growing use of functional brain-imaging techniques with simultaneous and sequential bilingual learners is also enhancing our knowledge of how unique aspects of dual-language processing develop. Although bilingual infants share many characteristics of language development with monolingual learners of the same languages, differences across groups have been noted for various aspects of language processing. Such differences should not be interpreted as delays caused by early bilingualism—they may only reflect additional areas being used for the unique aspects of dual-language processing. Differences in brain function and structure have also been noted in bilingual adults when compared to monolingual adults. There is good reason to expect differences between the brain development of ELL children and monolingual children, but the exact ones remain to be discovered from future research. As children acquire a second language, some degree of reorganization of brain function and structure is likely to occur. Research on bilingual language learning and processing suggests variability across learners and that monolingual models might not always be appropriate for bilingual learners. Methods that capitalize on children's first-language knowledge may be effective but also have limitations. Educators should take such information into account when deciding on appropriate instructional methods for bilingual children.

IMPLICATIONS FOR RESEARCH, PRACTICE, AND POLICY

The research reviewed in this chapter has shown that brain function and structure are shaped by the dynamic patterns of using one or more languages in one's daily life. Research using functional brain measures with young children is just beginning to flourish and can be expected to shed increasing light on relationships between language learning and brain development. Further research is needed to understand how individual differences across children in first-language development and brain organization relate to individual differences in second-language learning and processing.

Parents and teachers should respect their intuitions about children's readiness to learn when promoting language and literacy skills in young children. When working with young ELLs and children who are bilingual from birth, teachers should consider that these children might not be equally ready to learn the same things in each language. Different patterns of brain activity for processing each language are the consequence of different amounts of prior learning, but may also affect subsequent learning. ELL children who are in the process of becoming bilingual should not be expected to process information in ways that are identical to monolingual children. Educators can capitalize on the strengths of ELL children's skills in their first language, recognizing that children require adequate experience with a second language before they can use that language in the same ways as the first language.

REFERENCES

Aslin, R. N., & Mehler, J. (2005). Near-infrared spectroscopy for functional studies of brain activity in human infants: Promise, prospects, and challenges. *Journal of Biomedical Optics, 10*(1), 011009-1–011009-3.

Aslin, R. N., & Schlagger, B. L. (2006). Is myelination the precipitating neural event for language development in infants and toddlers? *Neurology, 66,* 304–305.

Bates, E., & Roe, K. (2001). Language development in children with unilateral brain injury. In C. A. Nelson & M. Luciana (Eds.), *Handbook of developmental cognitive neuroscience* (pp. 281–307). Cambridge, MA: MIT Press.

Bates, E., Thal, D., Finlay, B., & Clancy, B. (2003). Early language development and its neural correlates. In I. Rapin & S. Segalowitz (Eds.), *Handbook of neuropsychology: Vol. 6. Child neurology* (2nd ed., pp. 525—592). Amsterdam: Elsevier.

Best, C., & McRoberts, G. (2003). Infant perception of non-native consonant contrasts that adults assimilate in different ways. *Language and Speech, 46*, 183–216.

Bialystok, E. (2009). Bilingualism: The good, the bad, and the indifferent. *Bilingualism: Language and Cognition, 12*(1), 3–11.

Bialystok, E., Craik, F. I. M., Klein, R., & Viswanathan, M. (2004). Bilingualism, aging, and cognitive control: Evidence from the Simon task. *Psychology and Aging, 19*, 290–303.

Bialystok, E., & Hakuta, K. (1994). *In other words: The science and psychology of second-language acquisition.* New York: Basic Books.

Bosch, L., & Sebastián-Gallés, N. (2003). Simultaneous bilingualism and the perception of a language specific vowel contrast in the first year of life. *Language and Speech, 46*(2–3), 217–43.

Bruer, J. T. (2008). Critical periods in second language learning: Distinguishing phenomena from explanations. In. M. Mody & E. R. Silliman (Eds.), *Brain, behavior, and learning in language and reading disorders* (pp. 72—96). New York: Guilford Press.

Burns, T. C., Yoshida, K. A., Hill, K., & Werker, J. F. (2007). Bilingual and monolingual infant phonetic development. *Applied Psycholinguistics, 28*(3), 455–474.

Carlson, S. M., & Meltzoff, A. N. (2008). Bilingual experience and executive functioning in young children. *Developmental Science, 11*, 282–298.

Cheour, M., Alho, K., Ceponiene, R., Reinikainen, K., Sainio, K., Pohjavuori, M., et al. (1998). Maturation of mismatch negativity in infants. *International Journal of Psychophysiology, 29*(2), 217–226.

Cheour, M., Leppanen, P., & Kraus, N. (2000). Mismatch negativity (MMN) as a tool for investigating auditory discrimination and sensory memory in infants and children. *Clinical Neurophysiology, 111*, 4–16.

Clancy, B., & Finlay, B. (2001). Neural correlates of early language learning. In M. Tomasello & E. Bates (Eds.), *Language development: The essential readings* (pp. 307–330). Malden, MA: Blackwell.

Conboy, B. T., Brooks, R., Taylor, M., Meltzoff, A., & Kuhl, P. K. (2008, March). *Joint engagement with language tutors predicts brain and behavioral responses to second-language phonetic stimuli.* Poster presented at the biennial meeting of the International Society for Infant Studies, Vancouver, BC.

Conboy, B. T., Jackson-Maldonado, D., & Kuhl, P. K. (2009, November). *Speech perception in bilingual and monolingual infants.* Poster presented at the annual convention of the American Speech–Language–Hearing Association, New Orleans, LA.

Conboy, B. T., & Mills, D. L. (2006). Two languages, one developing brain: Effects of vocabulary size on bilingual toddlers' event-related potentials to auditory words. *Developmental Science, 9*(1), F1–F11.

Conboy, B. T., Rivera-Gaxiola, M., Silva-Pereyra, J. F., & Kuhl, P. K. (2008). Event-related potential studies of early language processing at the phoneme, word, and sentence levels. In A. D. Friederici & G. Thierry (Eds.), *Trends in language acquisition research series: Vol. 5. Early language development: Bridging brain and behaviour* (pp. 24–64). Amsterdam: Benjamins.

Conboy, B. T., Sommerville, J. T., Wicha, N., & Kuhl, P. K. (2010). *Language switching during word processing is linked to nonlinguistic cognitive control skills in bilingual toddlers: An event-related brain potentials study.* Manuscript in preparation.

Conboy, B. T., & Thal, D. J. (2006). Ties between the lexicon and grammar: Cross-sectional and longitudinal studies of bilingual toddlers. *Child Development, 77,* 712–735.

DeCasper, A. J., Lecanuet, J. P., Busnel, M. C., Granier-Deferre, C., & Maugeais, R. (1994). Fetal reactions to recurrent maternal speech. *Infant Behavior and Development, 17,* 159–164.

DeCasper, A. J., & Spence, M. J. (1986). Prenatal maternal speech influences newborns' perception of speech sounds. *Infant Behavior and Development, 9,* 133–150.

Dehaene-Lambertz, G., Hertz-Pannier, L., & Dubois, J. (2006). Nature and nurture in language acquisition: Anatomical and functional brain-imaging studies in infants. *Trends in Neurosciences, 29*(7), 367–373.

De Houwer, A. (2009). *Bilingual first language acquisition.* Bristol, UK: Multilingal Matters.

Dronkers, N. F., Wilkins, D. P., Van Valin, R. D., Jr., Redfern, B. B., & Jaeger, J. J. (2004). Lesion analysis of the brain areas involved in language comprehension. *Cognition, 92*(1–2), 145–177.

Evans Schmidt, M., Rich, M., Rifas-Shiman, S. L., Oken, E., & Taveras, E. M. (2009). Television viewing in infancy and child cognition at 3 years of age in a U. S. cohort. *Pediatrics, 123,* e370–e375.

Fennell, C. T., Byers-Heinlein, K., & Werker, J. F. (2007). Using speech sounds to guide word learning: The case of bilingual infants. *Child Development, 78*(5), 1510–1525.

Fenson, L., Dale, P. S., Reznick, J. S., Thal, D., Bates, E., Hartung, J., et al. (1993). *The MacArthur Communicative Development Inventories: User's guide and technical manual.* San Diego, CA: Singular Publishing Group.

Flege, J., & MacKay, I. (2004). Perceiving vowels in a second language. *Studies in Second Language Acquisition, 26,* 1–34.

García-Sierra, A., Diehl, R., & Champlin, C. (2009). Testing the double phonemic boundary in bilinguals. *Speech Communication, 51,* 369–378.

García-Sierra, A., Rivera-Gaxiola, M., Conboy, B., Romo, H., & Kuhl, P. K. (2009, February). *Social–cultural support for early bilingual language learning: A collaboration combining behavior, ethnography and neuroscience.* Paper presented at the second annual Inter-Science of Learning Centers conference, Seattle, WA.

Gathercole, V. C. M. (2007). Miami and North Wales, so far and yet so near: A constructivist account of morphosyntactic development in bilingual children. *International Journal of Bilingual Education and Bilingualism,10*(3), 224–247.

Gottlieb, G. (2007). Probabilistic epigenesis. *Developmental Science 10*(1), 1–11.

Grosjean, F. (1989). Neurolinguists, beware! The bilingual is not two monolinguals in one person. *Brain and Language, 36,* 3–15.

Hakuta, K. (2001). A critical period for second language acquisition? In D. Bailey, J. Bruer, F. Symons, & J. Lichtman (Eds.), *Critical thinking about critical periods* (pp. 193–205). Baltimore: Brookes.

Hari, R., Levänen, S., & Raij, T. (2000). Timing of human cortical functions during cognition: Role of MEG. *Trends in Cognitive Sciences, 4*(12), 455–462.

Heeger, D. J., & Reiss, D. (2002). What does fMRI tell us about neuronal activity? *Nature Reviews Neuroscience, 3*, 142–150.

Hickok, G., & Poeppel, D. (2004). Dorsal and ventral streams: A framework for understanding aspects of the functional anatomy of language. *Cognition, 92*, 67–99.

Imada, T., Zhang, Y., Cheour, M., Taulu, S., Ahonen, A., & Kuhl, P. K. (2006). Infant speech perception activates Broca's area: A developmental magneto-encephalography study. *NeuroReport, 17*, 957–962.

Jackson-Maldonado, D., Thal, D., Marchman, V., Fenson, L., Newton, T., & Conboy, B. (2003). *El Inventario del Desarrollo de Habilidades Comunicativas [The Communicative Development Inventory (Spanish version)]: User's guide and technical manual.* Baltimore: Brookes.

Kovács, M. A., & Mehler, J. (2009). Cognitive gains in 7–month-old bilingual infants. *Proceedings of the National Academy of Sciences, 106*(16), 6556–6560.

Krashen, S., & McField, G. (2005). What works?: Reviewing the latest evidence on bilingual education. *Language Learner 1*(2), 7–10, 34.

Kuhl, P. K. (2007). Is speech learning "gated" by the social brain? *Developmental Science, 10*, 110–120.

Kuhl, P. K., Conboy, B. T., Padden, D., Rivera-Gaxiola, M., & Nelson, T. (2008). Phonetic learning as a pathway to language: New data and native language magnet theory expanded (NLM-e). *Philosophical Transactions of the Royal Society B, 363*, 979–1000.

Kuhl, P. K., Stevens, E., Hayashi, A., Deguchi, T., Kiritani, S., & Iverson, P. (2006). Infants show a facilitation effect for native language phonetic perception between 6 and 12 months. *Developmental Science, 9*, F13–F21.

Kuhl, P. K., Tsao, F. M., & Liu, H. M. (2003). Foreign-language experience in infancy: Effects of short-term exposure and social interaction on phonetic learning. *Proceedings of the National Academy of Science, 100*(15), 9096–9101.

Levy, B. J., McVeigh, N. D., Marful, A., & Anderson, M. C. (2007). Inhibiting your native language: The role of retrieval-induced forgetting during second-language acquisition. *Psychological Science, 18*, 29–34.

Liu, H.-M., Kuhl, P. K., & Tsao, F.-M. (2003). An association between mothers' speech clarity and infants' speech discrimination skills. *Developmental Science, 6*(3), F1–F10.

López, L. M., & Greenfield, D. B. (2004). The cross-language transfer of phonological skills of Hispanic Head Start children. *Bilingual Research Journal, 28*, 1–18.

Luck, S. J. (2005). *An introduction to the event-related potential technique.* Cambridge, MA: MIT Press.

Marchman, V. A., Martínez-Sussmann, C., & Dale, P. S. (2004). The language-specific nature of grammatical development: Evidence from bilingual language learners. *Developmental Science, 7*(2), 212–224.

Mareschal, D., Johnson, M. H., Sirois, S., Spratling, M. W., Thomas, M. S. C., & Westermann, G. (2007). *Neuroconstructivism: How the brain constructs cognition.* Oxford, UK: Oxford University Press.

Mayberry, R. I., & Lock, E. (2003). Age constraints on first versus second language acquisition: Evidence for linguistic plasticity and epigenesis. *Brain and Language, 87,* 369–384.

Mechelli, A., Crinion, J. T., Noppeney, U., O'Doherty, J., Ashburner, J.,, Frackowiak, R. S., et al. (2004). Structural plasticity in the bilingual brain: Proficiency in a second language and age at acquisition affect grey matter density. *Nature, 431,* 757.

Mills, D. L., Coffey-Corina, S., & Neville, H. J. (1997). Language comprehension and cerebral specialization from 13 to 20 months. *Developmental Neuropsychology, 13,* 397–445.

Mills, D., & Conboy, B. T. (2009). Early communicative development and the social brain. In M. de Haan & M. R. Gunnar (Eds.), *Handbook of developmental social neuroscience* (pp. 175–206). New York: Guilford Press.

Mills, D., Plunkett, K., Prat, C., & Schafer, G. (2005). Watching the infant brain learn words: Effects of language and experience. *Cognitive Development, 20,* 19–31.

Moon, C. M., & Fifer, W. P. (2000). The fetus: Evidence of transnatal auditory learning. *Journal of Perinatology, 20,* S36–S43.

Nazzi, T., Bertoncini, J., & Mehler, J. (1998). Language discrimination by newborns: Toward an understanding of the role of rhythm. *Journal of Experimental Psychology: Human Perception and Performance, 24*(3), 1–11.

Patterson, J. L. (2002). Relationships of expressive vocabulary to frequency of reading and television experience among bilingual toddlers. *Applied Psycholinguistics, 23*(4),493–508.

Pearson, B. Z., Fernández, S., Lewedeg, V., & Oller, D. K. (1997). The relation of input factors to lexical learning by bilingual toddlers. *Applied Psycholinguistics, 18,* 41–58.

Perani, D., Abutalebi, J., Paulesu, E., Brambati, P. S., Cappa, S. F., & Fazio, F. (2003). The role of age of acquisition and language usage in early, high-proficient bilinguals: An fMRI study during verbal fluency. *Human Brain Mapping, 19,* 170–182.

Pujol, J., Soriano-Mas, C., Ortiz, H., Sebastián-Gallés, N., Losilla, J. M., & Deus, J. (2006). Myelination of language-related areas in the developing brain. *Neurology, 66,* 339–343.

Rivera-Gaxiola, M., Silva-Pereyra, J., & Kuhl, P. K. (2005). Brain potentials to native and non-native speech contrasts in 7– and 11–month-old American infants. *Developmental Science, 8,* 162–172.

Sundara, M., Polka, L., & Molnar, M. (2008). Development of coronal stop perception: Bilingual infants keep pace with their monolingual peers. *Cognition, 108,* 232–242.

Thal, D. J., Reilly, J., Seibert, L., Jeffries, R., & Fenson, J. (2004). Language development in children at risk of language impairment: Cross-population comparisons. *Brain and Language, 88,* 167–179.

Thierry G., Vihman M., & Roberts M. (2003). Familiar words capture the attention of 11–month-olds in less than 250 ms. *NeuroReport, 14,* 2307–2310.

van Praag, H., Kempermann, G ., & Gage F. H. (2000). Neural consequences of environmental enrichment. *Nature Reviews Neuroscience, 1,* 191–198.

Vihman, M. M., Thierry, G., Lum, J., Keren-Portnoy, T., & Martin, P. (2007). Onset of word form recognition in English, Welsh, and English–Welsh bilingual infants. *Applied Psycholinguistics, 28,* 475–493.

Werker, J. F., & Tees, R. C. (1984). Cross-language speech perception: Evidence for perceptual reorganization during the first year of life. *Infant Behavior and Development, 7,* 49–63.

Westermann, G., Mareschal, D., Johnson, M. H., Sirois, S., Spratling, M. W., & Thomas, M. S. C. (2007). Neuroconstructivism. *Developmental Science 10*(1), 75–83.

Zimmerman, F. J., Christakis, D. A., & Meltzoff, A. N. (2007). Associations between media viewing and language development in children under age 2 years. *Journal of Pediatrics, 151,*364–368.

2

The Process of Acquiring a First and Second Language

Kathryn Kohnert
Giang Pham

FOCUS POINTS

- Language acquisition is a product of ongoing interactions between internal child factors and the environment. These factors are described as MOM—the means, opportunities, and motive for language acquisition (Kohnert, 2009).

- Children enter elementary educational programs with several years of experience in language, although the quality and quantity of these early language experiences and resulting skill level vary considerably.

- Most minority first-language learners in the United States attend educational programs in which English is the primary language of instruction, thereby requiring children to simultaneously acquire spoken and written English.

- Consistent with the response-to-intervention (RTI) mandate, the process of English language acquisition is facilitated when educators provide children with multiple opportunities to engage with meaningful language through the combined use of enhanced teacher talk, peer-mediated learning activities, technology, and community collaborations.

- For minority language learners in the United States, positive long-term social, emotional, and academic outcomes are strengthened when home language skill is supported along with English.

CHAPTER PURPOSE

Children acquire language under a wide variety of circumstances. Some children learn only one language during childhood whereas others acquire two languages from infancy. Young, internationally adopted children quickly replace a single first language with a second language, becoming competent monolingual speakers of the language used in their new homes and community. Many other children learn a single home language beginning at birth (L1) and a second language (L2) in early childhood. In some cases L1 is the majority language of the community and L2 is acquired in formal immersion educational programs designed to promote proficiency in a "foreign" or second national language. In the United States many English-speaking families opt to enroll their children in educational programs in which French, Spanish, Hebrew, or Chinese is the language of instruction during the primary grades.

Our focus is on a different type of young L2 learners—children who acquire a single minority L1 at home with immersion in the majority community language (L2) beginning in childhood, often with attendance in formal educational programs. The use of the term *minority language* implies that there are fewer opportunities to develop and use these languages as well as less social value associated with skill in these first languages within the majority community. Minority L1 learners in the United States are from homes in which Spanish, Vietnamese, Somali, Hmong, Tagalog, Urdu, or one of hundreds of different languages is spoken. Both home and community languages play important, complementary, and continuous roles in these children's lives. L1 and L2 acquisition under these circumstances is highly variable in terms of factors that influence language development and the L1–L2 proficiency profile over time, presenting educators and policymakers with significant practical challenges. Although minority L1 learners in the United States are most often referred to in the educational literature as *English language learners* or *ELLs*, we also use the term *early sequential bilinguals* to emphasize the continued importance of L1 in addition to L2.

The purpose of this chapter is to describe major aspects of language acquisition in early sequential bilinguals. We focus on children in the United States who learn a minority L1 from birth, with consistent experience in English beginning with attendance in educational programs. In the first section we describe general interacting factors that affect language acquisition and then summarize findings related to patterns of language change in sequential bilinguals and relationships between L1 and L2. Next we link these conceptual frameworks and empirical findings to pedagogy, describing strategies educators may use to support skills in L1 and L2. We conclude with a summary of main points and a discussion of implications for research, practice, and policy.

REVIEW OF RESEARCH AND THEORY

Language Acquisition: Conceptual Framework and Empirical Evidence

Language is our most valuable, efficient, and effective communication tool. It consists of formal symbols—sounds, words, and grammatical inflections—combined in specific ways to communicate the range of human thoughts and feelings, from the mundane to the sublime. Even for monolingual children, language acquisition is an extended process, beginning at or before birth and continuing through adolescence. Different aspects of language acquisition come online at different developmental periods and progress at different rates. Young children first learn to talk, mapping linguistic symbols onto communicative functions in conventional ways, while interacting with others in their environment. By the time typically developing children from literate, middle-income families enter kindergarten at about age 5, they know several thousand words and most of the sounds and sound patterns of their native language, and they speak in long, largely grammatical sentences to express a wide range of social purposes (e.g., Hirsh-Pasek & Golinkoff, 2003). As language is mastered, it becomes a powerful tool for learning about the world (Shatz, 2007).

Spoken language acquisition, literacy, and academic achievement are fundamentally linked. Oral language is used throughout formal education programs to learn about world events, science, math, and even about language itself. Children with better oral language skills make faster progress in acquiring literacy skills during the early elementary school years (e.g., National Early Literacy Panel, 2006). Better readers do better in school and graduate at higher rates. Higher levels of education are linked to better vocational and economic outcomes, which benefit the community as well as the next generation of learners. As with spoken language, once children learn to read, they then use this facility with the printed word to explore and learn in other areas. With continued language and world experience, bidirectional links between spoken language and literacy are enhanced.

Proficiency or ability in a particular language is related to, but not quite the same as, general language proficiency. *General language profi-*

ciency refers to the ability to use a complex symbol system efficiently in conventional ways for meaningful communication. Reduced proficiency in a specific language, alongside relatively stronger or age-appropriate skills in another language, may be due to reduced experiences or opportunities to learn or use that language. At least three general factors interact to affect general proficiency in language as well as acquisition in specific first and second languages, such as Spanish and English. These three general factors are means, opportunities, and motive, or *MOM* (Kohnert, 2009). As a conceptual framework for L1 and L2 acquisition, MOM is summarized in Table 2.1. The first *M* refers to internal resources of the learner that affect language acquisition, including the integrity of cognitive, sensory, and neurobiological systems. Weaknesses in any of these systems may undermine the child's ability to acquire any or all languages efficiently. For example, congenital hearing loss, mental retardation, acquired brain injury, or subtle weaknesses in the underlying cognitive–linguistic processing system may present challenges to the timely acquisition of language. For bilingual children, weaknesses in basic internal mechanisms affect both L1 and L2 acquisition.

The *O* in *MOM* refers to opportunities, including the availability of rich language in the environment and diverse opportunities to develop or use a particular language for meaningful communicative interactions. For English-only learning children in the United States there are strong links between family income level (presumably correlated with educational and literacy levels) and the quantity and quality of language available in young children's home environment (e.g., Hoff, 2003). Language opportunities in the environment (i.e., input) exert a significant effect on

TABLE 2.1. Language Acquisition and MOM

M eans

Internal resources of learner: Integrity of cognitive, sensory, social, emotional, and neurobiological systems—any breach in the integrity of one or more of these systems may challenge language acquisition and use.

O pportunity

Social factors, including availability of rich language in the environment and diverse opportunities to develop and use a particular language for meaningful communicative interactions.

M otive

Interactions between internal and external resources, environmental needs, opportunities, as well as personal preferences that are linked to social contexts.

Note. The conceptual framework is adapted from Kohnert (2009).

the learning of important aspects of language. Hart and Risley (1995) found that children from "working-" and "professional-class" families received two to three times more input than children from families whose income qualified them to receive public assistance. Additionally, children who received greater language input also heard more praise and far fewer reprimands. In turn, children who received more and higher-quality input when they were younger had larger vocabularies and better academic achievement at school age (Hart & Risley, 1995). Similarly, Huttenlocher and colleagues found that preschool children attending Head Start programs produced more grammatically complex sentences when their teachers were trained to use more complex sentences and engage in child-directed discourse (Huttenlocher, Vasilyeva, Cymerman, & Levine, 2002). Multiple opportunities to hear and use quality language within responsive social contexts provide the exogenous elements critical to first-language acquisition. For sequential bilingual children, increased opportunities to use L1 or L2 for meaningful interactions facilitate ability in that linguistic code as well as elevate the general language foundation. When opportunities are insufficient, as is the case with environmental deprivation, the child's general language system may be weak. Limited opportunities or experiences in either L1 or L2 hinder development of that particular language, despite intact general language learning mechanisms (Table 2.1).

The final *M* in the *MOM* framework refers to motive. Motive reflects interactions between child-internal and -external resources; between environmental needs and opportunities as well as personal preferences interwoven within social contexts. For sequential bilingual children, motive and opportunities to use language for rich, meaningful interactions tend to go hand in hand. Often one language is needed with parents, siblings, and/or grandparents at home and a different language is needed with peers, teachers, and staff at school. Another important aspect of motive is the social status or prestige associated with particular languages. As the most valuable currency in the United States, English looms large in terms of motivation. In contrast, native home languages are often undervalued in the United States, which may undercut the motivation to use L1, at least for youth who are also shifting their primary sphere of social influence from family to peers and the broader community.

In summary, means, opportunity, and motive interact in complex ways to account for successful language acquisition (Kohnert, 2008, 2009). For sequential bilingual children, when MOM is sufficient, ability in both L1 and L2 will be developed and maintained. When one or more aspects of MOM are weak, either language—or both—may be affected. Reduced proficiency in both languages because of developmental delays, sensory deficits, or injury is not typical and comes under the purview of special education. Low proficiency in only one language because of reduced opportunities or motivation is sometimes a natural consequence of evolving circumstances. We return to this point in our summary of studies that have investigated patterns of L1 and L2 acquisition by children.

Rate, Manner, and Direction of Change in L1 and L2

For sequential bilingual children, rate and manner of L1 acquisition is expected to parallel that of monolingual children, given comparable social, economic, and health circumstances. This seems to be the case, at least until the introduction of L2. Once a majority L2 is introduced, a number of different paths have been observed in the minority home language. These paths include continued L1 growth but at a slower pace than is expected in monolingual children (e.g., Jia, Kohnert, Collado, & Aquino-Garcia, 2006); a leveling off or plateau in L1 ability (e.g., Kan & Kohnert, 2005); or a regression of previously attained L1 skills (e.g., Anderson, 2004; Jia & Aaronson, 2003; Francis, 2005). Factors that contribute to slowed rates of growth, plateaus, or regression in L1 include low social status of a minority L1 in the broader community, immersion in L2 in early childhood educational programs with few opportunities to use L1 outside the home, and relatively low ability in L1 at the time L2 is emphasized (see Kohnert, 2008, for discussion).

Research has consistently shown that young immigrants in the United States learn English within a single generation. Steady gains in English combined with slow or halted growth in L1 produce a shift in relative strength or dominance from the home language to L2. Precisely how long it takes for English to become the stronger language for minority L1 children in the United States seems to vary with the particular aspect of language measured, how it is measured, as well as the children's age and developmental stage when consistent experience with L2 begins. Long-term attainment studies that capture L1 and L2 proficiency after a minimum of 5 years' exposure to English have documented a switch in language dominance for pronunciation (Yeni-Komshian, Flege, & Liu, 2000) and grammatical proficiency (Jia, Aaronson, & Wu, 2002). Eilers and Oller (2003) showed that by fifth grade, early sequential Spanish–English bilinguals performed better on standardized tests in English than in Spanish. Kohnert and colleagues found a shift to greater skills in English in the processing of basic nouns for native Spanish-speaking children in California. This shift to better performance in English came earlier in the receptive mode (evident after 6–7 years of systematic English) than in production (evident only after approximately 10 years of systematic English) (Kohnert & Bates, 2002; Kohnert, Bates, & Hernandez, 1999). However, 3- to 5-year-old Hmong children who began learning English in preschool named more pictures in L2 (English) than L1 after only 1–2 years of experience with the broader community language (Kan & Kohnert, 2005).

Even when L2 becomes the child's relatively stronger language, it may not be the case that his or her English abilities will be directly comparable to those of monolingual speakers. For example, we found significant differences in the strategies used by Vietnamese–English-speaking school-age children to interpret sentences in English as compared to their monolingual-age peers (Pham & Kohnert, 2008). Nelson and colleagues found that classroom noise presented a greater challenge on an English listening task for typically developing second-grade ELLs as compared to monolingual English-only classmates (Nelson, Kohnert, Sabur, & Shaw, 2005). Other studies have demonstrated that 8- to 13-year-old Spanish–English bilinguals were slower or less accurate in naming pictures, identifying grammatical violations, and repeating English nonsense words as compared to typical monolingual English-age peers, despite performance within the normal range on some standardized language and academic measures in English (Kohnert, Windsor, & Yim, 2006; Windsor & Kohnert, 2004). Persisting discrepancies in language performance between ELLs and their English-only peers reflect fundamental differences in language experiences between these groups. Such experience-based discrepancies between monolingual and bilingual performance caution against using monolingual language norms as the criterion for identifying language-based learning impairments in bilingual children (see Kohnert, 2008, for alternative assessment methods).

Although some believe that exclusive ability in the mainstream community language is desirable for ELLs, sociologists have shown that increased ability in a minority home language (L1) in addition to proficiency in the community L2 increases academic aspirations and achievement in immigrant youth beyond those of peers who speak only English (Feliciano, 2001; Portes & Hao, 2002; see Schmid, 2001, for review). Failure to develop or maintain L1 may result in, among other things, loss of cultural identity, reduced contact with family members, lower academic aspirations, and diminished achievement in L2. It is also the case that greater proficiency in L1 is positively associated with English literacy skills, a point to which we return in the following section.

Relationships between L1 and L2

In educational settings the language is both the medium and content of instruction. Academic success is dependent on proficiency of spoken and written forms of the language used for instruction (National Early Literacy Panel, 2006). There is strong consensus among researchers, educators, policymakers, and parents that mastery of English in both spoken and written forms is essential to academic and vocational success in the United States. The more controversial question is how to best achieve these desired outcomes in English.

Despite the common finding of depressed L1 skills among typical ELLs, it should be noted that this is not a necessary or inevitable consequence of successful English acquisition. That is, progress in one language need not come at the expense of the other. The general language-processing system or "mechanism" is capable of acquiring two or more languages; opportunities and motivation are limiting factors for developing high levels of skill in a specific language. This point is well accepted for majority English-speaking children who attend foreign-language immersion educational programs. The same may be true for minority L1 learners when enriched opportunities to develop and use both home and community languages are provided. Indeed it seems that greater support for the home language may help, rather than hurt, long-term attainment of English. Studies in bilingual education show that language-minority school-age children provided with support or direct instruction in L1 have better long-terms outcomes in English as compared to peers who receive reading and instructional support only in L2 (e.g., for a meta-analysis, see Rolstad, Mahoney, & Glass, 2005; Thomas & Collier, 2002). This may be due to shared cognitive, conceptual, and linguistic skills across the two language systems.

The benefit of systematic L1 support on long-term outcomes in English seems particularly true for younger children who are still in the most dynamic stages of spoken language acquisition. Campos (1995) compared outcomes for four groups of children in the United States: low-income children from Spanish-speaking homes who attended either a Spanish-only or English-only preschool program and children from low- or middle-income English-speaking families who attended English preschool programs. Children's progress in literacy and academic achievement was followed from kindergarten through the middle grades. Across grades, performance was greatest for the English-only middle-class group, reflecting robust effects of socioeconomic background on school achievement. Importantly, minority L1 children who attended the Spanish-only preschool outperformed the other two low-income groups in English across test periods. It seems that the human brain is fully capable of acquiring proficiency in two or more languages, if the development and continued use of these languages is supported in the environment.

Miller and colleagues (2006) used a cross-sectional design to investigate relationships between spoken language and reading in children learning Spanish (L1) and English (L2). Participants included more than 1,500 children attending kindergarten, first, second, or third grade transitional English programs in Texas. Oral narratives were collected during a story retell task along with standardized measures of reading comprehension and word-reading efficiency. Regression analyses demonstrated strong within-language relationships between the oral language and reading measures. There were also significant positive cross-language relationships. For example, Spanish reading scores and Spanish oral language measures predicted English reading scores beyond the variance accounted for by grade or within-language measures. Similarly, López and Greenfield (2004) investigated the potential predictive relationship between Spanish (L1) oral language skills and English (L2) phonological awareness in 4- and 5-year-old children attending a Head Start preschool program. Results showed that, along with English oral proficiency, both Spanish oral language proficiency and phonological awareness were significant positive predictors of English phonological awareness. Although relationships between spoken and written language are strongest within a given language, it also seems that native language acquisition provides a template that aids in second-language acquisition, even though the structure of these units is different (Miller et al., 2006; see also Dickinson, McCabe, Clark-Chiarelli, & Wolf, 2004).

Bilingual education may be the ideal for some minority L1 speakers, but it is not the reality for most. For a variety of policy and practical reasons, the vast majority of minority L1 learners in the United States attend English-only instructional programs. For most children who speak Spanish, Vietnamese, Somali, or other minority languages at home, a key educational issue is how best to support the simultaneous acquisition and mastery of spoken language and literacy in English. At the same time, research reviewed here indicates that a stronger L1 base will facilitate, rather than hurt, positive language and academic outcomes in L2. Next we turn our attention to practical strategies educators may use to support the development of English in the academic setting as well as to promote interactions between home and school environments to support continued development and use of L1.

BEST PRACTICES

In this section we describe strategies to promote language learning within an RTI multi-tiered educational framework. RTI was proposed under the 2004 reauthorization of the Individuals with Disabilities Act to address educational needs of all children. Under RTI, Tier 1 focuses on providing high-quality evidence-based classroom education with ongoing monitoring of student progress. Tier 2 consists of an increased level of support for children who are lagging behind classroom peers, and Tier 3 is a referral to special education (for RTI overview, see Graner, Faggella-Luby, & Fritschmann, 2005). For minority L1 learners, high-quality classroom instruction includes frequent, varied, and meaningful opportunities to build language skills. This section groups strategies into four general categories: teacher talk, peer-mediated learning activities, technology, and community collaborations. Strategies within each of these general categories are designed to support the acquisition and use of English; selected strategies within some categories are directed at reinforcing and developing children's home languages. All strategies are within the scope of regular education or Tier 1 support.

Teacher Talk

One way to facilitate the acquisition of English for academic purposes is to increase the availability of quality teacher talk during key instructional times. Teachers should use clear, explicit instructions; modify the language level, as needed, to ensure comprehension; directly teach vocabulary connected with each lesson; and talk openly about the specific features of language needed to communicate in social as well as academic settings (e.g., August & Hakuta, 1997; National Council of Teachers of English, 2006). It is also important that this carefully constructed teacher talk is available to learners and not degraded by competing noise or unfavorable listening conditions.

The issue of classroom acoustics or listening conditions within instructional areas is not trivial. Because cognitive and auditory systems continue to develop through adolescence, children have more difficulty processing speech in unfavorable listening conditions than adults. Research has clearly demonstrated that for typically developing monolingual English-speaking children, classroom noise (defined as sounds extraneous to teacher talk) and sound reverberating or "echoing" off hard surfaces compromise the comprehension of speech, reduce scores on reading and spelling tests, and challenge children's ability to concentrate (e.g., Crandell, Smaldino, & Flexer, 2005). Children with weaker language skills, either due to disabilities or less experience in the language of instruction, are at an even greater disadvantage (e.g., Nelson et al., 2005).

Educators can work in collaboration with the school audiologist to implement a two-step plan to increase favorable language-listening conditions in the classroom. The first step is to identify and reduce sources of background noise. Factors that contribute to poor classroom acoustics include high ceilings; hard walls and floors; older heating and ventilation systems, noise from outside traffic, adjacent playgrounds, or cafeterias; as well as noise within the classroom. Nelson and colleagues (2005) suggest turning off optional equipment such as overhead projectors, computers, and fish tanks, fitting tennis balls under chair legs to reduce scraping noise on hard floors, and closing windows to reduce noise from outside traffic. Sound reverberation can be reduced by draping cloth materials on hard walls and from high ceilings and covering floors with rugs or carpets. The second step, again in collaboration with the school audiologist, is to advocate for the purchase and installation of a classroom sound field system to increase acoustic saliency of teacher talk during key instructional times. Administrators and classroom teachers have discussed how this relatively inexpensive system may enhance classroom learning for all students (e.g., *Classroom Acoustics*, 2000; Nelson, Soli, & Seltz, 2002). Also, inexpensive personal teacher microphones and preferential seating may be used to improve listening conditions for ELLs.

Peer-Mediated Learning Activities

Under an RTI framework, Tier 1 can include multiple grouping formats (Xu & Drame, 2008). Planned peer-based interactions can complement traditional teacher-mediated learning as a powerful way to multiply opportunities for meaningful and motivating language-based interactions. Peer-based learning activities vary in the way student pairs or groups are configured. In some cases children are arranged in dyads, and for other purposes small cooperative learning groups are formed. Examples of peer-based learning programs empirically validated for use with children learning in their L2 are classwide peer tutoring (CWPT; Greenwood, Arreaga-Mayer, Utley, Gavin, & Terry, 2001) and peer-assisted learning strategies (PALS; Fuchs, Fuchs, Hamlett, Phillips, & Bentz, 1994).

CWPT and PALS have three main common factors that contribute to their effectiveness. First, students work in pairs on a literacy-based task and alternate between the role of tutor and tutee within a single session. The experience of being both a tutor and tutee has academic and social benefits. The tutee receives immediate feedback and multiple opportunities to practice listening and using language. The role of tutor may increase self-confidence, a sense of responsibility for the other, and appropriate social behaviors for peer interaction (Utley & Mortweet, 1997). Second, students follow a planned script that precisely describes the sequence of activities, how to model language, and when and how to give feedback. The teacher monitors student understanding, facilitates pair work, and directs students to alternate roles after an allotted time period. Third, student pairs receive points for accuracy and effort that are summed at the end of the session. The tangible reward system encourages students to remain on task and give their best effort. Teachers have reported positive student progress as a result of implementing peer-mediated learning programs such as CWPT; students and teachers reported that it was relatively easy and fun to follow (Greenwood et al., 2001).

Both CWPT and PALS pair a student with low language proficiency with an average student, an average student with a high-performing student, or a student who has recently arrived in the United States with a high-performing bilingual student (Greenwood et al., 2001). Some peer-based instructional programs pair an older student with a younger student, particularly when students with disabilities are included (for a review, see Utley & Mortweet, 1997); others promote cooperative learning in small groups (Jacob, Rottenburg, Patrick, & Wheeler, 1996). Peer-mediated learning has been applied to a wide variety of content or skill areas such as reading, mathematics, spelling, language arts, second-language learning, and social language monitoring.

Technology

Another method for promoting frequent opportunities for listening and producing oral and written language is through the use of technology. Based on a survey of English as a second language (ESL) and bilingual programs (Meskill & Mossop, 2000), elementary school teachers reported using computer software to tutor vocabulary and written language skills such as letter recognition and spelling, and upper-grade levels targeted more advanced language skills, including decision making, predicting, and problem solving. Technology can also be used as a tool to enhance experiences with written language in English. Furthermore, there are many websites and software programs available in languages other than English that can be used to support skills in a home language and to reinforce links between home and school. For example, content-based software programs are available in Spanish for reading, science, and math for primary school–age children. These programs can be used as a complement to classroom instruction in English, with a "home language loan library" established to facilitate the sharing of learning tools across home and school environments. Students can also be taught to do Internet searches in other languages by changing the language of their search engine.

There are many advantages to using computer software to reinforce language learning. Children can work at their own pace, practice a skill many more times than in traditional teacher-directed activities, and receive immediate feedback about their responses. In addition, children are motivated to work on computers because learning becomes "alive" and interactive with multiple connections between visual, graphic, and audio information. Computers have a practical economic advantage as well, since one teacher can monitor students across many computers, rather than needing one-on-one human tutors for each student. However, all tools have their limitations, and computer technology is no exception. For example, computer software has not been widely used to facilitate social aspects of language such as turn taking and interpersonal communication skills (Westby & Atencio, 2002). There is the risk of children "mindlessly" completing computer activities without comprehending target concepts. Children may wander through a software program out of sequence or may have difficulty beginning and maintaining progress due to lack of adult monitoring and guidance. Westby and Atencio (2002) discuss factors to consider when implementing computer technology in the classroom. Teachers need to address whether students have enough prerequisite skills to benefit from computer mediation, how much monitoring is needed, and whether the computer software program is an effective medium for the target skill. As with all educational tools, judicious selection and use of software programs are needed.

Community Collaborations

Language-building opportunities extend beyond the classroom and involve strong connections between home, school, and the wider community. When parents are limited in English proficiency, both parents and teachers may feel uncomfortable or intimidated when attempting to interact (e.g., Lahman & Park, 2004). One way to establish an exchange of ideas is to organize small-group discussions for parents from the same language background. Parents may feel more comfortable speaking to other parents in their native language about school-related concerns, and one bilingual parent can be designated as the liaison to share concerns with the classroom teacher. Teachers may also ask parents, community members, or high school or college students in service-learning programs to read stories or teach songs to children in other languages. This practice supports language acquisition and also sends a clear message that the home language is valued by the academic community.

Educators can serve as an important link between families and the larger community. As part of an ongoing exchange of ideas, educators can introduce community resources such as local cultural organizations, public libraries, museums, and park and recreation programs. Outings sponsored by cultural organizations can help families preserve cultural traditions and establish social support networks. Many public libraries have storytelling events, reading clubs, children's books in many languages, computer software, and videos that support language learning. Local museums and parks often provide free events and programs that help expand children's world knowledge and their experiences within the larger community. The goal here is not to provide an exhaustive list of how to support the continued use of the primary home language but rather to underscore the need to do so. Once the "why" is understood, creative educators will likely be able to engage colleagues, community professionals, and parents to determine additional opportunities best suited for their students and families.

SUMMARY OF MAIN IDEAS

A general shift to relative dominance in English is considered the norm for minority L1 learners in the United States. As with monolingual learners, language acquisition takes place over an extended period of time, in the context of rich opportunities and support. Due to fundamental differences in language experiences, sequential bilingual children are unique language processors and may not be directly comparable to monolingual children on some language tasks.

It is also important to note that relatively stronger skills in English (as compared to L1) may not translate into the absolute levels of language needed for high literacy and academic achievement when sufficiently rich language opportunities are not available. That is, the seemingly inevitable shift to greater skills in English for minority L1 learners in the United States does not necessarily mean that English attainment is as good as it needs to be. This is also true of monolingual English speakers from disadvantaged backgrounds (e.g., Hart & Risley, 1995; Hoff, 2003). On the other hand, with continued opportunities to develop and use English, minority L1 speakers are fully capable of becoming extraordinarily high achievers in the community language.

Although there is significant documentation indicating that bilingual education may improve outcomes for language minority sequential bilinguals, most of these learners in the United States attend English-only educational programs. In these programs children need to simultaneously acquire spoken and written English. Consistent with the MOM framework (means, opportunities, motives), this demanding process is facilitated when teachers provide children with multiple opportunities to engage with meaningful language. Carefully constructed teacher talk presented in favorable listening conditions can be combined with teacher-implemented peer-mediated learning programs, additional practice opportunities using selected software programs, and collaborations with colleagues in the school as well as in the broader community. Documenting children's responses to enhanced learning conditions is consistent with Tier 1 of RTI (Graner et al., 2005).

There is no question that high proficiency in both spoken and written English is essential to academic and vocational success for all children in the United States. However, it is also true that the need for English does not negate the continuing relevance of the home language for minority L1 learners. Support and opportunities to develop and use L1 strengthen self-identity, social relationships, and long-term academic outcomes in English (L2). In addition, proficiency in world languages by U.S. residents is seen as an essential national resource: Minority L1 children are an extraordinary potential source of multilingual competency if effective methods for supporting both home and community languages are available.

IMPLICATIONS FOR RESEARCH, PRACTICE, AND POLICY

Teachers are faced with the extraordinary challenge of using English to facilitate literacy and world knowledge in children who may not have a strong foundation in the language of instruction. To meet this challenge, teachers need additional training and support. Administrators can assist by providing professional development opportunities for teachers to learn about typical first- and second-language-acquisition processes, cultural competency, and specific ways to promote language learning (Xu & Dame, 2008). Basic information on spoken as well as written language and the process of language acquisition in diverse learners should also be included as a core component in professional training programs. Additional training for educators on relationships between language and learning should benefit English-only speaking students who do not have the strong spoken language foundation needed to support advanced literacy and academic skills. That is, although teachers are presented with significant challenges with respect to their role in facilitating language for academic purposes, additional training in this area also provides tremendous opportunities for reducing academic achievement gaps in ELLs and other at-risk learners.

Collaborative teams can be formed within schools to develop (1) policies for shared technology needs (e.g., selecting software, advocating for sound field amplification systems in key classrooms), (2) approaches to increase bidirectional interactions between school and linguistically diverse home environments, and (3) methods to meet all three tiers in the RTI framework (e.g., classroom teacher, speech–language pathologist, ESL teacher). Empirical validation of all recommended practices is needed to inform interdisciplinary understanding of links between environmental language and learning in early sequential bilinguals. Even more importantly, documenting individual student performance as a function of specific educator-implemented strategies is consistent with RTI mandates as well as best educational practices. Documenting potential cascading effects across individual students will provide powerful ammunition with which to advocate for policies within school systems that recognize and support teachers' fundamental role in promoting language acquisition.

General research is also needed on language acquisition in a broader range of minority L1 learners. For example, although we know about the strong cross-language relationships between selected aspects of spoken and written language in Spanish–English learners, we know very little about language acquisition in children who speak Somali, Hmong, or Urdu as a first language and English as L2. Also, given that RTI is a relatively recent mandate, there is little empirically validated information on the best ways to address its basic tenets. Comparative research studies investigating outcomes from different approaches to RTI are needed, with careful attention to both program components and child language and cultural characteristics.

REFERENCES

Anderson, R. (2004). First language loss in Spanish-speaking children. In B. Goldstein (Ed.), *Bilingual language development and disorders in Spanish–English speakers* (pp. 187–211). Baltimore: Brookes.

August, D., & Hakuta, K. (Eds.). (1997). *Improving schooling for language-minority children: A research agenda.* Washington, DC: National Academy Press.

Campos, S. J. (1995). The Carpentería preschool program: A long-term effects study. In E. E. Garcia & B. McLaughlin (Eds.), *Meeting the challenge of linguistic and cultural diversity in early childhood education* (pp. 34–48). New York: Teachers College Press.

Classroom acoustics: A resource for creating learning environments with desirable listening conditions. (2000). Retrieved November 15, 2008, from asa.aip.org/classroom/booklet.html.

Crandell, C. C., Smaldino, J. J., & Flexer, C. (2005). *Sound–field amplification: Applications to speech perception and classroom acoustics* (2nd ed.). New York: Thomson Delmar Learning.

Dickinson, D., McCabe, A., Clark-Chiarelli, N., & Wolf, A. (2004). Cross-language transfer of phonological awareness in low-income Spanish and English bilingual preschool children. *Applied Psycholinguistics, 25,* 323–347.

Feliciano, C. (2001). The benefits of biculturalism: Exposure to immigrant culture and dropping out of school among Asian and Latino youths. *Social Science Quarterly, 82,* 865–879.

Francis, N. (2005). Research findings on early first language attrition: Implications for the discussion on critical periods in language acquisition. *Language Learning, 55*(3), 491–531.

Fuchs, L. S., Fuchs, D., Hamlett, C. L., Phillips, N., & Bentz, J. (1994). Classwide curriculum- based measurement: Helping general educators meet the challenge of student diversity. *Exceptional Children, 60,* 518–537.

Graner, P. S., Faggella-Luby, M. N., & Fritschmann, N. S. (2005). An overview of responsiveness to intervention: What practitioners ought to know. *Topics in Language Disorders, 25*(2), 93–105.

Greenwood, C., Arreaga-Mayer, C., Utley, C., Gavin, K., & Terry, B. (2001). Classwide peer tutoring learning management system: Applications with elementary-level English language learners. *Remedial and Special Education, 22*(1), 34–47.

Hart, B., & Risley, T. (1995). *Meaningful differences in the everyday experiences of young American children.* Baltimore: Brookes.

Hirsch-Pasek, K., & Golinkoff, R. M. (2003). *Einstein never used flash cards.* New York: Rodale.

Hoff, E. (2003). The specificity of environmental influence: Socioeconomic status affects early vocabulary development via maternal speech. *Child Development, 74,* 1368–1378.

Huttenlocher, J., Vasilyeva, M., Cymerman, E., & Levine, S. (2002). Language input and child syntax. *Cognitive Psychology, 45,* 337–374.

Jacob, E., Rottenberg, L., Patrick, S., & Wheeler, E. (1996). Cooperative learning: Context and opportunities for acquiring academic English. *TESOL Quarterly, 30*(2), 253–280.

Jia, G., & Aaronson, D. (2003). A longitudinal study of Chinese children and adolescents learning English in the United States. *Applied Psycholinguistics, 24,* 131–161.

Jia, G., Aaronson, D., & Wu, Y. (2002). Long-term language attainment of bilingual immigrants: Predictive variables and language group differences. *Applied Psycholinguistics, 23,* 599–621.

Jia, G., Kohnert, K., Collado, J., & Aquino-Garcia, F. (2006). Action naming in Spanish and English by sequential bilingual children and adolescents. *Journal of Speech, Language, and Hearing Research, 49,* 588–602.

Kan, P. F., & Kohnert, K. (2005). Preschoolers learning Hmong and English: Lexical–semantic skills in L1 and L2. *Journal of Speech, Language, and Hearing Research, 48,* 372–378.

Kohnert, K. (2008). *Language disorders in bilingual children and adults.* San Diego, CA: Plural.

Kohnert, K. (2009). Bilinguals with primary language impairment. In K. De Bot & R. Schrauf (Eds), *Language development over the life-span* (pp. 146–170). Mahwah, NJ: Erlbaum.

Kohnert, K., & Bates, E. (2002). Balancing bilinguals: II. Lexical comprehension and cognitive processing in children learning Spanish and English. *Journal of Speech, Language, and Hearing Research, 45,* 347–359.

Kohnert, K., Bates, E., & Hernandez, A. E. (1999). Balancing bilinguals: Lexical–semantic production and cognitive processing in children learning Spanish and English. *Journal of Speech, Language, and Hearing Research, 42,* 1400–1413.

Kohnert, K., Windsor, J., & Yim, D. (2006). Do language-based processing tasks separate children with primary language impairment from typical bilinguals? *Journal of Learning Disabilities Research and Practice, 21,* 19–29.

Lahman, M., & Park, S. (2004). Understanding children from diverse cultures: Bridging perspectives of parents and teachers. *International Journal of Early Years Education, 12*(2), 131–142.

López, L. M., & Greenfield, D. B. (2004). The cross-language transfer of phonological skills of Hispanic Head Start children. *Bilingual Research Journal, 28,* 1–18.

Meskill, C., & Mossop, J. (2000). Technologies use with ESL learners in New York State: Preliminary report. *Journal of Educational Computing Research, 22*(3), 265–284.

Miller, J. F., Heilmann, J., Nockerts, A., Iglesias, A., Fabiano, L., & Francis, D. J. (2006). Oral language and reading in bilingual children. *Learning Disabilities Research and Practice, 21,* 30–43.

National Council of Teachers of English. (2006). *Position paper on the role of English teachers in educating English language learners.* Retrieved November 15, 2008, from *www.ncte.org/about/over/positions/level/gen/124545.htm.*

National Early Literacy Panel. (2006). *Synthesizing the scientific research on development of early literacy in young children.* Retrieved November

15, 2008, from *www.nifl.gov/partnershipforreading/family/ncfl/NELP-2006Conference.pdf.*

Nelson, P., Kohnert, K., Sabur, S., & Shaw, D. (2005). Classroom noise and children learning through a second language: Double jeopardy? *Language, Speech, and Hearing Services in Schools, 36,* 219–229.

Nelson, P., Soli, S., & Seltz, A. (2002). *Classroom acoustics: II. Acoustical barriers to learning.* Melville, NY: Acoustical Society of America.

Pham, G., & Kohnert, K. (in press). Sentence interpretation among typically developing Vietnamese–English bilingual children. *Applied Psycholinguistics.*

Portes, A., & Hao, L. (2002). The price of uniformity: Language, family, and personality adjustment in the immigrant second generation. *Ethnic and Racial Studies, 25,* 889–912.

Rolstad, K., Mahoney, K., & Glass, G. V. (2005). The big picture: A meta-analysis of program effectiveness research on English language learners. *Educational Policy, 19*(4), 572–594.

Schmid, C. L. (2001). Educational achievement, language minority students, and the new second generation. *Sociology of Education, 74,* 71–87.

Shatz, M. (2007). Revisiting *A Toddler's Life* for the toddler years: Conversational participation as a tool for learning across knowledge domains. In C. A. Brownell & C. B. Kopp (Eds.), *Socioemotional development in the toddler years: Transitions and tranformations* (pp. 241–260). New York: Guilford Press.

Thomas, W. P., & Collier, V. P. (2002). *A national study of school effectiveness for language minority students' long-term academic achievement.* Santa Cruz: Center for Research on Education, Diversity, and Excellence, University of California, Santa Cruz.

Utley, C., & Mortweet, S. L. (1997). Peer-mediated instruction and interventions. *Exceptional Children, 29*(5), 1–23.

Westby, C., & Atencio, D. (2002). Computers, culture, and learning. *Topics in Language Disorders, 22*(4), 70–87.

Windsor, J., & Kohnert, K. (2004). In search of common ground: Part I. Lexical performance by linguistically diverse learners. *Journal of Speech, Language, and Hearing Research, 47,* 877–890.

Xu, Y., & Drame, E. (2008). Culturally appropriate context: Unlocking the potential of response to intervention for English language learners. *Early Childhood Education, 35,* 305–311.

Yeni-Komshian, G. H., Flege, J. E., & Liu, S. (2000). Pronunciation proficiency in the first and second languages of Korean–English bilinguals. *Bilingualism: Language and Cognition, 3,* 131–149.

$\underline{3}$

Language Choice
and Competence

*Code Switching and Issues of Social
Identity in Young Bilingual Children*

Iliana Reyes
Susan Ervin-Tripp

FOCUS POINTS

- Language choice and code switching are a normal part of children's language development and are a communicative tactic for young multilingual children.

- Code switching, as a rhetorical and stylistic tool, is not a sign of a deficit but of enrichment.

- Variety and complexity in code switching develop with age as the child's skills and linguistic competence in the two languages increase.

- Language choice and code switching can serve as social identity tools for participation in home and community (e.g., school) interactions in both minority and dominant groups.

- Code switching has a role as a teaching and learning tactic in classroom language and literacy practices.

CHAPTER PURPOSE

The purpose of this chapter is to describe how children make use of their multiple languages, and in particular, how children use switches between languages, or code switching, for local and affective communicative purposes and for displaying different social identities. In addition, we explore how these children, growing up between different linguistic and cultural identities, construct hybrid spaces as part of their discourse negotiation with teachers and peers. In this chapter we address the following points: We first describe the language strategies used by bilingual children in all face-to-face communication. We then analyze children's code switching as an aspect of their language development that reflects the linguistic practices modeled at home and in the community. We end by explaining how the development of bilingual competencies supports the development of literacy and social and educational success in young children.

RESEARCH AND THEORY

Growing Up Bilingual

From the start, children in multilingual communities notice who speaks what. They choose the form of speech that they assume can be understood on the basis of how their addressees look, where they are, or what they speak (Genesee & Nicoladis, 2007). When very young children use a word from the "wrong" language for a monolingual hearer, it fills a gap, occurring when they do not know a word or lack immediate access to that word. Another explanation is that children are utilizing code switching as a rhetorical and stylistic tool, which demonstrates their later sophisticated sociolinguistic competence in their two languages.

From an early age, children notice who is bilingual in their community, and they notice switching between languages by the bilingual speakers around them (Paradis & Nicoladis, 2007). Thus, they learn from their parents, siblings, and peers how to make use of both languages in conversation, and with whom. Comeau, Genessee, and Lapaquette (2003) found that young bilingual children could adjust their rates of code mixing, following the lead of an adult interlocutor, to keep the same frequency of switching. Thus, community and school practices can enhance or inhibit switching languages, or code switching, as a form of communication.

Just what is code switching? The form code switching takes seems to depend on three factors: (1) how well a speaker knows both languages, (2) whether the languages are grammatically similar, and (3) relative language prestige. When languages are very different in type, or when a new learner does not know both languages well, a word or phrase is usually inserted (Deuchar, Muysken, & Want, 2007). We are all familiar with borrowed words in English; for example, *rodeo* was borrowed from Spanish. Confirming what Jørgensen (1998) found with young Turkish immigrants, we have found in some of our studies with young English language learners (7- and 10-year-old children) that they start speaking their second language by inserting English phrases or words such as *okay* or *dude* into their first-language (L1) sentences (Ervin-Tripp & Reyes, 2005; Reyes, 2004). However, these early insertions are frequently exclamations and tags that are only loosely connected grammatically.

Code Switching and Language Development

As speakers become more competent in another language, they can switch languages at phrase or clause boundaries or between sentences or turns. Code switching by children reflects what they hear between adults in a bilingual community. In the Puerto Rican communities studied by Poplack (1980) and Zentella (1997), code switching is so common as to be a regular style of talk. But in Ontario, English is the dominant variety, so most English speakers are unlikely to understand French (Paradis & Nicoladis, 2007). The consequence is that most code switching there has special functions, as we will see, and Ontario bilinguals, by 3 or 4 years old, are likely to switch during speech with Francophones but not with Anglophones.

Code switching is grammatically constrained, such that switches between languages occur at points of syntactic concordance. Bilingual children have learned two grammatical systems, often quite different from each other, but they locate the points where switching is possible (Genesee & Nicoladis, 2007). Typically it is between sentences or at matched points in utterances, such as at interjections, clause boundaries, noun phrases, side remarks, or afterthoughts. Code switching is never random, and it requires competence in more than one syntactic system to go beyond inserting words. When languages are similar, like English and Spanish, switching can occur fairly freely in competent speakers (Deuchar et al., 2007; Poplack, 1981; Zentella, 1997).

Why does code switching occur in children's speech? Since recording of natural conversations of bilinguals began (Auer, 1998; Fantini, 1985; Gumperz, 1972; Reyes, 2004), analysts have observed that code switching between the same participants is due to specific dynamics in the conversation, some similar to those that affect prosody and speech styles. But even adult speakers are not good at reporting what they do, and often they are unaware of their code-switching practices (Blom & Gumperz, 1972), so we must analyze recordings.

When we record the monolingual (English) peer talk of schoolchildren, we find that they use markers such as vocatives and *well, hey, but, look, okay,* as well as prosodic changes in loudness and rate, repetition, and style changes (e.g., baby talk). The functions of these discourse markers (which, of course, bilingual children use too) are to shift footing by changing genre, topic, perspective, or speech act; to mark episodes such as roles, quotes, or evaluations in a story; to attract attention, grab a turn, elaborate, insist, or emphasize (Andersen, Brizuela, DuPuy, & Gonnerman, 1999; Ervin-Tripp & Reyes, 2005; Gardner-Chloros, 2000). In code switching another marker is added that can signal many of the same conversational functions with some added meanings.

Jørgensen (1998) argued that before age 8, children were most sensitive to interlocutor skill and to setting (e.g., classroom vs. playground) in their language choice. From an early age, code switching is used by children to select participants and to mark changes of setting and situation (e.g., fantasy, role play) (Ervin-Tripp & Reyes, 2005; Garcia-Sánchez, 2009; Sebba & Wootton, 1998). Interactional and discursive functions of children's code switching, such as differentiating between negotiation of the play and in-character play, marking byplay, teasing, displaying power or anger, and marking topic changes, emphasis, requests, story evaluations, and punchlines have been described (e.g., Cromdal, 2005; Ervin-Tripp & Reyes, 2005; Halmari & Smith, 1994; Paugh, 2005).

Does the particular language used in the switch make a difference, or is a switch all that matters, as in the above examples? Language choice can influence who gets included in an interaction, such that bilinguals have an advantage in controlling participation and exclusion. Children pick up on community-function specifics; for example, in Jørgensen 's project, Turkish–Danish bilinguals spoke Danish for public academic talk, but for affective talk and insults, they used Turkish. Jørgensen (1998) found that even grade-school children could use multiple language sources and mimic stylized stereotypical immigrant Danish, expressing an attitude to a language variety.

What might come later is the kind of code switching noticed in adolescents and adults where a particular language is used to mark familiarity or distance or to change cultural assumptions in interpreting meaning (Gumperz, 1972). Rampton (1998) considers this a kind of figurative switching so that listeners have to search for meaning in ambiguity. Studies of multilingual communities have shown that "crossing" occurs, such that even partial knowledge of other languages can allow allusion, joking, and power plays.

Code Switching and Context

Children's use of code switching in contexts such as the home or school may indicate that they want to establish themselves as members of a particular speech community. Learning and switching among multilingual peers may symbolize identification with multiple speech communities, as noted by Jørgensen and by Rampton in informal peer contexts. Zentella (2008, p. 5) describes this phenomenon from the speaker's perspective: "They speak both because they are both." Similarly, Auer (1998) has argued that in the second generation of immigrants, code switching may designate the "we" code. It is important to emphasize that parental strategies, peer practices, and school and community attitudes and practices will highly influence the linguistic abilities and practices of a bilingual child, in whom the possibilities are numerous (Fantini, 1985).

Young preschoolers from an early age use their two languages both to communicate with others in the classroom and to start making sense of print around them (Kenner, 2004; Roca, 2005). Reyes and colleagues have observed language and literacy use by Latino preschoolers in a predominantly English classroom (Reyes, Soltero, & Azuara, 2006). Although English was the medium of instruction, both teachers at times used code switching into Spanish for clarification purposes and when explaining to children the instructions for classroom lessons. The children constantly made use of code switching when playing and interacting with peers, answering the teacher, and making connections between vocabulary in English and in their native language. In the following exchange, a teacher asks children about their journal entries after a visit to the zoo (all names used are pseudonyms).

> TEACHER: ¿Qué dibujaste? (What did you draw?)
>
> MIGUEL: Una *giraffe*. (A giraffe.)
>
> TEACHER: Una *giraffe*? (A giraffe?)
>
> MIGUEL: Sí, una jirafa y tiene el cuello largo. (Yes, a giraffe with a long neck.)
>
> TEACHER: ¿Qué otro animal estaba ahí cerca de la jirafa? (What other animal did you see near the giraffe?)
>
> MIGUEL: El oso, el oso polar. (The bear, the polar bear.)
>
> LAURA: *Yes the polar bear* estaba nadando. (The polar bear was swimming.)

This example illustrates how children's use of the two languages allows them to make connections between their background experiences and knowledge presented in the school context. During our observations, the children continued to use Spanish to make sense of classroom discourse as they developed English. Since the teachers also used Spanish, the children knew they were understood. Most importantly, the children began to develop spontaneous biliteracy through daily interactions at home and school, in which they transferred their knowledge from one language to another. Despite the emphasis on English formal instruction during most classroom activities, these emergent bilingual children continued to use their native language, Spanish, to make connections between what they heard and observed during instructional activities in English (e.g., story time, journal time, circle time) and their own experiences in Spanish. Normally, the teaching of reading is based on oral fluency. But when this requirement is violated, and children are expected to learn to read in a second language before they understand the meaning of the words they are reading, code switching with a teacher or among themselves can be a bridge to understanding the meaning of the text.

In addition to code switching by children, some studies have shown that teachers also use switching to encourage and motivate students to participate in classroom activities. The findings from Guthrie and Guthrie's (1987) study in California showed that a teacher in an English–Chinese bilingual classroom code-switched during reading lessons for several purposes: (1) for translation; (2) as a "we code" to establish and maintain solidarity and membership in their group (presented previously by Gumperz, 1982); (3) to provide instructions for the lesson; (4) for clarification and introduction of new vocabulary for the lesson; (5) and to check students' understanding. The use of the native language benefited the children while enhancing their reading skills and learning content.

In a related research study, Hughes, Shaunessy, Brice, Ratliff, and Alvarez McHatton (2006) acknowledged code switching as a reflection of competence and proposed that educators need to reconsider code switching as a possible indicator of the potential of bilingual children to participate in special programs for gifted children. The rationale for this is that children must master highly developed cognitive and linguistic competence in order to successfully code-switch. Moreover, Hughes and colleagues invited educators to consider code switching as an important part of children's language assessments, since it could help teachers identify and differentiate between language or learning issues that a young English language learner (ELL) may be experiencing. Therefore, both Hughes and colleagues and Valdés's (2003) recent study of young immigrant child interpreters who use code switching as a strategy challenge an earlier perspective that code switching comes from deficits leading to language interference. Instead, these findings, among others, point to the enhanced linguistic skills that bilingual children bring to classrooms. In addition, code switching appears in sophisticated literature, since it is a major component of bilingual adult communication.

Beyond Language Competence: Code Switching and Identity

Despite the advances made by recent research on immigrants and language choice, the field is still in its infancy in exploring the connections between identity and culture in relation to language use among emergent bilingual children. Children's choice to use a particular language can signal a particular affiliation with a group and consequently a particular linguistic identity. Some research (e.g., Iannacci, 2008; Kenner, 2004) indicates that children from ethnic backgrounds different from the dominant one are constantly involved in a process whereby they construct and reconstruct their identities according to the social situation.

For families that speak more than one language, maintaining connections to speakers of the same language means that they will not only maintain and continue to grow their heritage, but also may continue to share with their children traditions and beliefs that are part of their cultural communities. A crucial means to do this is through children's use of their home language and the display of its relation to their family linguistic identity and their cultural values. Thus children in ethnolinguistic communities use multiple codes for multiple identities (Zentella, 2008).

In a study with adult Hispanic immigrants, Cashman (2004) followed a group of women playing Mexican *lotería* (similar to the Bingo game). The participants used code switching into their heritage language as a membership categorization device. From this study and others with adults, we learn that language choice cannot be simply described as an in-group/out-group dichotomy because members of speech communities talk "into being" different social and linguistic identities (Cashman, 2004; De Fina, 2007). Therefore, bilinguals are not merely recipients of cultural models; instead they actively explore new ways of "doing being bilingual" and use their languages to display gender, class, and ethnic identities. Many times these new repertoires of identity include diverse linguistic and cultural practices, creating a "hybrid" space (Zentella, 2008, p. 6) where bilingual speakers merge their two languages and interact with speakers of these two languages.

Iannacci (2008) considers that children live in a situation of *in-betweenness* when they face a conflict between the language they know best and the one required for use in the school context. He states that this situation could be "disorienting and often disruptive to young children's development of a positive and additive ethnic linguistic identity" (p. 125). The author shows how code switching was used in the classroom by two young children, Inés and Akil, whose home languages were Spanish and Arabic, respectively. At school they spoke mainly English as part of their English as a second language (ESL) classes, but they used their home language to negotiate some classroom activities. For them, code switching was used as a social indexing device that indicated another identity apart from that of the dominant culture and language of the classroom. Fortunately, as a result of this study, the teacher wanted to be more supportive of fostering the linguistic and cultural diversity of the children by providing a multilingual and multicultural environment for them.

Garcia-Sánchez (2009) found that Moroccan immigrant 4- to 8-year-old girls in Spain could enact with dolls fantasy roles drawn from TV in Spanish, whereas they switched to Moroccan Arabic for negotiation, plot construction, commentary, interaction with others, and conflict. In this case, the language choice matters for expressing different identities. The Spanish these girls used in play was a stylized register of Spanish, distinct from what they spoke in daily life but drawn from TV. The dolls represented values and roles unavailable to them and culturally distant, as their Arabic commentary indicated. The language switching represented different identities they could recognize around them.

Jørgensen (1998) argues that at the face-to-face level between children, the larger dominance and prestige in the community is not as important as local dynamics. Code switching has local effects via accommodation and distance. It symbolically expresses convergence and divergence in code with other speakers. Studies from Britain have also documented the role of languages for immigrant children from various ethnolinguistic backgrounds, including Asian, Arabic, Bengali, and Bulgarian. Mills (2001) reports that the languages helped the children she studied have a multiple identity, such as British and Pakistani.

An important factor for bilingual children is community support, which of course includes school support. Mills (2001) mentions that some immigrants feel that they don't fit in anywhere, but in a rich cultural environment such as the Puerto Rican community described by Zentella (1997), this sense of displacement doesn't happen. They see themselves as forming a new variety. This has happened in Britain with Asians too. "The children had views on language maintenance that endorsed the crucial role of their languages in forming their identities" (Mills, p. 391). They found it important to speak to relatives in the family language, where good manners demand accommodation to elders. They also reported switching in relation to moods of happiness or anger. The children experienced multiple identities to which their languages contributed, and they were attached to the cultures associated with the languages.

In another study with young children in England, Pagett (2006) found that parents had a strong aspiration for their children to learn and to maintain their home language because they recognized the importance of L1 maintenance for their children's future jobs that might require bilingual competencies, thus helping them in the global economy. However, these same immigrant families reported that they did not want to be "different outside (the home)" and therefore spoke in English to each other when shopping or going about in the community. Children would often switch to English when entering school grounds and during instruction that was conducted in English. Some children treated the home language like a private secret, to be used only in seclusion:

> I feel it embarrassing [to speak to her mother in Mongolian at school]; it's just a feeling in my stomach, really weird feeling. I pretend not to hear it [when her mother speaks to her in Mongolian in front of her friends] (Pupil 4). (in Pagett, 2006, p. 139)

Wong Fillmore (2000) has discussed a similar dilemma that many minority families and children in the United States face as they try to understand the conflicting messages they receive from school teachers and administrators about the importance of their home language:

> They [children] quickly discover that in the social world of the school, English is the only language that is acceptable. The message they get is this: "The home language is nothing; it has no value at all." If they want to be fully accepted, children come to believe that they must disavow the low status language spoken at home. (pp. 207–208)

Despite ambivalent feelings about the use of the family native language described by some of the children in these studies, the authors reported code switching, and they also found the use of what Pagett (2006) labeled *bilingual parallel code*—a practice between parents and their children at home. While parents speak the family home language, the children use the community's dominant language. Children themselves report switching to English most of the time because of preference but other times because it appears rude to exclude others (Reyes, 2004).

In conclusion, code switching by adults and peers in the community can support bilingual children's development of bilingual competence to align positively with peers and form groups to which they like to belong. Because of this positive perspective on language switching, teachers as well have been observed to use code switching and to become more sensitive to the use of children's abilities in and outside the classroom context (Díaz-Rico, 2004; Iannacci, 2008).

BEST PRACTICES

In this section, we consider some of the instructional practices that support young ELL students in their learning. We present the following teaching practices that integrate an *additive* approach to the use of native language instruction for emergent bilingual children as they develop competencies in both their L1 and L2, rather than losing L1.

Encouraging L1 Use and Code Switching as Part of Classroom Discourse

When teachers encourage L1 use in classrooms, they foster students' comfort in using code switching without having any repercussions in the development of their academic discourse. If children feel more comfortable in one language, then teachers should allow them to use that language. By allowing native language use and code switching as part of classroom discourse practices, teachers are helping children reduce anxiety when making the transition into a new linguistic environment. Moreover, this strategy might help students establish group solidarity when interacting with other children who share their home language in the classroom (Iannaci, 2008; Reyes, 2004).

Teaching Vocabulary and Cognates

When children are allowed to use their native language and to code-switch between the two languages as part of lesson activities, they are provided with the opportunity to improve vocabulary in their L2 by making connections to their vocabulary knowledge in their L1. A helpful practice is to generate a list of words that are commonly used in the classroom by children and teachers (e.g., *bathroom, coats, lunch*) and use these words as part of labels and announcements in the classroom. If these labels and signs are posted around the classroom, students will be able to associate and learn specific words within a meaningful context.

An additional strategy is to teach ELLs who speak languages related to English those words that are similar in both sound and meaning in both of their languages. These words are known as *cognates*, because in addition to the shared meaning they are also phonetically similar. For example, as part of a science lesson focusing on the topic of time, teachers working with ELLs from a Spanish-speaking background could introduce cognates that are relevant to the study lesson (e.g., time/*tiempo*, hour/*hora*, minutes/*minutos*, seconds/*segundos*). The goal is for students to become aware of the linguistic similarities that might exist between their two languages and for them to become junior ethnographers as they explore language (see also Brisk, Chapter 7, this volume, on including instruction on relevant aspects of English while teaching various subjects).

Using L1 for Letter–Sound Identification

The use of L1 to compare letter–sound relationship similarities and differences in the two languages will help children differentiate between them. From an early age bilinguals can identify differences between languages and begin making hypotheses about how print is associated with sounds in different languages (Reyes & Azuara, 2008). This strategy helps children develop metalinguistic awareness of how language is structured and how two languages compare to each other. Of course, character and syllabary orthographies would require a more complex comparison (see Newman, Chapter 5, this volume).

Scaffolding Language

From a sociocultural constructivist perspective, teachers can support students' language and literacy development by helping them focus attention on specific parts of the task. ELL students benefit from having teachers or more advanced peers analyze an activity into different steps. For example, teachers or peers can ask questions that will help the ELL students to think and verbalize while completing a particular task in class. In addition, teachers can build on students' linguistic resources by inviting them to bring in a first-language word each day that is particularly meaningful to them, and all students in the class can learn this word and talk about its meaning and cultural connotations (Cummins, 2000).

Díaz-Rico (2004) encouraged teachers to practice a set of "formulaic expressions" with their students that can be used during most day-to-day interactions so that they feel comfortable in routine language use (e.g., "Hi, how are you?" "More, please"). This practice might help children use different strategies, such as repeating words they hear, using verbal attention getters to initiate interaction, appealing for assistance, asking the speaker to clarify or repeat, and using formulaic expressions that function as a unit in common pragmatic contexts.

Seeking Out Families as Resources for Knowledge

Parents should be teachers' number one allies in support of children's linguistic development. Because parents and primary caregivers in immigrant communities sometimes need support in understanding and navigating the educational system in the United States, teachers should share with parents their expectations for children's educational plans. They should encourage the parents to learn how to make use of the home language in support of English development. More specifically, parents and family members should be encouraged to continue speaking and reading in their most comfortable language; this way, children from a young age will develop appreciation for and value their family's heritage language.

Teachers should also make explicit to the parents how the use of the two languages, including code switching, is accepted in the classroom as a linguistic tool to communicate with children. They can also encourage parents to help with various activities in the classroom. For example, bilingual parents can help create dual-language books in children's native languages as part of a class project. Or, teachers can invite parents to bring magazines or material from home to share as part of the classroom's multiliteracy activities (Kenner, 2004). In many indigenous communities, the elders should be invited to share their cultural knowledge and values with the younger generation (Reyhner, 1997). This way, families can learn from each other's cultural and linguistic knowledge and model to all students their appreciation for others' languages.

Another effective practice for teachers is to learn about their students' cultural and linguistic background by making home visits to their families. When teachers become familiar with students' backgrounds, they become more effective at creating a socioculturally supportive learning environment that affirms the cultural and linguistic resources for all students. Families should be actively sought as resources for knowledge generation throughout the school year.

Getting Support in Linguistically Heterogeneous Classrooms

A major factor to be considered when implementing these best practices is the competence of the school personnel in the languages known by the children, and the number of languages involved. The practices described above would work in classrooms where the vast majority of students come from a single linguistic group (as in the Southwest where Spanish is spoken by a majority of immigrant families). However, in places such as San Francisco or New York, where several different languages are spoken in the same classroom, there is a great need to search for general practices that can help improve the education of all children. Moreover, it would be unfair to teachers (and also unrealistic) to expect them to learn many languages or cultural practices when children come from such diverse backgrounds. However, a possible solution is to invite children's relatives and other members of their community to join the classroom. Relatives can serve as language resources to the classroom by sharing or reading stories in the native language (see previous section on "Seeking Out Families as Resources for Knowledge"). Family and community members could serve as visible and audible funds of knowledge for children in the school context (González, Moll, & Amanti, 2005).

An important goal for the implementation of these different practices should be to increase the status and prestige of the students' heritage languages in the classroom. In addition to utilizing the L1 for instructional support, students also learn to view their home language and culture as having an important place in the classroom. The goals of these practices should be to make available to students different "identities" that they can develop and feel comfortable in adopting at school (Iannaci, 2008).

SUMMARY OF MAIN IDEAS

For a long period of time in the United States, code switching was viewed as a deficiency rather than as an important linguistic tool available to bilingual speakers (Amastae & Elías-Olivares, 1982). The studies reviewed in this chapter provide evidence from a different ideological orientation in which code switching is seen as a positive and useful linguistic practice. In addition, these studies point to the complexity of issues involved in children's development of bilingual competence and their connection to code switching and identity.

From a language competence perspective, code switching and language choice by children are indicators of their bilingual abilities. As children become more competent in another language, they can switch languages at different levels (e.g., between sentences or turns) and for different sociolinguistic functions (e.g., for clarification purposes, explanation, for use of a "we" code). In addition, how easy and freely code switching is used depends on whether the languages are grammatically similar and on the child's perception of the prestige each language has in a specific community. From a social and identity perspective, children's code switching at home or school serves as a tool to participate and become members of different speech communities. Children's use of code switching to negotiate membership may depend on whether they find themselves in situations in which they feel they can use their home language comfortably or feel inhibited in using it. There is a great need for research in this area to further understand the connections between identity, culture, and language use among emergent bilingual children. Because bilingual speakers are often not aware themselves of such choices, or even of switching, a challenge in this area is for research to identify the particular reasons that children use one language versus another.

Finally, from a pedagogical perspective, code switching can be used by both teachers and students as part of their classroom discourse practices. Specifically, teachers can support students' learning by modeling code switching as part of the classroom discourse practices, thereby creating a linguistic environment in which children feel comfortable using their native language in the school context. In addition, teachers can actively seek out families and parents as resources for generating knowledge throughout the school year. When teachers become familiar with students' backgrounds, they become more effective at creating a socioculturally supportive learning environment that affirms a range of cultural and linguistic resources for all students. The implementation of these practices will not only help students learn, but it will increase the status and prestige of their heritage languages as part of classroom day-to-day discourse.

IMPLICATIONS FOR RESEARCH, PRACTICE, AND POLICY

Several implications can be drawn from the work reviewed on code switching and language choice by young children. First, research in this area can contribute studies that include children and families from different language groups to see if the same practices can be used within a variety of linguistic communities. Moreover, research can point to more effective teaching strategies to use with children who are learning English as their second, and sometimes as their third, language.

Second, we encourage teachers and educators to move beyond deficit-oriented definitions and understand code switching from a sociocultural perspective. We have seen that code switching is used by speakers as a linguistic tool that allows them to create complex communication and multiple literacies (Iannacci, 2008; Zentella, 1997). Children's development of bilingual communicative competence advances their literacy knowledge in both their first and second languages (see Bedore, Peña, & Boerger, Chapter 4, and Bialystok & Peets, Chapter 6, this volume, for further studies on literacy). In states where English has been made the sole official language and where pro-English monolingual policies have been passed, using code switching as a viable pedagogical tool has been assumed to be counterproductive and has been severely curtailed. Teachers often contribute to the marginalization of heritage languages, typically unknowingly, by accepting one single hegemonic standard. Administrators and teachers need to participate in ongoing dialogue to understand students' development in both their L1 and L2 in order to implement effective practices so that students' growth in a major resource skill—their home language—is not threatened by school reinforcement of English as the official language.

Whenever possible, administrators should support teachers in these efforts by sponsoring specific training to obtain bilingual and/or ESL credentials. This advanced training would provide teachers with the knowledge necessary to work with a diverse population, and it would motivate them to learn from each other and share insights.

Related to this approach, in terms of policy, responsive teachers should question and contest language policies and discourses present in our classroom settings where assimilation is directly or indirectly promoted as part of mainstream learning. The expectation of English monolingualism, often taken for granted and viewed unproblematically in general, should be challenged by teachers and parents. Language programs (e.g., dual-language education, heritage language programs) and literacy strategies should reflect the specific needs of the student population. In particular, the suppression rather than the promotion of L1 spoken and literate skills should be viewed as loss of a major national resource.

Finally, parents should be encouraged to support their children's learning by making use of code switching and the L1 as part of their linguistic strategies. As Troike (2008) said, "Encouraging code switching as a pedagogical and parenting strategy may therefore actually contribute to the development of both languages, though care should be taken that one language does not come to dominate and inhibit the development of the other" (p. 146). It is with the support provided by adults and peers around them that children will have a positive experience and may reclaim their linguistic and cultural identity.

REFERENCES

Amastae, J., & Elías-Olivares, L. (Eds.). (1982). *Spanish in the United States: Sociolinguistic aspects*. New York: Cambridge University Press.

Andersen, E., Brizuela, M., DuPuy, B., & Gonnerman, L. (1999). Cross-linguistic evidence for the early acquisition of discourse markers as register variables. *Journal of Pragmatics, 31*(10), 1339–1351.

Auer, P. (Ed.). (1998). *Code-switching in conversation: Language, interaction and identity*. London: Routledge.

Blom, J. P., & Gumperz, J. J. (1972). Social meaning in linguistic structures: Codeswitching in Norway. In J. J. Gumperz & D. Hymes (Eds.), *Directions in sociolinguistics* (pp. 407–434). New York: Holt, Rinehart, & Winston.

Cashman, H. R. (2004). Identities at play: Language preference and group membership in bilingual talk in interaction. *Journal of Pragmatics, 37,* 301–315.

Comeau, L., Genesee, F., & Lapaquette, L. (2003). The modeling hypothesis and child bilingual codemixing. *International Journal of Bilingualism, 7,* 113–128.

Cromdal, J. (2005). Bilingual order in collaborative word processing: On creating an English text in Swedish. *Journal of Pragmatics, 37*(3), 329–353.

Cummins, J. (2000). *Language, power, and pedagogy: Bilingual children in the crossfire*. Clevedon, UK: Multilingual Matters.

De Fina, A. (2007). Code-switching and the construction of ethnic identity in a community of practice. *Language in Society, 36,* 371–392.

Deuchar, M., Muysken, P., & Want, S.-L. (2007). Structured variation in codeswitching: Towards an empirically based typology of bilingual speech patterns. *International Journal of Bilingual Education and Bilingualism, 10*(3), 298–340.

Díaz-Rico, L. T. (2004). *Strategies for teaching English learners* (2nd ed.). Needham Heights, MA: Allyn & Bacon.

Ervin-Tripp, S. & Reyes, I. (2005). From child code-switching to adult content knowledge. *International Journal of Bilingualism, 9*(1), 85–102.

Fantini, A. E. (1985). *Language acquisition of a bilingual child: A sociolinguistic perspective*. San Diego, CA: College-Hill Press.

Garcia-Sánchez, I. (2009). *Moroccan children in a time of surveillance: Navigating sameness and difference in contemporary Spain*. Unpublished doctoral dissertation, University of California, Los Angeles.

Gardner-Chloros, P. (2000). Parallel patterns: A comparison of monolingual speech and bilingual codeswitching discourse. *Journal of Pragmatics, 32*, 1305–1341.

Genesee, F., & Nicoladis, E. (2007). Bilingual first-language acquisition. In E. Hoff & M. Shatz (Eds.), *Blackwell handbook of language development* (pp. 324–342). Malden, MA: Blackwell.

González, N., Moll, L. C., & Amanti, K. (Eds.). (2005). *Funds of knowledge: Theorizing practices in households, communities, and classrooms.* Mahwah, NJ: Erlbaum.

Gumperz, J. J. (1972). The communicative competence of bilinguals: Some hypotheses and suggestions for research. *Language in Society, 1*(1), 143–154.

Gumperz, J. J. (1982). *Discourse strategies.* Cambridge, UK: Cambridge University Press.

Guthrie, L. F., & Guthrie, G. P. (1987). Teacher language use in a Chinese bilingual classroom. In S. R. Goldman & H. T. Trueba (Eds.), *Becoming literate in English as a second language* (pp. 205–231). Norwood, NJ: Ablex.

Halmari, H., & Smith, W. (1994). Code-switching and register shift: Evidence from Finnish–English child bilingual conversation. *Journal of Pragmatics, 21*(4), 427–445.

Hughes, C. E., Shaunessy, E. S., Brice, A. R., Ratliff, M. A., & Alvarez McHatton, P. (2006). Code switching among bilingual and limited English proficient students: Possible indicators of giftedness. *Journal for the Education of the Gifted, 30*(1), 7–28.

Iannacci, L. (2008). Beyond the pragmatic and the liminal: Culturally and linguistically diverse students' code-switching in early-years classrooms. *TESL Canada Journal, 25*(2), 103–123.

Jørgensen, J. N. (1998). Children's acquisition of code-switching for power wielding. In P. Auer (Ed.), *Code-switching in conversation; Language, interaction and identity* (pp. 237–258). New York: Routledge.

Kenner, C. (2004). *Becoming biliterate: Young children learning different writing systems.* Stoke-on-Trent, UK: Trentham Books.

Mills, J. (2001). Being bilingual: Perspectives of third-generation Asian children on language, culture, and identity. *Journal of Bilingual Education and Bilingualism, 4*(8), 383–402.

Pagett, L. (2006). Mum and Dad prefer me to speak Bengali at home: Code switching and parallel speech in a primary school setting. *Literacy, 40*(3) 137–145.

Paradis, J., & Nicoladis, E. (2007). The influence of dominance and sociolinguistic context on bilingual preschoolers' language choice. *International Journal of Bilingual Education and Bilingualism, 10*(3), 277–297.

Paugh, A. L. (2005). Multilingual play: Children's code-switching, role play, and agency in Dominica, West Indies. *Language in Society, 34*, 63–86.

Poplack, S. (1980). "Sometimes I'll start a sentence in Spanish *y termino en español*": Toward a typology of code-switching. *Linguistics, 18*(7), 581–618.

Poplack, S. (1981). Syntactic structure and social function of codeswitching. In R. P. Duran (Ed.), *Latino language and communicative behavior* (pp. 169–184). Norwood, NJ: Ablex.

Rampton, B. (1998). Crossing: Language and ethnicity among adolescents. In P. Auer (Ed.), *Code-switching in conversation: Language, interaction and identity* (pp. 290–317). New York: Routledge.

Reyes, I. (2004). Functions of code switching in schoolchildren's conversations. *Bilingual Research Journal, 28*(1), 77–98.

Reyes, I., & Azuara, P. (2008). Emergent biliteracy in young Mexican immigrant children. *Reading Research Quarterly, 43*(4), 374–398.

Reyes, I., Soltero, L., & Azuara, P. (2006, December). *The development of emergent biliteracy in preschool children.* Paper presented at the annual meeting of the National Reading Conference, Los Angeles.

Reyhner, J. (Ed.). (1997). *Teaching indigenous languages* (pp. v–xii). Flagstaff: Northern Arizona University.

Roca, A. (2005). Raising a bilingual child in Miami: Reflections on language and culture. In A. C. Zentella (Ed.), *Building on strength: Language and literacy in Latino families and communities* (pp. 110–118). New York: Teachers College Press; Covina: California Association for Bilingual Education.

Sebba, M., & Wootton, T. (1998). We, they, and identity: Sequential versus identity-related explanation in code-switching. In P. Auer (Ed.), *Code-switching in conversation: Language, interaction and identity* (pp. 262–290). London: Routledge.

Troike, R. (2008). Code-switching. In J. M. González (Ed.), *Encyclopedia of bilingual education* (pp. 142–147). Thousand Oaks, CA: Sage.

Valdés, G. (2003). *Expanding definitions of giftedness: The case of young interpreters of immigrant communities.* Mahwah, NJ: Erlbaum.

Wong Fillmore, L. (2000). Loss of family languages: Should educators be concerned? *Theory into Practice, 39*(4), 203–221.

Zentella, A. (1997). *Growing up bilingual: Puerto Rican children in New York.* Malden, MA: Blackwell.

Zentella, A. (2008). Preface. In M. Niño-Murcia & J. Rothman (Eds.), *Bilingualism and identity.* Philadelphia: Benjamins.

PART II

LANGUAGE AND LITERACY PRINCIPLES AND PRACTICES IN SCHOOL

4

Ways to Words
Learning a Second-Language Vocabulary

Lisa M. Bedore
Elizabeth D. Peña
Karin Boerger

FOCUS POINTS

- Bilingual children's vocabulary is distributed across two languages, and the underlying semantic base is larger than the lexicon of either language.

- Because bilingual children tend not to have large proportions of overlapping vocabulary, we should not expect them to provide the same responses in both languages.

- Depth and breadth of vocabulary knowledge are both important to academic success. Lexical and semantic knowledge in each language can facilitate the development of breadth and depth across bilingual learners' languages.

- Vocabulary lessons need to explicitly address multiple aspects of vocabulary learning, including the ways that words sound, word meaning, and word use.

- Teachers and speech–language pathologists can collaborate to improve vocabulary knowledge by focusing as a team on the vocabulary children will use in the classroom and by teaching children strategies to acquire new vocabulary independently.

- To facilitate efficient recall of the vocabulary, educators need to ensure that children have multiple exposures to new vocabulary and that they link their vocabulary across languages. Teachers can accomplish this by identifying translation equivalents and cognates.

CHAPTER PURPOSE

The purpose of this chapter is to review theoretical perspectives on vocabulary acquisition as they apply to children who are exposed to two languages either simultaneously or sequentially. We consider how current research on vocabulary development in these children in the early school years fits within these theoretical frameworks. Evaluating research in this way can help us develop principled approaches to assessing and teaching vocabulary to bilingual and English language learning (ELL) children, both with and without language impairment.

A young child's vocabulary links his or her world knowledge or conceptual system with his or her ability to communicate effectively through sentences and discourse. To learn words, children need to attend to the sound sequences that comprise them (e.g., /dog/ vs. /log/), determine if they know that word, and then either retrieve (and perhaps refine) the meaning for that word or figure out what the word means (for a review, see Bloom, 2000). Words are also building blocks for more complex language. For example, children need to acquire about 50 words before they begin to combine them into sentences. Children's receptive vocabulary size is a key predictor of reading success. Vocabulary concepts and specific word knowledge helps children compare words they sound out with the words they know in order to extract meaning from print. What is unique about bilingual word learning, regardless of the age at which one begins to acquire the second language, is that bilinguals have a single conceptual system but vocabulary specific to each of their languages; they know words in their first language (L1) as well as their second language (L2).

Word-Learning Theory and Bilinguals

Several theories address different aspects of word learning, such as how children acquire words initially and how they develop full meanings of words (Clark, 1993; Hollich, Golinkoff, & Hirsh-Pasek, 2007; Hollich et al., 2000; Maguire, Hirsh-Pasek, & Golinkoff, 2006; Merriman & MacWhinney, 1999). One common feature of these proposals is recognition that learners must be able to efficiently identify sound sequences of words and extract lexical items from the speech stream (Bloom, 2000; Jarvis, Merriman, Barnett, Hanba, & Van Haitsma, 2004; Merriman & Marazita, 1995). Researchers also agree that children commonly make several assumptions about the meaning of new words until or unless they have evidence that contradicts these basic assumptions. For example, children are more likely to assume that words are nouns referring to objects than verbs or adjectives referring to actions or attributes (Golinkoff et al., 2000; Golinkoff, Jacquet, Hirsh-Pasek, & Nandakumar, 1996). They also assume that new words refer to previously unnamed objects and to whole objects rather than their parts (Clark, 1993; Golinkoff et al., 1996). Finally, children resist learning multiple words with precisely the same meanings (Golinkoff et al., 1996). Most of these proposals focus on monolingual development but can be extended to bilingual word learning. Bilingual and ELL children also need to develop strategies that will permit them to acquire multiple words for the same concepts and transfer knowledge across their languages.

Several models address cross-language transfer of knowledge (MacWhinney, 2005). Early models of lexical organization and transfer worked on the assumption that bilinguals had and used the same words in both of their languages (Kormos, 2006). But as it has become clear that knowledge of each bilingual's lexicon reflects his or her experience in that language, this original model has been gradually modified. A current version of this model is expressed in work focusing on the developmental hypothesis (Kroll & de Groot, 1997; Kroll & Tokowicz, 2005; Potter, So, von Eckardt, & Feldman, 1984), which incorporates both the word-association model—in which words in the L2 are mediated through the L1 to access the conceptual system—and the concept mediation model—in which words in the L2 are linked directly to the conceptual system. In the developmental hypothesis it is proposed that there is a shift in strategies as individuals increase their fluency in an L2 from word association to conceptual mediation. Thus, in early stages of L2 acquisition, if a child hears a word in the L2, the meaning will be accessed via the word in the L1 and its connection to the concept. Over development children gradually learn to transfer word knowledge between the first and second languages at the lexical level. As learners become more proficient in their L2, they gain the ability to acquire vocabulary via either language or the links between the lexicon of both languages and between the lexicon, and underlying semantic representations or concepts gain strength. This model will help us understand how children move from being able to learn vocabulary in their L1 to being able to learn vocabulary in either language.

The unified model (MacWhinney, 2005) is discussed here to complement our understanding of what learners do when processing linguistic information to learn an L2. This model emphasizes that there are multiple cues to meaning in language input. Some cues provide converging information and are highly reliable, whereas other cues may compete and thus be somewhat less reliable. Cues that bilinguals and ELLs need to attend to include word order—for example, English follows a subject–verb–object order so the first word or phrase in a sentence is likely to be a noun. They also need to attend to the chunks in which words occur. Thus, it would be beneficial to hear a verb such as *draw* in multiple utterances to learn the full range of uses, such as the intransitive "he *draws* well," the transitive "he *drew* the car," and the alternate meaning "he *drew* the winning ticket." None of these models, however, specifically addresses the fact that young sequential bilinguals who are educated in a language other than their home language will likely shift dominance to that language.

Here we consider how current literature on vocabulary learning in sequential bilingual children who are in the process of learning an L2 fits within Kroll's developmental model (Kroll & Tokowicz, 2005), and how the mechanisms proposed in the unified model might be used to facilitate vocabulary learning across two languages (MacWhinney, 2005). Data on vocabulary learning and production support the initial and end points of the developmental model. We also discuss how the developmental model can be extended, by taking into account some of the mechanisms proposed in the unified model, to show how knowledge of the two languages interacts to increase the breadth and depth of children's vocabulary overall. However, the developmental model might need to be adapted to account for the shift to an L2 that is better developed than the L1, since it is a common situation for sequential bilinguals who are educated in an L2, as is the norm in the United States. Based on the developmental hypothesis, we can develop educational and intervention strategies to maximize the development of breadth and depth in vocabulary development.

REVIEW OF RESEARCH AND THEORY

Initially links between the L2 lexicon and underlying L2 semantic representations are weak or nonexistent (Kroll & Tokowicz, 2005). Figure 4.1 illustrates a common pattern of early vocabulary production in an L2 or early bilingual acquisition. The child has more lexical items in L1 than in L2, but the underlying concepts for all of the lexical items are represented. The child's stronger language is highlighted in gray. As illustrated here, children who are in the process of becoming bilingual often have low rates of overlap between the lexicons of their languages, suggesting awareness of the concepts for which they have lexical items in each language (Pearson & Fernández, 1994; Peña, Bedore, & Zlatic-Giunta,

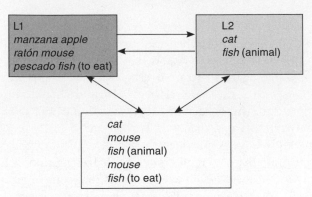

FIGURE 4.1. Early in L2 vocabulary acquisition the links between L2 and underlying concepts are weak, and there is little overlap with LI. Based on Kroll's (Kroll & de Groot, 1997) concept mediation model.

2002). The underlying semantic concepts for the lexicon across each of the languages represent the child's knowledge better than the lexicon of either language individually (Bedore, Peña, García, & Cortez, 2005). However, the fact that there is little overlap in the lexicon suggests that the learner has some level of awareness that these concepts are already represented by words in his or her lexicon. This awareness may inhibit the child from adding new words in one language that he or she has in the other language. If learners were unaware of the translation equivalence of word pairs, they would have more overlap.

Learning New Words

To the extent that the initial phase of vocabulary learning depends on phonological processing skills in the L2, it seems particularly challenging for bilingual children. Although these children need to learn the sound patterns and meanings of L2 words, they are exposed to fewer exemplars in each language compared to monolinguals (Kohnert & Bates, 2002; Oller, Pearson, & Cobo-Lewis, 2007). Bilingual children's mismatches or word-use errors suggest that sometimes they fail to form fully accurate phonological representations (Peña & Bedore, 2008) and that they sometimes produce phonologically related items when attempting to recall vocabulary. The following examples come from our database of language samples with sequential Spanish–English bilinguals who began to learn English in prekindergarten classes. A first grader called a *rhinoceros* by an invented name, [rinocornio] (rhinocorn), in Spanish when asked to name zoo animals. A second grader started his story with "It was a beautiful *shiny* day," when the picture illustrated a sunny day. Another second grader called a *boat* a [bark]. This error seems to represent English phonological structure overlaid on the Spanish word *barco*, for *ship*. Errors such as these are relatively rare and suggest that children are developing a sufficiently detailed representation of the sound system as they learn vocabulary in their L2. At the same time the errors reflect the semantic knowledge from which these bilingual children draw when they cannot call up the correct phonological representation of the target word. The fact that these errors exist suggests that sometimes it may be difficult for children to recognize L2 vocabulary when it is not accurately stored or when the representation is not fully formed. Incomplete or shallow representations could be problematic when children participate in receptive vocabulary activities, wherein they need to select a picture that corresponds to a word. An example of this is a child who selects *girl* (her) instead of *ear* when asked to respond to the word *heard*. The response is clearly an error; weak phonological representation interferes with the child's ability to respond correctly.

Transfer between L1 and L2

One interesting question about the early stages of L2 vocabulary acquisition is the extent to which children are aware of the links between the L1 and the L2. Some work exploring the developmental model and the concept mediation model suggested that the route from semantic representation to the L2 lexicon occurs via the L1. However, children's avoidance of the translation equivalents suggests some awareness of which concepts are associated with each language (Bedore et al., 2005; Pearson & Fernández, 1994; Peña et al., 2002). These differences could be due to the fact that children need to add new words *and* concepts to their semantic system. Adults, on the other hand, already have an established conceptual system and lexicon that can aid in learning new words in another language. Figure 4.2 shows that as bilingual children add vocabulary and increase breadth they continue to add few overlapping lexical items across languages. All of the concepts are still represented, and items could be added to the conceptual level from either language. The lexicons for both languages are highlighted in gray here because there is a balance between the languages in vocabulary size at this point. The types of words that sequential bilinguals who use one language at home and another at school add to each of their vocabularies may also differ because of the differences in experiences and because concepts are lexi-

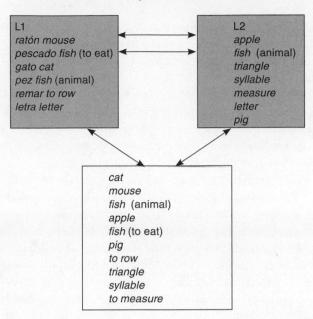

FIGURE 4.2. Sequential bilinguals may add different lexical items to their vocabularies based on their home language and school language experiences.

calized differently across languages (Choi, McDonough, Bowerman, & Mandler, 1999). Studies focusing on the ways that children develop an initial representation of word meanings provide some insights into why words tend to be added in one language but not the other.

When children learn new words, they tend to assume that the new words refer to previously unnamed objects and whole objects rather than to parts. Furthermore, they resist learning multiple words with precisely the same meanings. Five-year-olds only accepted another name for an object when it was clear that the new label came from another language (Au & Glusman, 1990). Davidson and Tell (2005) studied bilingual and monolingual children's interpretation of novel (invented) words that referred to a familiar or an unfamiliar object. Bilingual 5- and 6-year-olds were less likely to use a new label for an object (familiar or unfamiliar) than younger bilingual children or monolingual children. But all of the children were more likely to accept a new label when it was clearly different from other familiar objects because it had a salient spare part attached. When the investigators followed up by asking the children to identify the specific referent (the whole object or the spare part) of the new label, bilingual children were more likely to select the whole object than the spare part, in contrast to the monolingual children, who selected the spare part.

Pragmatic constraints may also influence bilingual children's willingness to accept another label for a familiar object. Diesendruck (2005) used "monolingual" and "bilingual" puppets to teach Hebrew–English preschool-age bilinguals new labels for already named novel creatures. Children were much more likely to accept a second label for the creature when they were interacting with a bilingual puppet. These studies suggest that even though bilingual children are aware that objects can have two names, they may be conservative in applying them.

Production data from our work provide insight into the kinds of distinct words and translation equivalent forms that children are likely to employ. Kindergarten-age Spanish–English sequential bilinguals were asked to name objects in categories (e.g., "Tell me all the foods you can eat at a birthday party") (Bedore et al., 2005; Peña et al., 2002). In this category-generation task some elements tended to be common across languages, such as *cake* and *ice cream*. Other items were language and culture specific. Thus among the most common Spanish responses were *rice* and *beans*, whereas in English children tended to include *hamburgers* and *hotdogs* on their list. In more recent work we have continued to employ the same task with second and third graders and college-age bilinguals. The pattern of limited overlap is robust even as students are able to generate an increasing number of items. *Cake* is a common element in college-age Spanish–English students' responses as well as those of other language pairs, including Hindi–English and Russian–English. School-age students and college-age students generate more items in each of their languages. They also seem to generate more items that overlap across the two languages in comparison to younger children. But, there are still more nonoverlapped items overall. Some categories (e.g., food, clothing) show more language-specific responses, yielding relatively few overlapped or translation-equivalent responses.

Increasing Vocabulary Size

For children to use vocabulary fluently, they need to have continued exposure to words so as to ultimately increase the size of their lexicon. This is called *breadth of vocabulary knowledge*. When children learn about additional meanings of words or more about the contexts and/ or sentences structures in which new words can be used, they increase vocabulary depth (Vermeer, 2001). What is unique about bilingual language acquisition is that children's input (and their resulting linguistic knowledge) is spread across languages. Because language input is spread across two languages, it may be challenging to form an initial representation of a new word—particularly before phonological representations are sufficiently developed to facilitate the recognition of new words. Spreading word knowledge across two languages supports the development of breadth. It may also take longer for bilingual learners to gain depth of knowledge because they reencounter the words less often, given that their linguistic experience is distributed across two languages (Gollan, Montoya, Cera, & Sandoval, 2008). The other unique aspect of bilingual vocabulary acquisition is that children may have multiple lexical items corresponding to a single concept. The development of breadth and depth across the two lexicons is illustrated in Figure 4.3. As children's experiences with each language grow, the lexicon of each is enriched by knowledge of the other. For example, the idea that an animal and food name differ in one language (e.g., *pez–pescado*) may transfer to the other. Children may also recognize some of the similari-

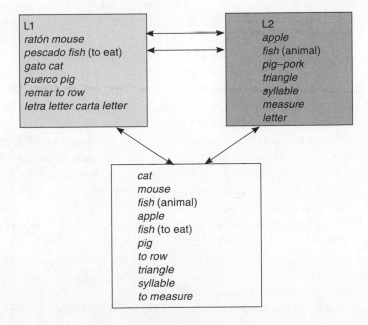

FIGURE 4.3. As children's experiences with each language grow, the lexicon of each is enriched by knowledge of the other.

ties between names for objects, especially cognates, and add additional meanings to words they have in the lexicons. As above, there is still relative balance between the languages in terms of vocabulary size; thus both are highlighted.

A strong vocabulary base may also support efficient word-learning strategies in bilingual children. Kan and Kohnert (2007) taught Hmong–English bilingual preschoolers novel words in each of their languages. Children's ability to learn new words in a short teaching task was associated with higher receptive vocabulary scores in each of their languages. This finding suggests that accumulated vocabulary knowledge (as measured by the children's receptive vocabulary) supports the addition of new words to the lexicon or vocabulary breadth.

Depth or richness of meaning in bilingual children is facilitated by exposure to the multiple contexts of word use. Silverman (2007) provided vocabulary intervention focusing on vocabulary in literature-based contexts for kindergarten-age bilinguals for one semester. Bilingual children demonstrated growth at the same rate on standardized vocabulary measures as their monolingual classmates. These gains held to the end of the year. Although the researcher did not specifically test the richness of the children's representations, the fact that children were taught in context-rich activities suggests that teaching can target depth. Error data from second- and third-grade sequential bilinguals in our dataset provide insight into some of the ways in which children may make associations across languages that facilitate depth of knowledge. One example is the child who refers to a school *principal* as a *director* (perhaps based on the Spanish cognate *director*, which could be used for a school *principal*). The word *director* in English is not as precise, but it is certainly related. Another error is to provide a description such as the "circle with antennas" to describe a spaceship. Being able to provide a description when a child does not have a specific lexical item available may be communicatively effective in demonstrating knowledge. In this case the child may be relying on words acquired in school (e.g., the concept *circle* is particularly likely to be taught in school) or cognates, as both of the words are cognates in Spanish and English. Thus by having two lexicons available, children may be able to associate knowledge and work their way toward richer representation of words that are not yet well established in their L2 lexicon, as in the examples illustrated here.

The process of language loss is well documented in bilingual children and typically involves lack of access to low-frequency structures or low-frequency words in the case of vocabulary (Anderson, 2001; Restrepo & Kruth, 2000; Schiff-Meyers, 1992). Figure 4.4 represents a possible

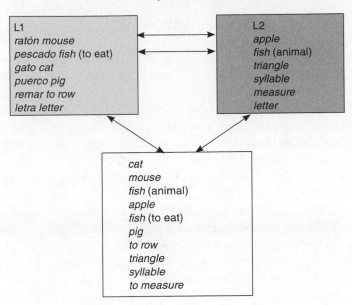

FIGURE 4.4. As the second language becomes stronger children may lose access to L1 vocabulary but not underlying concepts.

scenario in which children may have weaker representations in the L1. The weakening status of the language is represented by the lighter shading of the L1 lexicon, and the weakening items are represented in gray text, but the knowledge is not entirely lost, given that the child retains the semantic representation at the underlying conceptual level and perhaps acquires the word in the other language. When children are educated in their L2, and it becomes stronger than the L1, a shift in balance between the two lexicons may develop. Children do not necessarily lose underlying concepts, but as the L2 becomes stronger, children may lose access to words in the L1. Examples are highlighted in gray. A case study comparing a child with language impairment and a classmate with typical language skills shows that the child with language impairment showed more significant language loss (Restrepo & Kruth, 2000). But studies with children who move from place to place have provided documentation that loss may be temporary (e.g., Faingold, 1999). This is a topic that bears further investigation because there is a tendency to stop using the L1 with children who have trouble using that language and increase the amount of L2 use (Merino, 1983). Long-term vocabulary growth may be facilitated by continued use of the L1 even if it is temporarily frustrating.

BEST PRACTICES

Teachers and speech–language pathologists (SLPs) understand the importance of increasing oral vocabulary knowledge in ELL students to support academic language skills, but they have little research to inform their instructional practices. However, emerging studies of vocabulary acquisition in school-age bilingual children and studies that explicitly evaluate vocabulary instruction provide information that informs best practices on vocabulary development, particularly for those children in the transitional period, moving from Spanish to English instruction in the schools.

ELL children are most likely to benefit from instruction that increases both vocabulary breadth and depth. Three of the most important approaches to effectively teaching Spanish-speaking children English vocabulary are (1) to provide repeated exposure to words in multiple contexts; (2) to utilize the children's knowledge of their L1 to learn English words, particularly by studying cognates; and (3) to teach children explicitly about words by directly teaching vocabulary words and definitions and by discussing their parts of speech, roots, and morphological components.

Often teachers present new vocabulary to ELL students in decontextualized formats, in the same manner that it is presented to children who speak English as a first language. Teachers often present a weekly list of key, grade-level words with their corresponding definitions and/or spellings for children to memorize. Teachers then test the children on the words at the end of the week without providing explicit links between the listed words and the curriculum. At the week's end it is unlikely that the classroom curriculum reviews those words; rather, it progresses to a new set. The intent is to expose children to many new words throughout the course of a school year to increase the breadth of their vocabulary. This approach may not provide sufficient exposure for bilingual children. By progressing through word sets without review or explicit curricular links, ELL students who speak their L1 outside of school will have only superficial exposure to these words—unlike English monolingual children, who are likely to have repeated exposure.

Traditionally, through the treatment approach called a *pullout* model, SLPs have written and carried out language goals somewhat independent of the children's classroom curricula. This method is likely to decontextualize vocabulary teaching. For example, when teaching younger children, a common goal might be this: "Child will identify and categorize 10 items correctly from the following categories—animals, foods, transportation—with 80% accuracy after a model." The SLP then teaches these vocabulary items by engaging the child in categorization activities. Often the only context of the activity is the task of categorizing, rather than using the words from a category in a meaningful way, such as in interactive storybook reading or play-based engagement with the vocabulary words. Generally, there is little attempt to integrate the weekly treatment objectives with the vocabulary taught in the classroom. For older children, SLPs often use vocabulary-building programs. These programs are not typically used by the classroom teacher, nor are there opportunities for targeting words that overlap with the classroom curriculum. Furthermore, there is variability between vocabulary-building curricula: Some programs utilize recommended best practices, whereas others do not. Lastly, not all programs are specially designed for ELL children.

The results of recent studies suggest that, rather than teach vocabulary words in a single-faceted, decontextualized manner, teachers and SLPs should create a variety of contexts in which the children can learn and use vocabulary words, and instruction should be multidimensional. Carlo and colleagues (2004) tested an instructional strategy in which teachers presented only 12 vocabulary words a week across multiple text genres within one topic. The program lasted 15 weeks, with reviews of previous vocabulary items every fifth week. It also included exercises in root-word analysis, morphological relationships, comprehension monitoring, and cognate work. At the end of the program children demonstrated improvements in vocabulary knowledge and comprehension. Another study by Calderon and colleagues (2005), this time completed with third graders in the transitional period, included many similar components with an additional preteaching exercise on a DVD. Children participated in extensive vocabulary instruction exercises in both reading and oral exercises that focused on cognate instruction, root and morphological analysis, translational information, and phonological awareness and pronunciation, among others. At the end of the 6-week study, the experimental group showed an improvement in English vocabulary and, surprisingly, in Spanish vocabulary as well. This short but focused intervention potentially provided benefits for children's reading comprehension in both of their languages. Silverman (2007) also demonstrated that multidimensional vocabulary instruction for kindergartners was more effective than unidimensional instruction. Through storybook reading, she provided definitions and explanations of words, asked questions about word meanings, provided opportunities for children to act out words, pronounce the words, observe the word spelling, and compare the words to other words. She also provided opportunities for children to repeat and review the words. The ELL children in her study learned target words at a similar rate as the English monolingual children.

Overall, vocabulary instruction must be multifaceted and focused on both increasing the breadth and depth of children's knowledge. One technique should not be taught at the exclusion of others; rather, multiple approaches, across multiple formats with frequent review, should be employed with each new vocabulary word. What might this look like? Take the example of vocabulary instruction within a science unit. Children in early elementary grades learn how to conduct experiments about the world around them. One typical activity for children is to observe how water takes up volume in its different states of matter. Table 4.1 displays some possible examples for employing different instructional dimensions to a key set of vocabulary within such a science unit. The table is not exhaustive, but it demonstrates how one set of contextually relevant words might be taught across multiple domains with multiple techniques. The identified target vocabulary words for this unit are *prediction, investigation, observation, conclusion, liquid, solid, gas,* and *volume*.

When treating ELL students who have language impairment, SLPs should work within the context of the classroom curriculum with the teacher's input. Though the pullout model was previously favored, there is momentum on a national level to the response-to-intervention (RTI) model of treatment. In the RTI model, SLPs are expected to allocate more time in the classroom working with children who already have identified needs as well as with children who are considered at risk. While SLPs are encouraged to spend more time in the classrooms working with a range of students, they also can effectively utilize one-on-one or small-group instruction with students who require more attention. SLPs might introduce vocabulary words before they are introduced in class so that children become familiar with them, and they might provide another text genre or experiential learning opportunity in order to increase children's exposure to the class vocabulary words. SLP treatment could take many forms, but most important is to *align instruction with the classroom curriculum*.

These strategies build on the research discussed above in two ways. First, repeated exposures help children all the way through the learning process by increasing the salience of cues (MacWhinney, 2005) and by increasing the connections between words and concepts (Kroll & Toko-wicz, 2005). Repetition helps develop stronger phonological representations on the words so that they can be retrieved and processed more effi-

TABLE 4.1. Teaching Scripts That Contextualize Vocabulary Teaching

Dimension	Vocabulary	Sample teaching scripts
Cognates	*liquid* *solid* *volume* *investigation*	TEACHER: "Cognates are words that look the same or sound the same in two languages. Many times, when words look the same and sound the same, they also have the same meaning. The word *liquid* in English is a cognate of the word *liquido* in Spanish. They sound similar but they look even more alike (*teacher writes words on board*)"
Parts of speech	*prediction* *investigation*	TEACHER: "Verbs are action words. Nouns are people, places, or things. Some words, if you change them just a little, can change from verbs to nouns and back again. Our vocabulary words, *prediction* and *investigation*, are nouns. If we change the last syllable—the part of the word that sounds like *tion*, to a *t* sound—these nouns become verbs."
Simple definitions	*prediction* *observation*	TEACHER: "Sometimes the best way to learn a new word is to begin by defining it with a simple word we already know. You all know what the word *guess* means. We make a guess when we are not sure of the answer. We play the game Guess Who? and try to figure out who touched our thumb when our eyes were closed. A *prediction* is like a guess. It is a guess about what is going to happen."
Writing activity	*prediction* *liquid* *solid* *gas* *volume*	WORKSHEET: "My prediction is that when water is a _____, it will take up _____ volume." "My observation is that when water is a _____, it takes up _____ volume." "Conclusion: _____."
Applications	*liquid* *solid* *gas*	TEACHER: "In our school there are many forms of matter. We have liquids, solids, and gases in our school. We're going to take a walk and see if we can find each different kind of matter in our school. You will write down observations in your field notebook, and we will talk about our conclusions when we return to class."
Orthography (comparing words) and word repetition out loud	*prediction* *investigation* *observation* *conclusion*	TEACHER: "We talked about how, if we make little changes to some words, they can change from nouns to verbs. When we made those changes, we kept the root of the words and changed the ending. Let's look at all of our scientific process nouns (*teacher writes them on the board*). Do you notice anything about the endings of these nouns?" "Three of the nouns have the same four letters in their ending, but one is different. Let's see if they all sound the same or if they sound different.

ciently. Repeated contexts help ensure that children will recall the word in the future. A pitfall of distributed vocabulary knowledge is the resulting decrease in opportunities to hear the same words in each language. Here we deliberately create opportunity to reinforce knowledge, which is especially critical for children with language impairment. Repeated use helps children acquire deeper knowledge of the words in their lexicon. Second, making deliberate comparisons between the languages reinforces links between the lexicons of each language (Kroll & Tokowicz, 2005) and links the lexicon to other linguistic domains (MacWhinney, 2005). This is a skill that may emerge gradually on its own for typically developing children, but because of their generally weaker processing skills may be unavailable to the child with language impairment. Making this more apparent will speed the process for typically developing children and perhaps make it accessible for children with language impairment.

With the movement toward an RTI model, there may be more opportunity in the future for SLPs to provide optimal vocabulary instruction. The RTI model allows for increased collaboration between general and special educators. Ideally, for vocabulary instruction, an SLP will know which word corpus is being taught in a classroom and find ways to bolster children's learning by providing multiple contexts in which to experience the words and to find effective explicit ways to teach word meanings. The SLP can also provide consultation with the classroom teacher to identify effective strategies or best practices for children who are falling behind in the classroom.

SUMMARY OF MAIN IDEAS

In the sections above we discussed research of vocabulary learning and production as it related to the developmental hypothesis (Kroll & Tokowicz, 2005). One question that has been addressed in work on the developmental hypothesis is the extent to which concepts are initially mediated through L1 knowledge. Data on the initial phases of learning suggests that, at least for early sequential bilinguals who are typically still learning their L1, the lexicons and the underlying semantic representations are linked. This linkage is supported by the relatively low rates of overlap observed in children's learning and production of vocabulary. Pragmatic, linguistic, and experiential constraints all work against overlap, unless there is a specific need for it. Speech production errors, where children use similar but incorrect words, suggest that the links between form and meaning may be weak because children do not yet have a strong representation of the word. Weak word representations decreases ability to associate words and meaning rapidly and efficiently during this time when they are still learning about the phonological and phonotactic systems of the L2.

Breadth and depth of vocabulary knowledge are both important to academic success. As children develop the interactive links between L1, L2, and conceptual knowledge, as shown in Figures 4.2 and 4.3, it appears that practice using vocabulary enriches vocabulary knowledge. Thus, the more words children already know, the more words they are likely to learn. But having experience using both may help children make connections between the languages. Thus the source of growth is by no means restricted to L2 exposure at school.

IMPLICATIONS FOR RESEARCH, PRACTICE, AND POLICY

The developmental model highlights the relationship between underlying semantic knowledge and the lexicon. Semantic knowledge supports development across languages and is crucial for the effective acquisition of new vocabulary. However, the lexicon in either of the bilingual's lexicons may not be a good indicator of his or her total vocabulary knowledge. The more experience children have processing cues, the better they will become at learning new vocabulary.

The most important implication for assessment research is the need to develop tools that reflect children's semantic knowledge overall. Measures that focus on the lexical level (in either language) are likely to be a mismatch relative to the learner's total vocabulary knowledge. The research tasks discussed here, such as category-generation measures, can provide insight into semantic knowledge because they do not require the knowledge of specific lexical items (e.g., "Tell me the foods you can eat for lunch" can be answered as appropriately with *sandwich, apple,* and *cheese* as with *enchiladas, rice,* and *orange*). This task has been successfully incorporated into the Bilingual English Spanish Assessment (Peña, Gutierrez-Clellen, Iglesias, Goldstein, & Bedore, 2009). Measures that adequately reflect depth of knowledge in addition to breadth are also needed.

A key teaching implication also relates to the need to incorporate overall semantic knowledge to facilitate vocabulary growth. There have been relatively few studies of educational or intervention strategies for vocabulary growth, but these studies illustrate that systematic instruction can lead to change in both languages. We need to study further how to build L2 vocabulary. When there is support for both languages, teaching the same vocabulary in both languages is most likely unnecessary, since children typically do not systematically add the same words in each language. However, in situations where there is no L1 support, providing parents with the vocabulary (in their L1 and L2) that their children are learning in school may help support lexical and semantic development and provide important information to parents about what their children are learning. If such a strategy were explored, we would most likely find that parents would benefit from support in implementing vocabulary teaching by either giving them specific activities along with the vocabulary or providing ideas about the ways in which vocabulary could be taught.

Policy implications also emerge from the recognition of the importance of maintaining a strong base of knowledge for the acquisition of both languages. Even when maintenance of the L1 is not an educational goal, it should be recognized as an important support system for the development of the L2. We need to continue to evaluate the outcomes of programs that provide bilingual education or later transition programs. Recognizing that these programs are not always practical or feasible, given the range of languages spoken in the United States and the availability of personnel, we need to identify educational practices and policies that help children maintain their knowledge base across languages. Educating parents to maintain the home language may be one approach to this challenge, as many parents tend to, or are advised to, speed their children's transition to English. Supplementary instruction in the L1 may also be a way to help maintain children's semantic knowledge base.

REFERENCES

Anderson, R. (2001). Lexical morphology and verb use in child first language loss: A preliminary case study investigation. *International Journal of Bilingualism, 5*(4), 377–401.

Au, T. K.-F., & Glusman, M. (1990). The principle of mutual exclusivity in word learning: To honor or not to honor? *Child Development, 61*, 1474–1490.

Bedore, L. M., Peña, E. D., García, M., & Cortez, C. (2005). Conceptual versus monolingual scoring: When does it make a difference? *Speech, Language, Hearing Services in Schools, 36*, 188–200.

Bloom, P. (2000). *How children learn the meanings of words*. Cambridge, MA: MIT Press.

Calderón, M., August, D., Slavin, R., Duran, D., Madden, N., Cheung, A., et al. (2005). Bringing words to life in classrooms with English-language learners.

In E. H. Hiebert & M. L. Kamil (Eds.), *Teaching and learning vocabulary: Bringing research to practice* (pp. 115–136). Mahwah, NJ: Erlbaum.

Carlo, M. S., August, D., McLaughlin, B., Snow, C. E., Dressler, C., Lippman, D. N., et al. (2004). Closing the gap: Addressing the vocabulary needs of English language learners in bilingual and mainstream classrooms. *Reading Research Quarterly, 39*(2), 188–215.

Choi, S., McDonough, L., Bowerman, M., & Mandler, J. (1999). Early sensitivity to language-specific spatial categories in English and Korean. *Cognitive Development, 14,* 241–268.

Clark, E. V. (1993). *The lexicon in acquisition.* New York: Cambridge University Press.

Davidson, D., & Tell, D. (2005). Monolingual and bilingual children's use of mutual exclusivity in the naming of whole objects. *Journal of Experimental Child Psychology, 92*(1), 25–45.

Diesendruck, G. (2005). The principles of conventionality and contrast in word learning: An empirical examination. *Developmental Psychology, 41*(3), 451–463.

Faingold, E. D. (1999). The Re-emergence of Spanish and Hebrew in a multilingual adolescent. *International Journal of Bilingual Education and Bilingualism, 2*(4), 283–295.

Golinkoff, R. M., Hirsh-Pasek, K., Bloom, L., Smith, L. B., Woodward, A. L., Akhtar, N., et al. (2000). *Becoming a word learner: A debate on lexical acquisition.* Oxford, UK: Oxford University Press.

Golinkoff, R. M., Jacquet, R. C., Hirsh-Pasek, K., & Nandakumar, R. (1996). Lexical principles may underlie the learning of verbs. *Child Development, 67*(6), 3101–3119.

Gollan, T. H., Montoya, R. I., Cera, C., & Sandoval, T. C. (2008). More use almost always means a smaller frequency effect: Aging, bilingualism, and the weaker links hypothesis. *Journal of Memory and Language, 58*(3), 787–814.

Hollich, G. J., Golinkoff, R. M., & Hirsh-Pasek, K. (2007). Young children associate novel words with complex objects rather than salient parts. *Developmental Psychology, 43*(5), 1051–1061.

Hollich, G. J., Hirsh-Pasek, K., Golinkoff, R. M., Brand, R. J., Brown, E., Chung, H. L., et al. (2000). Breaking the language barrier: An emergentist coalition model for the origins of word learning. *Monographs of the Society for Research in Child Development, 65*(3, Serial No. 262).

Jarvis, L. H., Merriman, W. E., Barnett, M., Hanba, J., & Van Haitsma, K. S. (2004). Input that contradicts young children's strategy for mapping novel words affects their phonological and semantic interpretation of other novel words. *Journal of Speech, Language, and Hearing Research, 47*(2), 392–406.

Kan, P. F., & Kohnert, K. (2008). Fast mapping by bilingual preschool children. *Journal of Child Language, 35*(3), 495–514.

Kohnert, K., & Bates, E. (2002). Balancing bilinguals: II. Lexical compehension and cogitive processing in children learning Spanish and English. *Journal of Speech, Language, and Hearing Research, 45,* 347–359.

Kormos, J. (2006). *Speech production and second language acquisition*. Mahwah, NJ: Erlbaum.

Kroll, J. F., & de Groot, A. M. B. (1997). Lexical and conceptual memory in the bilingual: Mapping form to meaning in two languages. In J. F. Kroll & A. M. B. de Groot (Eds.), *Tutorials in bilingualism: Psycholinguistic perspectives* (pp. 169–199). Mahwah, NJ: Erlbaum.

Kroll, J. F., & Tokowicz, N. (2005). Models of bilingual representation and processing: Looking back and to the future. In J. F. Kroll & A. M. B. de Groot (Eds.), *Handbook of bilingualism* (pp. 531–555). Oxford, UK: Oxford University Press.

MacWhinney, B. (2005). A unified model of language acquisition. In J. F. Kroll & A. M. B. de Groot (Eds.), *Handbook of bilingualism* (pp. 49–67). Oxford, UK: Oxford University Press.

Maguire, M. J., Hirsh-Pasek, K., & Golinkoff, R. M. (2006). A unified theory of word learning: Putting verb acquisition in context. In K. Hirsh-Pasek, R. Michnick, & R. M. Golinkoff (Eds.), *Action meets word: How children learn verbs* (pp. 364–391). Oxford, UK: Oxford University Press.

Merino, B. J. (1983). Language development in normal and language handicapped Spanish-speaking children. *Hispanic Journal of Behavioral Sciences, 5*(4), 379–400.

Merriman, W. E., & MacWhinney, B. (1999). Competition, attention, and young children's lexical processing. In B. MacWhinney (Ed.), *The emergence of language* (pp. 331–358). Mahwah, NJ: Erlbaum.

Merriman, W. E., & Marazita, J. M. (1995). The effect of hearing similar-sounding words on young 2–year-olds' disambiguation of novel reference. *Developmental Psychology, 31*(6), 973–984.

Oller, D. K., Pearson, B. Z., & Cobo-Lewis, A. B. (2007). Profile effects in early bilingual language and literacy. *Applied Psycholinguistics, 28*(2), 191–230.

Pearson, B. Z., & Fernández, S. C. (1994). Patterns of interaction in the lexical growth in two languages of bilingual infants and toddlers. *Language Learning, 44*(4), 617–653.

Peña, E. D., & Bedore, L. M. (2008). Bilingualism and language impairment in children. In R. Schwartz (Ed.), *Handbook of child language disorders* (pp. 281–307). New York: Psychology Press.

Peña, E. D., Bedore, L. M., & Zlatic-Giunta, R. (2002). Category generation performance of young bilingual children: The influence of condition, category, and language. *Journal of Speech, Language, and Hearing Research, 41*, 938–947.

Peña, E. D., Gutierrez-Clellen, V. F., Iglesias, A., Goldstein, B., & Bedore, L. M. (2009). *Bilingual English Spanish assessment*. Manuscript in preparation.

Potter, M. C., So, K.-F., von Eckardt, B., & Feldman, L. B. (1984). Lexical and conceptual representation in beginning and proficient bilinguals. *Journal of Verbal Learning and Verbal Behavior, 23*(1), 23–38.

Restrepo, M. A., & Kruth, K. (2000). Grammatical characteristics of a Spanish–English bilingual child with specific language impairment. *Communication Disorders Quarterly, 21*(2), 66–76.

Schiff-Meyers, N. B. (1992). Considering arrested language development and language loss in the assessment of second language learners. *Language, Speech, and Hearing Services in the Schools, 23*(1), 28–33.

Silverman, R. D. (2007). Vocabulary development of English-language and English-only learners in kindergarten. *Elementary School Journal, 107*(4), 366–383.

Vermeer, A. (2001). Breadth and depth of vocabulary in relation to L1/L2 acquisition and frequency of input. *Applied Psycholinguistics, 22*(2), 217–234.

5

The Role of Phonology in Orthographically Different Languages

Ellen H. Newman

FOCUS POINTS

- Phonological awareness is considered the *sine qua non* of reading development in English speakers, but the importance of this skill in languages other than English is not as straightforward.

- Recently, researchers have proposed a universal model of reading acquisition that captures the role phonology plays in different orthographies as a means of explaining the role of phonological awareness in reading cross-culturally (e.g., Ziegler & Goswami, 2005).

- Based on this model, three specific dimensions of one's language and writing systems—availability, consistency, and granularity—are identified as critical for understanding the role of phonological awareness in predicting reading in a particular language and for understanding differences in the transfer of phonological skills during literacy acquisition from a first language to a second language (e.g., Oller & Jarmulowicz, 2007).

- To better prepare English language learners for reading in English, it is important that educators provide instruction that optimizes the cross-linguistic transfer of phonological skills, based on a thorough understanding of these three linguistic dimensions.

CHAPTER PURPOSE

The purpose of this chapter is to use our understanding of the role phonology plays in learning to read in different orthographies to inform instructional practices for English-language learners' reading acquisition.

Both research and practice underscore the importance of phonological awareness in learning to read in English, but there is conflicting evidence as to the importance of this skill in languages other than English. In the current chapter I review a recent theory of reading acquisition in order to help reconcile the competing research findings. The theory of psycholinguistic grain size proposes that there are three dimensions of the spoken and written systems of a language that explain differences in the importance of phonological skills in reading development across languages and cultures. Based on the framework presented in this theory, I highlight ways in which phonological skills may transfer across linguistic domains for children learning to read in a non-native language. The chapter ends with suggestions for ways to use this understanding to develop classroom practices geared to enhance English language learners' English literacy skills.

REVIEW OF RESEARCH AND THEORY

I'd rather clean the mold around the bathtub than read.
—FOURTH-GRADE STUDENT (in Juel, 1988)

Although perhaps unbelievable to some fourth graders, historically the purpose of writing was not to torture children but simply to "convey or record information through a constellation of visual symbols" (Adams, 1990, p. 13). The symbols that writing systems have used to convey meaning have (for the most part) advanced from pictographs or logographs to abstract symbols representing either full syllables or the individual sounds in a language (Adams, 1990). In this evolution, sounds became intimately linked to symbols, meaning became more abstracted, and writing became a transcription of the sounds of the language at its most elemental. "Although writing systems are, in general terms, systems for communication, what they actually communicate is the spoken language—as opposed to communicating nonverbal ideas and meanings" (Katz & Frost, 1992, p. 67). Thus, in today's languages a large component of learning to read is mastering the particular system that connects the sounds and symbols of a language.

Over the past 50 years research has focused on identifying the underlying skills that give children insight into the rules of this transcription, with particular attention to the phonological skills that enable phonological recoding[1] in English-speaking children (e.g., Share, 1995). However, until recently little research has examined the role of phonology in learning to read in *different* orthographies (although there are important exceptions—e.g., Katz & Frost, 1992), an oversight that has kept our knowledge of reading and our models of reading remarkably Anglocentric (Share, 2008). Not all spoken languages or writing systems are the same, and not all languages use the same rules for linking sounds and symbols. Thus, it is important to explore the relationship between the spoken and written systems in different languages and examine the similarities and differences in reading acquisition cross-culturally in order to move toward a universal model of reading acquisition.

Predictors of Reading in English-Speaking Children: The Role of Phonological Awareness

Research on reading acquisition in English has underscored the importance of phonological skills as a benchmark of children's reading development (e.g., Torgesen, Wagner, & Rashotte, 1994). Historically, three phonological skills have proved important predictors of emergent reading: phonological awareness (identification and manipulation of sound units), phonological working memory (storage of sound units), and phonological rapid access (speed of processing and access to sound units; e.g., Wagner & Torgesen, 1987). Each of these three skills has been suggested to represent a separate underlying ability (e.g., Torgesen, Wagner, Rashotte, Burgess, & Hecht, 1997). However, of this triumvirate, phonological awareness has triumphed as the single, strongest predictor of reading ability for English-speaking children, explaining more than 50% of individual differences in later reading ability even when controlling for age, IQ, and vocabulary (e.g., Lonigan, Burgess, & Anthony, 2000). This finding has led many to claim that phonological awareness—specifically, children's metalinguistic awareness of the sounds in their language—is the most important causal factor in reading ability (e.g., Adams, 1990; but see Castles & Coltheart, 2004). However, the understanding of *why* phonological awareness is such a powerful predictor of reading in English has, until recently, been typified by fairly course-grained explanations.

English is an alphabetic language that uses letters to represent the phonemes of the language. Furthermore, although the mappings are not always one to one between the letters and the sounds (e.g., c = /s/ in *city* or /k/ in *cat*) or between the sounds and the letters (e.g., /eɪt/ = *ate* or *eight*), there are inductive regularities in the grapheme–phoneme relations (Ziegler & Goswami, 2005). These symbol–sound properties of English are proposed to underlie the strong relationship between phonological awareness and reading in English-speaking children. Given the seeming transparency of this relationship, researchers have endorsed phonological awareness, particularly phoneme-level awareness, as the key to learning to read and as a panacea to remediating reading difficulties in English speakers—and, by default, in all alphabetic languages. However, cross-linguistic research reveals inconsistencies with this monolithic endorsement, inconsistencies that prove important for refining our understanding of *why* and *when* phonological awareness is related to reading universally.

Predictors of Reading Cross-Linguistically: The Fate of Phonological Awareness

Although initial cross-linguistic research supported the status of phonological awareness as the gold standard of reading predictors for alphabetic languages (e.g., Cossu, Shankweiler, Liberman, Katz, & Tola, 1988), recent cross-linguistic research has revealed *differences* in the predictive power of phonological awareness depending on the particular alphabetic script. For example, in a recent comparative study of phonological awareness and reading in five languages (Smythe et al., 2008), phonological awareness was found to be the strongest predictor of reading ability in grade 3 for English-speaking children and a less strong predictor for Hungarian-speaking children, although both languages are alphabetic. Furthermore, there are differences in the level of phonological awareness (phoneme, onset–rime, or syllable) that relate to reading in different alphabetic languages (e.g., Nag, 2007). Lastly, there has been a growing body of research showing the importance of phonological awareness in nonalphabetic scripts, such as Chinese, Korean, Japanese, and Arabic (e.g., al Mannai & Everatt, 2005; Mann, 1986; McBride-Chang & Ho, 2005). These findings bring to the forefront two questions: (1) What is the role of phonological awareness in predicting reading cross-linguistically? (2) More generally, what is the nature of phonology in learning to read in different orthographies?

Universal Models of Reading Acquisition: The Role of Phonology and Orthography

To date, there are four general theories of reading, theories that attempt to identify both universal and language-specific features of the correlates of reading ability (Katz & Frost, 1992; Perfetti, Liu, & Tan, 2005; Seymour, 2006; Ziegler & Goswami, 2005). The commonality in these four theories is that there is a complex interplay between phonology, morphology, orthography, and (to a lesser extent, e.g., Frost, 2005) semantics in word reading and that the relative contributions of each in the process of single-word identification depends on the configuration of a culture's spoken and written language and the mapping between these two systems. Here I outline one of the most representative theories for reading acquisition—the theory of psycholinguistic grain size (PGST; Ziegler & Goswami, 2005), as a method for understanding how the properties of one's spoken and written language and the mapping between these two affect the skills that predict reading acquisition within a particular language. Through this review, I highlight the different roles that phonology plays in learning to read in a variety of different orthographies.

According to proponents of PGST, there are three dimensions of a linguistic system that determine which skills predict reading ability in a particular language: (1) the linguistic grain size (or *granularity*) at which phonology is mapped to orthography in a particular language (i.e., syllable, onset-rime, phoneme), (2) the *consistency* of this mapping, and (3) the *availability* of this linguistic level in the spoken language (Ziegler & Goswami, 2005). Although proposed as a universal model of reading acquisition, these particular features determine the type of phonological awareness that is important in learning to read and the strength of the relationship between phonological awareness and reading ability in a particular language.

There is strong evidence that the *granularity*, or the level at which the sounds of a language map to the graphemes of the language, is an important linguistic factor for understanding the role of phonological skills in reading acquisition. In alphabetic languages the mapping between the sounds of the language and the letters of the alphabet most typically occurs at the level of the phoneme. This level of mapping makes phoneme-level awareness an extremely important skill in predicting reading outcomes, as evidenced in most Indo-European languages such as Italian (e.g., Cossu et al., 1988), Turkish (e.g., Durgunoglu & Oney, 1999), and English (e.g., Torgeson, Wagner, & Rasnotte, 1994). In alphabetic languages where the mapping occurs at a larger grain size, such as the syllable, phenome-level awareness is not as important as predicting reading development. For example, Kannada, a south Indian Dravidian language, is considered an alphasyllabary wherein the sounds map to graphemes at the level of the syllable, in units called *akshara* (Nag, 2007). Although phoneme-level information is contained within the *akshara* units, early graphophonic knowledge in this language consists of learning the name–sound correspondences only at the level of the syllable, as demonstrated by young reader's early sensitivity to syllabic units, but not to phonemic units (Nag, 2007).

The importance of granularity has also been evidenced by research in nonalphabetic languages, such as Chinese (e.g., Siok & Fletcher, 2001) and Japanese (specifically, Kanji; e.g., Mann, 1986). In Chinese, which has a morphosyllabic structure rather than an alphabetic structure (McBride-Chang, 2004), syllable-level awareness develops early and is a strong predictor of reading ability in Mandarin- and Cantonese-speaking children (e.g., McBride-Chang, 2004), whereas there has been little to no evidence of a role for phoneme-level awareness in learning to read Chinese (e.g., Huang & Hanley, 1997).

There is also evidence that the *consistency* of the sound–symbol mappings in a language influences the rate of development of phonological awareness and the strength of the relationship between phonological awareness and reading. In Spanish, a *shallow* language (i.e., one with a highly regular symbol–sound mapping), phoneme-level awareness develops early and is related to reading ability for a short period of time (Anthony et al., 2006), particularly relative to French, a language with a higher degree of spelling inconsistencies, or English, a language with a higher degree of pronunciation *and* spelling inconsistencies (e.g., Duncan, Cole, Seymour, & Magnan, 2006). In Hebrew, a *deep* language (i.e., one in which only partial phonological information can be retrieved from the unvoweled orthography), phoneme-level awareness develops more slowly and is related to reading later in elementary school (e.g., Levin & Korat, 1993). Thus, the degree of consistency in a language's mapping appears to affect the rate and timing of reading acquisition.

Importantly, there is an interaction between the *consistency* and *granularity* of a language. The consistency of a particular language's grapheme–phoneme mappings can vary depending on the particular phonological level under examination. And, the level at which a language maps graphemes to phonemes (its *granularity*) may not be the level at which the mapping is the most consistent (its *consistency*). For example, although English maps letters at the level of the phoneme and thus phoneme-level awareness is important, good onset-rime skills can also exploit regularities in the system at the level of the onset-rime that are not captured in a direct one-to-one mapping at the level of the phoneme (Treiman, Mullennix, Bijeljac-Babic, & Richmond-Welty, 1995). Thus sensitivity to subsyllabic and phonemic divisions (e.g., ability to segment *school* into /sk/ and /u:l/ as well as /s/ /k/ /u:/ /l/) within words is an important precursor to gaining alphabetic insight—a proposal with strong empirical support (e.g., Bryant, 1998).

The final tenet of PGST is that languages differ in whether their spoken features serve to highlight or obscure phonological features important for reading. It is this *availability* of these features that is related to the development of phonological awareness and its relationship to reading within a language. One must have mental representations of the phonemes necessary for learning to read in one's language (e.g., Liberman, 1998). For example, Saiegh-Haddad (2007) found that in Arabic-speaking children levels of phonological awareness differed by type of phoneme tested. She examined phoneme-level awareness in Arabic-speaking children speaking two different regional dialects—one with nearly complete phonological overlap with the written language, the other with differences between the sounds of their language and the sounds represented in the orthography. Children speaking the dialect with incomplete phonological overlap performed more poorly than the children speaking the dialect with complete overlap, and these differences stemmed from a greater difficulty manipulating the non-native phonemes represented in the orthography of literary Arabic.

An additional aspect of *availability* is the manner in which the spoken language may or may not accentuate phonological features that are relevant for the transcription of the spoken language into writing. For example, in Malayian children who speak Indonesian, a language with mostly bi- and multisyllabic words and clear syllable boundaries, syllable awareness develops early and is important for learning to read and spell (Winskel & Widjaja, 2006). There is also evidence that the syllabic complexity of a language may affect phoneme-level awareness. Specifically, in a cross-linguistic comparison of English and 12 other European languages, Seymour, Aro, and Erskine (2003) found that children who learned languages with simple syllable structures (no consonant clusters or multiletter grapheme–phoneme correspondences), such as Finnish, were faster and more accurate at reading a list of simple nonwords than children who learned languages with complex syllable structures, such as English (Seymour et al., 2003). The authors of this study proposed that complex syllable structure in a language may serve to obscure the level of the phoneme (Seymour et al., 2003). However, other researchers have argued that syllabic complexity makes phonemes more salient (Caravolas & Bruck, 1993). Regardless of the direction of influence, there is mounting evidence that the structure of the spoken language affects children's developing awareness of the sounds within their language, and there is an interaction between this

availability and the *granularity* of the language that influences children's reading development.

Thus, PGST provides explanations for previous inconsistencies in reading research by demonstrating how the phonological and orthographic properties of a language affect *which* skills are related to reading acquisition and *when* they are related over the course of development. This review demonstrates that close examination of the dimensions of *availability, consistency,* and *granularity* of a particular language provides a clarification of the role of phonology in learning to read, and the role of phonological awareness in learning to read this language. Given these language-specific dimensions of reading acquisition, it is of the utmost importance for teachers in multilingual classrooms to have an understanding of how the properties of a child's *first* and *second* language affect the course of his or her reading development. To do this, educators must both understand the task of learning to read in English and how this task may vary depending on whether or not English is the child's native language.

Implications for Second-Language Learners

Hints on Pronunciation for Foreigners

... A moth is not a moth in mother
Nor both in bother, broth in brother,
And here is not a match for there
Nor dear and fear for bear and pear,
And then there's dose and rose and lose—
Just look them up—and good and choose,
And cork and work and card and ward,
And font and front and word and sword,
And do and go and thwart and cart—
Come, come, I've hardly made a start!
A dreadful language? Man alive.
I'd mastered it when I was five.
      —ANONYMOUS LETTER PUBLISHED IN THE
LONDON SUNDAY TIMES (January 3, 1965)

English is an alphabetic language that is considered orthographically deep (Katz & Frost, 1992). Letters map to individual sounds, but the consistency of this mapping is fairly poor, with some estimates suggesting that 33% of monosyllabic words contain inconsistent letter–sound relationships (Stone, Vanhoy, & VanOrden, 1997). However, the consistency of the mapping is improved at the level of the rime,[2] and this consistency

appears to be directly related to the accuracy and speed of children's lexical processing (Treiman et al., 1995). Thus for the child learning to read in English, phoneme (e.g., Wagner et al., 1994) and onset-rime awareness (Maclean, Bryant, & Bradley, 1987) are highly predictive skills of reading ability, *but* awareness at these levels may develop later and more slowly in English-speaking children than in children exposed to languages where there is a more consistent mapping between the letters and sounds (e.g., Spanish or Italian; Ziegler & Goswami, 2005) or where the spoken languages clearly emphasize phoneme-level processing (e.g., Turkish; Durgunoglu & Oney, 1999). Furthermore, because of the imperfect mapping between letters and sounds in English, it is argued that for English speakers to become fluent readers, they must develop two distinct systems for reading (the dual-route model; Coltheart, Rastle, Perry, Langdon, & Ziegler, 2001): one using phonological recoding strategies appropriate for reading regular words, and a second, more holistic approach for reading irregular words (where phonological recoding strategies fail). Although discussion of the dual-route model is beyond the scope of this chapter (for an analysis of the generalizability of the model, see Share, 2008), the key point to consider is that children's reliance on phonological recoding strategies, and by extension the importance of phonological awareness as a proxy of the child's understanding of this process, will vary by language learned. Thus, in order to understand literacy acquisition in second-language (L2) children, it is important to consider how the native or first language (L1) of an L2 learner may or may not be congruent with these properties of English.

A growing body of research has examined the conditions under which learning or skills appear to transfer from one's first language to a second language (see Bialystok & Peets, Chapter 6, this volume) and has found that the degree of cross-linguistic transfer depends on (1) the languages being learned, (2) the type of skills examined, and (3) the degree of a child's proficiency in both languages (Bialystok, McBride-Chang, & Luk, 2005).

Transfer Depends on the Languages Learned

The degree of cross-linguistic transfer for phonological awareness seems to depend on the correspondence between the two languages on the three dimensions of the language systems identified in the PGST model: *availability, consistency,* and *granularity.* For example, research has shown strong positive transfer for phoneme-level awareness in Latin-based alphabetic languages such as Spanish and English (Bialystok, Majumder, & Martin, 2003). In contrast, research has shown no or limited transfer

between alphabetic and nonalphabetic languages such as Chinese (e.g., Bialystok, Luk, & Kwan, 2005; but see Gottardo, Yan, Siegel, & Wade-Woolley, 2001).

One cause for differences in the degree of transfer of phonological skills is the *consistency* of the mapping between the sounds and letters in each language. For example, first-grade Spanish–English bilinguals outperformed English monolinguals on phoneme-level manipulation tasks (Bialystok et al., 2003). One explanation is that Spanish-speaking children develop phoneme-level awareness earlier and faster than English speakers, due to near-perfect mapping between sounds and symbols in Spanish, and this skill transfers to English performance.

A second cause for differences in the degree of transfer between L1 and L2 is the *granularity* of the mappings in the two languages. Transfer occurs where there is congruency between the level of awareness necessary for learning to read in one's L1 system and the L2. In Chinese, characters map to sounds at the level of the syllable (or morpheme), but not at the level of the phoneme (McBride-Chang, 2004). Thus, syllable-level awareness is of great importance in helping children identify the regularities between the sounds and symbols of the Chinese script (McBride-Chang, 2004). Correspondingly, Mandarin-speaking children learning English have shown higher levels of syllable awareness in English relative to their monolingual Chinese- or English-speaking peers (McBride-Chang, Bialystok, Chong, & Li, 2004).

Lastly, the phonological characteristics of one's native language appear to affect the degree to which literacy-related skills transfer between the child's L1 and L2. For example, Wade-Woolley (as cited in Akamatsu, 2006) explored the effect of familiarity of different syllable structures in children's native languages on their ability to perform phoneme segmentation from these same structures in English (L2). Specifically, she compared Japanese English as a second language (ESL) students to Russian ESL students on their ability to segment phonemes in syllable structures that were common for Russian speakers but uncommon for Japanese speakers. The structure of the L1 spoken language appeared to have a strong effect on performance of this phonological awareness task in the L2, with Japanese ESL participants performing worse on the phoneme segmentation of English syllables composed of structures that were uncommon in their native language than Russian ESL participants, for whom the syllable structures were familiar (Wade-Woolley, as cited in Akamatsu, 2006). Thus, the properties of the spoken and written structures of a child's L1 and L2 systems dictate when and how there is transfer in skill or learning of phonological awareness from an L1 to an L2.

Transfer Depends on the Skills Measured

However, not all skills are equal or are equally transferable cross-linguistically. In fact, Bialystok and colleagues have argued that the skills of phonological awareness and decoding are distinct in ways that are important to understanding L2s' reading development (Bialystok, McBride-Chang, et al., 2005). For example, in English not all words can be decoded using grapheme–phoneme understanding. Thus, at one level, children must have the ability decode grapheme–phoneme correspondences, and this ability appears to be highly related to phonological awareness. However, they must also know when and where to use these phonological recoding strategies. Interestingly, there appears to be a relationship between children's *approach* to reading and the properties of the language. For example, in Urdu, which has a highly consistent or regular orthography, bilingual Urdu–English speakers perform as well as monolingual English speakers on decoding regular English words but not irregular English words (Mumtax & Humprheys, 2002). This difference may stem from an overreliance by Urdu speakers on phonological recoding strategies that are effective for reading their completely consistent Persian–Arabic voweled script but are inadequate for decoding irregular English words such as *heir*. Thus, not only must one consider the type of skill but also the relative importance of the skill in the two languages in order to understand the nature of the cross-linguistic transfer.

Phonological skills show transfer across languages; however, the importance of phonological skills for learning to decode vary depending on the language. In this way, children's decoding abilities in the two languages may appear unrelated, although they show transfer of phonological skills across these languages (e.g., Bialystok et al., 2005).

Transfer Depends on the Level of Proficiency

The degree of transfer between L1 and L2 also depends on the child's level of proficiency in each language. On the one hand, the level of the child's preliteracy skills in their *native language* will naturally limit the degree of transfer of these skills to the L2. And, this level will vary not just by age, but also based on the properties of the language and the schooling practices of the particular culture. Children who are learning languages that preference the phoneme more directly (either in sound or script) or children who are learning to read in cultures where literacy training begins earlier will develop phonological and preliteracy skills earlier than children learning languages or living in cultures without these traits.

On the other hand, the level of children's proficiency in the *second language* can also limit the transfer in literacy skills between L1 and L2. Although so far in this discussion I have glossed over the distinction between bilingual children and second language learners (or English language learners, in particular), this proves a meaningful distinction when considering how second language learning affects literacy acquisition. For example, Bialystok and colleagues (2005) found that children with low L2 proficiency demonstrated a closer relationship between reading development in L1 and L2 than children with greater L2 proficiency. They hypothesized that children with more rudimentary second language skills may apply a similar reading strategy to both reading systems regardless of its appropriateness, whereas developing biliteracy requires mastering the particular approach required in each language system.

Outlined above are ways in which literacy acquisition in an L2 may benefit from language and literacy learning in a child's L1. In order to understand literacy development in English language learners and to prepare to educate these English language learners, it is important to consider (1) the language-specific factors identified by the PGST, (2) the type of skill being examined, and (3) level of proficiency of the child in both their L1 and L2.

BEST PRACTICES

Educators preparing to teach English language learners need to understand the different linguistic backgrounds that children bring to the classroom. This knowledge should include understanding the spoken and written properties of a child's native language and how that language compares to English along the dimensions of granularity, consistency, and availability. A summary of these dimensions for a selection of languages found in classrooms across the United States can be found in Appendix 5.1 at the end of this chapter. Although this is an overly simplistic representation of these languages, it can be used to identify features of a child's native language that may affect his or her literacy development in English. Below are additional suggestions for how to tailor instruction to optimize cross-linguistic transfer of phonological skills.

Granularity

The congruency in granularity between a child's native language and English will affect the level of phonological transfer and should be targeted through appropriate instruction. For example, children coming from languages where sounds map at the level of the syllable or the onset-rime (e.g., Chinese children) will find phoneme-level awareness very challenging. For these children it is important to provide training that focuses on explicit and extensive instruction with phoneme-level manipulations. Furthermore, one could couple this targeted training with a more implicit approach that capitalizes on features of the English spoken language to highlight phoneme-level awareness. For example, some research suggests that learning words composed of complex consonant clusters may serve to increase phoneme-level awareness (Cheung, Chen, Lai, Wong, & Hills, 2001), or that learning morphological rules that lie at the level of the phoneme may help increase phoneme-level awareness (Durgunoglu & Oney, 1999). Thus, practice forming plurals or learning the past tense of regular verbs can serve a secondary purpose of providing children with practice in isolating phonemes in English. In this way, educators can use the naturally occurring interaction between *granularity* and *availability* to help increase the transfer of phonological skills to the child's L2.

Letter names and letter sounds are a particularly powerful way to tune children to phoneme-level distinctions. Furthermore, there appear to be systematic regularities in the order in which children learn letters, regularities that should be used to guide classroom instruction. Children show an advantage for learning letters when there is a close phonological linkage between the name and sound (unlike letter *w*), and of these letters children show a learning preference for those where the relevant phonological information is at the beginning (/b/ in /biː/) than at the end of the letter name (/f/ in /ɛf/; Treiman, Pennington, Shriberg, & Boada, 2008). Thus, one important strategy for teaching phoneme-level awareness in ELL children may be to teach letter–name and letter–sound knowledge in a principled way that takes advantage of the phonological regularities in the name–sound relationships in the alphabet.

Consistency

Differences in the level of consistency in the sound–symbol mappings between the child's native language and English may also affect the likelihood of phonological transfer skill. Since children learning to read in more consistent orthographies demonstrate a stronger reliance on phonological skills than those in less consistent orthographies, children with highly consistent L1s may show an overreliance on phonological recoding strategies and need to be taught about the inconsistencies in English sound–letter mappings explicitly. If children are too young to understand these complex rules, educators can, at a minimum, draw children's attention to the irregular words in English (particularly as these are typically high-frequency words as well) in intentional and systematic ways.

Availability

In some instances, children may not possess the necessary phonological knowledge for learning to read in English. For example, children's phonological inventories may not include all the phonemes present in English. Many children learning English as an L2 struggle with the *r* sound, which is absent from many other languages, and may try to adapt this sound to a similar sound in their native language (Oller & Jarmulowicz, 2007). An incomplete understanding or representation of a phoneme has been shown to interfere with the development of phonological awareness and phonological recoding strategies (e.g., Liberman, Shankweiler, & Liberman, 1989). Because there are individual differences in phoneme-level awareness that stem from children's native language experiences, additional practice with non-native phonemes will help them gain representations of these sounds and the subsequent ability to manipulate them in more traditional phonological awareness tasks.

Through a careful comparison of the language systems in a child's L1 and L2, continuities and discontinuities in literacy acquisition can be identified and the way in which phonological skills may be complementary can be highlighted. Understanding in advance the expectations, knowledge, and skills that a child brings to learning to read in an L2 will allow a careful tailoring of instruction to best meet his or her needs.

Classroom Application

Beyond devising didactic strategies that speak specifically to the degree of congruency between literacy acquisition in a child's L1 and L2, I suggest an additional tool for promoting phonological understanding in the classroom. Training of phonological awareness in U.S. classrooms typically centers on teaching children the sounds of the letters and how to segment and blend words. These are clearly seminal skills for learning to read in English, and they are more powerful when learned in tandem than in isolation (Bus & IJzendoorn, 1999). However, the use of spelling has also long been recognized as an important tool for promoting alphabetic insight but one that is not always considered in the arsenal of tools for teaching phonological awareness. Children's early spelling efforts have been found to be a good proxy of their level of phonological awareness (Mann, Tobin, & Wilson, 1987). Furthermore, some have recently argued that practice with spelling before phonological mastery can contribute to growth in orthographic awareness and the consolidation of phono-orthographic information into a lexical form—both found to be important for reading acquisition (Shahar-Yames & Share, 2008).

A recent training study found that children who received instruction in invented spelling were able to read more novel words post-training than children who received instruction in phonological awareness. In this study, children in the invented spelling condition received individualized feedback about their misspellings, feedback that was designed to increase the accuracy of their spelling incrementally (for more detail, see Ouellete & Senechal, 2008). The study was designed to capitalize on the systematic development seen in invented spelling, such that children move from recoding words using nonalphabetic markings, to capturing the initial sounds in the words, then the final sounds, and lastly the full sound inventory (Gentry & Gillet, 1993). Given the success of this method for promoting growth in reading skills, it could be an additional tool useful in preparing ELLs to read in English and one that could be used well in concert with more traditional phonological training methods.

SUMMARY OF MAIN IDEAS

Heralded in research as the single strongest causal predictor of reading ability (e.g., Adams, 1990), phonological awareness has been promoted by federal and state policy as one of the five essential components of reading development, and its training has become instantiated in the classroom through federal and state mandates (e.g., National Reading Panel, 2000; Snow, Burns, & Griffin, 1998). However, the role of phonological awareness, so important for readers of English, is more complicated when we consider languages other than English. In this chapter I reviewed a universal theory of reading that explores both universal and language-specific features of reading development, with particular attention to the role of phonological awareness in reading. By understanding the three dimensions of this theory—(1) the linguistic level at which sounds are mapped to symbols, (2) the consistency of the mapping, and (3) the availability of the relevant linguistic grain size in the spoken language—educators can understand better the timing and development of phonological awareness in native English speakers. Furthermore, with a clear understanding of these properties across languages, educators can better understand how the different linguistic backgrounds of their ELL pupils can and will influence their literacy development in English. Based on this understanding, educators working with ELLs can adopt clear strategies to promote phonological development and reading acquisition in English.

IMPLICATIONS FOR RESEARCH, PRACTICE, AND POLICY

Due to the national endorsement of phonological awareness and the inclusion of phonemic awareness as one of the "big-five" components of reading development (National Reading Panel, 2000; Snow et al., 1998), teaching phonological awareness has become a mainstay of early elementary education. However, this endorsement has lead to a fairly homogeneous treatment of phonological awareness in the classroom that has overlooked the ways in which the task of acquiring phonological skills may vary depending on the child's L1 experiences. Thus, one important addendum to this national mandate is to understand how the role of phonological awareness may vary in reading acquisition and how a child's language status may dictate which phonological skills he or she will struggle to acquire.

In this review I have shown how the role of phonological awareness in learning to read varies depending on the properties of the language being learned. Furthermore, based on this understanding, there are differing levels of cross-linguistic transfer for phonological skills depending on the congruence between the two languages and the specific ways in which educators capitalize on these commonalities. Although this is a start, more research is needed on how, when, and under what conditions creating cross-linguistic connections will prove advantageous for non-native speakers learning to read in English. For example, Bialystok (2007) has argued that although there can be positive or negative transfer in phonological skills prior to the onset of reading, literacy tuition may neutralize these differences in bilingual children. An important extension of this is to examine whether the results apply also to ELLs, particularly given the high comorbidity between language-learning status and low socioeconomic backgrounds (Hammer & Miccio, 2006).

An important implication of this research for educators is that although policy is an effective method for operationalizing research findings on a large scale, the development of these policies often comes late to the field and fails to represent the nuances in the research. Given the rapidly changing demographics of the typical U.S. classroom, educators cannot wait for research to be translated into policy. Thus, the onus is on researchers and educators alike to ensure that there are open and clear paths of continuing communication from the labs at universities to classrooms around the nation.

NOTES

1. Phonological recoding is the ability to translate a graphemic form (symbol) into a phonological (sound-based) code used for retrieving words (Share, 1995).
2. In an extensive analysis of monosyllabic words (of the form consonant–vowel– consonant, or CVC; e.g., *b–a–t*), Treiman and colleagues (1995) noted that the consistency of the vowel pronunciation was particularly low (with there being, on average, three different pronunciations for each vowel), but that this consistency was significantly improved when considered together with the final consonant (1.32 different pronunciation possibilities).

REFERENCES

Adams, M. J. (1990). *Beginning to read: Thinking and learning about print.* Cambridge, MA: MIT Press.

Akamatsu, N. (2006). Literacy acquisition in Japanese–English bilinguals. In R. M. Joshi & P. G. Aaron (Eds.), *Handbook of orthography and literacy* (pp. 481–496). Mahwah. NJ: Erlbaum.

al Mannai, H., & Everatt, J. (2005). Phonological processing skills as predictors of literacy amongst Arabic-speaking Bahraini children. *Dyslexia, 11,* 269–291.

Anthony, J. L., Williams, J. M., McDonald, R., Corbitt-Shindler, D., Carlson, C. D., & Francis, D. J. (2006). Phonological processing and emergent literacy in Spanish-speaking preschool children. *Annals of Dyslexia, 56,* 239–270.

Bialystok, E. (2007). Acquisition of literacy in bilingual children. *Language Learning, 57*(Suppl. 1), 45–77.

Bialystok, E., Luk, G., & Kwan, E. (2005). Bilingualism, biliteracy, and learning to read: Interactions among languages and writing systems. *Scientific Studies of Reading, 9,* 43–61.

Bialystok, E., Majumder, S., & Martin, M. (2003). Developing phonological awareness: Is there a bilingual advantage? *Applied Psycholinguistics, 24,* 27–44.

Bialystok, E., McBride-Change, C., & Luk, G. (2005). Bilingualism, language proficiency, and learning to read in two writing systems. *Journal of Educational Psychology, 97*, 580–590.

Bryant, P. E. (1998). Sensitivity to onset and rhyme does predict young children's reading: A comment on Muter, Hulme, Snowling, and Taylor (1997). *Journal of Experimental Child Psychology, 71*, 29–37.

Bus, A. G., & van IJzendoorn, M. H. (1999). Phonological awareness and early reading: A meta-analysis of experimental training studies. *Journal of Educational Psychology, 91*, 403–414.

Caravolas, M., & Bruck, M. (1993). The effect of oral and written language input on children's phonological awareness: A cross-linguistic study. *Journal of Experimental Child Psychology, 55*, 1–30.

Castles, A., & Coltheart, M. (2004). Is there a causal link from phonological awareness to success in learning to read? *Cognition, 91*, 77–111.

Cheung, H., Chen, H.-C., Lai, C. Y., Wong, O. C., & Hills, M. (2001). The development of phonological awareness: Effects of spoken language experience and orthography. *Cognition, 81*, 227–241.

Coltheart, M., Rastle, K., Perry, C., Langdon, R., & Ziegler, J. (2001). DRC: A dual route cascaded model of visual word recognition and reading aloud. *Psychological Review, 108*, 204–256.

Cossu, G., Shankweiler, D., Liberman, I. Y., Katz, L., & Tola, G. (1988). Awareness of phonological segments and reading ability in Italian children. *Applied Psycholinguistics, 9*, 1–16.

Duncan, L. G., Cole, P., Seymour, P. H. K., & Magnan. A. (2006). Differing sequences of metaphonological development in French and English. *Journal of Child Language, 33*, 369–399.

Durgunoglu, A. Y., & Oney, B. (1999). A cross-linguistic comparison of phonological awareness and word recognition. *Reading and Writing, 11*, 281–299.

Frost, R. (2005). Orthographic systems and skilled word recognition processes in reading. In M. J. Snowling & C. Hulme (Eds.), *The science of reading: A handbook* (pp. 272–295). Malden, MA: Blackwell.

Gentry, J. R., & Gillet, J. W. (1993). *Teaching kids to spell.* Portsmouth, NH: Heinemann.

Gottardo, A., Yan, B., Siegel, L. S., & Wade-Woolley, L. (2001). Factors related to English reading performance in children with Chinese as a first language: More evidence of cross-language transfer of phonological processing. *Journal of Educational Psychology, 93*, 530–542.

Hammer, C. S., & Miccio, A. W. (2006). Early language and reading development of bilingual preschoolers from low-income families. *Topics in Language Disorders, 26*(4), 302–317.

Huang, H. S., & Hanley, J. R. (1997). A longitudinal study of phonological awareness, visual skills, and Chinese reading acquisition among first-graders in Taiwan. *International Journal of Behavioral Development, 20*, 249–268.

Juel, C. (1988). Learning to read and write: A longitudinal study of fifty-four children from first through fourth grade. *Journal of Educational Psychology, 80*, 437–447.

Katz, L., & Frost, R. (1992). The reading process is different for different orthographies: The orthographic depth hypothesis. In R. Frost & L. Katz (Eds.), *Advances in psychology: Vol. 94. Orthography, phonology, morphology, and meaning* (pp. 67–84). Oxford, UK: North-Holland.

Levin, I., & Korat, O. (1993). Sensitivity to phonological, morphological, and semantic cues in early reading and writing in Hebrew. *Merrill–Palmer: Quarterly Journal of Developmental Psychology, 39,* 213–232.

Liberman, A. M. (1998). When theories of speech meet the real world. *Journal of Psycholinguistic Research, 27,* 111–122.

Liberman, I., Shankweiler, D., & Liberman, A. (1989). *The alphabetic principles and learning to read.* Bethesda, MD: National Institute of Child Health and Human Development.

Lonigan, C., Burgess, S., & Anthony, J. (2000). Development of emergent literacy and early reading skills in preschool children: Evidence from a latent-variable longitudinal study. *Developmental Psychology, 36,* 596–613.

MacLean, M., Bryant, P. E., & Bradley, L. (1987). Rhymes, nursery rhymes, and reading in early childhood. *Merrill–Palmer Quarterly: Journal of Developmental Psychology, 33,* 255–282.

Mann, V. A. (1986). Phonological awareness: The role of reading experience. *Cognition, 24,* 65–92.

Mann, V. A., Tobin, P., & Wilson, R. (1987). Measuring phonological awareness through the invented spellings of kindergarten children. *Merrill–Palmer Quarterly: Journal of Developmental Psychology, 33,* 365–391.

McBride-Chang, C. (2004). *Children's literacy development.* New York: Oxford University Press.

McBride-Chang, C., Bialystok, E., Chong, K. Y., & Li, Y. (2004). Levels of phonological awareness in three cultures. *Journal of Experimental Child Psychology, 89,* 93–111.

McBride-Chang, C., & Ho, C. S. (2005). Predictors of beginning reading in Chinese and English: A 2–year longitudinal study of Chinese kindergartners. *Scientific Studies of Reading, 9,* 117–144.

Mumtax, S., & Humphreys, G. W. (2002). The effect of Urdu vocabulary size on the acquisition of single word reading in English. *Educational Psychology, 22,* 165–190.

Nag, S. (2007). Early reading in Kannada: The pace of acquisition of orthographic knowledge and phonemic awareness. *Journal of Research in Reading, 30,* 7–22.

National Reading Panel (NRP). (2000). *Teaching children to read: An evidence-based assessment of the scientific research literature on reading and its implications for reading instruction: Reports of the subgroups.* Bethesda, MD: National Institute of Child Health and Human Development.

Oller, D. K., & Jarmulowicz, L. (2007). Language and literacy in bilingual children in the early school years. In E. Hoff & M. Shatz (Eds.), *Blackwell handbook of language development* (pp. 368–386). Oxford, UK: Blackwell.

Ouellette, G. P., & Senechal, M. (2008). A window into early literacy: Exploring the cognitive and linguistic underpinnings of invented spelling. *Scientific Studies of Reading, 12,* 195–219.

Perfetti, C., Liu, Y., & Tan, L. H. (2005). The lexical constituency model: Some implications of research on Chinese for general theories of reading. *Psychological Review, 112,* 43–59.

Saiegh-Haddad, E. (2007). Linguistic constraints on children's ability to isolate phonemes in Arabic. *Applied Psycholinguistics, 28,* 607–625.

Seymour, P. H. K. (2006). A theoretical framework for beginning reading in different orthographies. In R. M. Joshi & P. G. Aaron (Eds.), *Handbook of orthography and literacy* (pp. 441–462). Mahwah, NJ: Erlbaum.

Seymour, P. H. K., Aro, M., & Erskine, J. M. (2003). Foundation literacy acquisition in European orthographies. *British Journal of Psychology, 94,* 143–174.

Shahar-Yames, D., & Share, D. L. (2008). Spelling as a self-teaching mechanism in orthographic learning. *Journal of Research in Reading, 31,* 22–39.

Share, D. L. (1995). Phonological coding and self-teaching: *Sine qua non* of reading acquisition. *Cognition, 55*(2), 151–218.

Share, D. L. (2008). On the Anglocentricities of current reading research and practice: The perils of overreliance on an "outlier" orthography. *Psychological Bulletin, 134,* 584–615.

Siok, W. T., & Fletcher, P. (2001). The role of phonological awareness and visual–orthographic skills in Chinese reading acquisition. *Developmental Psychology, 37,* 886–899.

Smythe, I., Everatt, J., Al-Menaye, N., He, X., Capellini, S., Gyarmathy, E., et al. (2008). Predictors of word-level literacy amongst grade 3 children in five diverse languages. *Dyslexia, 14,* 170–187.

Snow, C. E., Burns, M. S., & Griffin, P. (1998). *Preventing reading difficulties in young children.* Washington, DC: National Academy Press.

Stone, G. O., Vanhoy, M., & VanOrden, G. C. (1997). Perception is a two-way street: Feedforward and feedback phonology in visual word recognition. *Journal of Memory and Language, 36,* 337–359.

Torgesen, J. K., Wagner, R. K., & Rashotte, C. A. (1994). Longitudinal studies of phonological processing and reading. *Journal of Learning Disabilities, 27,* 276–286.

Torgesen, J. K., Wagner, R. K., Rashotte, C. A., Burgess, S., & Hecht, S. (1997). Contributions of phonological awareness and rapid automatic naming ability to the growth of word-reading skills in second- to fifth-grade children. *Scientific Studies of Reading, 1,* 161–185.

Treiman, R., Mullennix, J., Bijeljac-Babic, R., & Richmond-Welty, E. D. (1995). The special role of rimes in the description, use, and acquisition of English orthography. *Journal of Experimental Psychology, General, 124,* 107–136.

Treiman, R., Pennington, B. F., Shriberg, L. D., & Boada, R. (2008). Which children benefit from letter names in learning letter sounds? *Cognition, 106,* 1322–1338.

Wagner, R. K., & Torgesen, J. (1987). The nature of phonological processing and its causal role in the acquisition of reading skills. *Psychological Bulletin, 101*, 192–212.

Winskel, H., & Widjaja, V. (2005). Phonological awareness, letter knowledge, and literacy development in Indonesian beginner readers and spellers. *Applied Psycholinguistics, 28*, 23–45.

Ziegler, J. C., & Goswami, U. (2005). Reading acquisition, developmental dyslexia, and skilled reading across languages: A psycholinguistic grain size theory. *Psychological Bulletin, 131*, 3–29.

APPENDIX 5.1 Varied Properties
of Selected Languages

The table below is a grossly simplified representation of the properties of 10 different languages commonly found in U.S. classrooms around the nation. It includes large generalizations about phonology and spelling in ways that ignore many nuances of the languages. However, these generalizations are based on common understandings of the important properties of these languages in the reading literature and are presented in a way that should be useful for adapting classroom instruction to the needs of non-native English speakers. The following is a note to the reader on consistency:

1. In the literature, the consistency of a script is also referred to as the *regularity* or *transparency* of a script. In this chart, the term indicates the closeness of the mapping between the sounds and symbols of a language at the level at which this mapping occurs in the particular language (e.g., phoneme) and not at other levels that are possible (e.g., rime or syllable).

2. Two types of consistency have been shown to affect children's development of phonological awareness: grapheme-to-phoneme (G to P) consistency and, less directly, phoneme to grapheme (P to G) consistency (e.g., Caravolas, 2006; but see also Massaro & Jesse, 2005).

3. Ratings of consistency are difficult to define (Caravolas, 2006). Thus, I try to provide an *overall* rating of consistency for a language *relative to English*, a rating derived from how the literature talks about both the P to G and G to P consistency for that language. For languages where I did not find direct cross-linguistic comparisons or for languages where the comparison is debated, I include only a very general overview of the G to P and P to G relationships.

For a more detailed table or for a fuller list of references, please e-mail *eehamilt@ gmail.com*.

	Properties of the language		Granularity	Consistency	Availability	Reading instruction
	Script					
English	**Latin alphabet** 26 letters, 44 phonemes		Phoneme	**Grapheme to phoneme (G-P):** *low consistency* **Phoneme to grapheme (P-G):** *inconsistent*	Complex syllable structure	Mixed methods: Phonics and whole-word instruction
Italian	**Latin alphabet** 21 Latin letters, diacritics[a]		Phoneme	G to P: *high consistency. A highly consistent language.*	Open and simple syllable structure	Mixed methods used from kindergarten
Spanish	**Latin alphabet** 29 letters: 26 Latin, ñ, ch, ll, diacritics		Phoneme	G to P: *high consistency.* More consistent than English, but less than Italian.	Open and simple syllable structure	Mixed methods used
German	**Latin alphabet** 30 Latin, 3 with diacritics, ß		Phoneme	G to P: *high consistency.* More consistent than English and French, but less than Spanish or Italian.	Complex syllable structure, consonant clusters (> English)	Slow-advancing phonics program from first grade
French	**Latin alphabet** 26 Latin, 5 diacritics, 2 ligatures, œ, æ		Phoneme	G to P: *consistent.* More consistent than English but less than Italian, Spanish, German.	Complex syllable structure	Mixed methods used
Polish	**Latin alphabet** 32 letters: 23 Latin, 9 with diacritics		Phoneme	G to P: *high consistency*—mostly 1:1, some 1:2, but nasal vowels are 1:many P to G: *inconsistent,* 1:many	Complex syllable structure, many consonant clusters	

130

Arabic	**Aramaic alphabet** 28 letters	Phoneme	**G to P**[b]: Vowelized form: *high consistency* Partially vowelized: *less consistency* **P to G:** *inconsistent*, 1:many	Root words made of mostly consonants	Learn using vowelized form, unvowelized introduced after grade 1
Farsi (Persian)	**Persian alphabet** 32 letters: 28 Arabic, 4 Persian	Phoneme	**G to P:** Vowelized form: *high consistency* Partially vowelized: *less consistency* **P to G:** *inconsistent*, 1:many	Similar to Arabic	Similar to Arabic
Korean	**Hangul–Korean alphabet:** 24 Latin letters, 27 clusters	Syllable	**G to P:** *high consistency*—some irregularities, most resolved by context **P to G:** *high consistency*	Simple syllable structure, no onset clusters, few in word final position	Taught how to combine consonant–vowel chart with final consonants
Mandarin Chinese	**Not an alphabetic script**	Syllable	**G to P:** Character–syllable mapping[c]: sound component is *60% inconsistent*	Simple syllable structure, 2 consonants in word final position	Whole-word reading, but some phonemic coding (not in Hong Kong)

[a]An ancillary symbol added to a letter to change the sound of the letter or to indicate sounds not conveyed by the basic alphabet.

[b]Arabic and Farsi use two different scripts: one representing all sounds (used for children learning to read), the other representing only some sounds (mainly consonants).

[c]Chinese characters are composed of a sound component and a meaning component.

REFERENCES

Caravolas, M. (2006). Learning to spell in different languages: How orthographic variables might affect early literacy. In R. M. Joshi & P. G. Aaron (Eds.), *Handbook of orthography and literacy* (pp. 497–512). Mahwah, NJ: Erlbaum.

Goswami, U., Gombert, J. E., & de Barrera, L. F. (1998). Children's orthographic representations and linguistic transparency: Nonsense word reading in English, French, and Spanish. *Applied Psycholinguistics, 19*, 19–52.

Joshi, R. M., & Aaron, P. G. (Eds.). (2006). *Handbook of orthography and literacy.* Mahwah, NJ: Erlbaum.

Landerl, K., Wimmer, H., & Frith, U. (1997). The impact of orthographic consistency on dyslexia: A German–English comparison. *Cognition, 63,* 315–334.

Massaro, D., & Jesse, A. (2005). The magic of reading: Too many influences for quick and easy explanations. In T. Trabasso, J. Sabatini, D. Massar, & R. Calfee (Eds.), *From orthography to pedagogy* (pp. 37–63). Mahwah, NJ: Erlbaum.

Rahbari, N., & Senechal, M. (2009). Lexical and nonlexical processes in the skilled reading and spelling of Persian. *Reading and Writing, 22,* 511–530.

Saiegh-Haddad, E., & Geva, E. (2008). Morphological awareness, phonological awareness, and reading in English–Arabic bilingual children. *Reading and Writing, 21,* 481–504.

Smythe, I., Everatt, J., & Salter, R. (Eds.). (2004). *International book of dyslexia: A cross language comparison and practice guide.* West Sussex, UK: Wiley.

Trabasso, T., Sabatini, J., Massar, D., & Calfee, R. (Eds.). (2005). *From orthography to pedagogy.* Mahwah, NJ: Erlbaum.

Treiman, R. (1993). *Beginning to spell.* New York: Oxford University Press.

6

Bilingualism and Cognitive Linkages

Learning to Read in Different Languages

Ellen Bialystok
Kathleen F. Peets

FOCUS POINTS

- Children enter school with a wide variety of language skills in one or more languages, and depending on linguistic, social, and educational factors, the children are considered to be English language learners or bilinguals. These linguistic profiles play an important role in children's acquisition of literacy in the school language.

- Children's oral language skills, including vocabulary size, grammatical sensitivity, and narrative skills, are central to acquiring literacy. These linguistic achievements are acquired differently by children learning more than one language than by monolinguals, sometimes to the detriment of English language learners or bilingual children.

- Bilingual children, and to some extent English language learners, have been shown to have precocious development of a set of cognitive skills, called *executive control*, that is central to literacy and school achievement and potentially benefits bilingual children relative to their monolingual peers.

CHAPTER PURPOSE

The purpose of this chapter is to examine the effect of bilingualism on children's ability to learn to read in the language of schooling. We also examine the implications of this process for the ability to become biliterate, reading in both the home and the school languages.

Literacy builds on developments in children's language and cognitive abilities and emerges in the context of experience with the specific type of language encountered in print. All of these factors are essential for learning to read. Our review focuses on three aspects of this profile. The first is a discussion of the context of bilingualism and learning to read. We discuss varieties of bilingualism and how these relate to the specific issue of English language learners (ELLs). Although there are important overlaps, these concepts are not the same: Children who are bilingual may or may not be ELLs, and ELLs may or may not be bilingual. We also discuss the importance of considering the relation between the child's two languages in understanding the effect of language background on early literacy success. The second section deals with the linguistic basis of learning to read and examines how the prerequisite skills of language proficiency, including vocabulary knowledge, narrative and discourse competence, and metalinguistic ability, particularly phonological awareness, are affected by bilingualism and therefore impact on the development of literacy. Finally, we describe the role of nonverbal cognitive skills in the acquisition of literacy and consider how differences between monolinguals and bilinguals in the development of these abilities might affect learning to read.

We use the evidence presented in the three sections to discuss how language background provides a crucial basis for children's development of literacy in any language and propose suggestions for effective pedagogical procedures.

REVIEW OF RESEARCH AND THEORY

Language Experience and Bilingualism

Our ordinary conversational means for describing people's language experience perpetuates a fiction so compelling that we accept the description as a meaningful category. We talk as though being bilingual, or being a language learner, or being literate in a language is an identifiable state with objective criteria and stable characteristics. Our faith in these descriptions as reliable and valid categories extends to education, where such categories are used to classify children and place them in various instructional programs, and to research, where experimental designs are built around the objective of uncovering the unique profile for members of the respective categorical groups. Practically, these approaches are useful and allow educational practice and research enquiry to proceed, producing outcomes that are largely positive. Theoretically, however, the categories are elusive, with individual variation within a category sometimes as great as that between two individuals from different categories.

There are prototypical experiences that correspond to these defining categories in that they reflect combinations of home and school language use and functional and literate ability to operate in one or both of the languages to which children are exposed. But the differences are important as well: Different homes use multiple languages in different ways, to different extents, with different family and extended family members. These languages are sometimes supported by a community of speakers, sometimes by print and other media, and sometimes by the school. The relationship between the two languages used in the home can be close, as in dialect or family relationships between the two languages, or different to such an extent that the languages are not even recorded in the same writing system. Finally, a child growing up in a home with some configuration of these values can learn one or both of the home languages to varying degrees of proficiency. When the child enters school, all of this matters greatly, although no simple classification could possibly reflect the detail carried by all these dimensions.

One distinction that captures some of the variation in these situations is in the difference between children designated as ELLs and children who are bilingual, a distinction important for both educational practice and research. The basis of the distinction is largely in the relation between proficiency in the two languages, but socioeconomic factors are also relevant. In general, one assumes somewhat equivalent proficiency for bilinguals but unbalanced competence for ELLs. However, when schooling is carried out in one of those languages, the direction of asymmetry between the two languages of a language learner becomes *relevant* for education but largely *irrelevant* for research. In other words, from the perspective of cognitive and linguistic development, the important consideration is that children are acquiring two different systems, a situation that has been shown to have broad implications for development; from the perspective of education, only children's competence in the language of schooling is considered to be important. Our view, however, is that even in educational contexts, the totality of children's language competence and the extent to which children are proficient in languages outside the language of school should be considered as well, as these experiences have documented effects on children's language, cognitive, and academic achievement.

Extensive research has demonstrated the linguistic costs and cognitive benefits of bilingualism for children's development (reviewed in Bialystok, 2001). In the most general terms, bilingual children usually experience slower language development with smaller vocabularies in each language (Bialystok & Feng, in press; Oller & Eilers, 2002) but superior development of cognitive processes relating to the important executive functions of control and selective attention (Carlson & Meltzoff, 2008). Control and selective attention are two aspects of executive functioning, a set of abilities that also includes switching and working memory. These executive control abilities develop throughout childhood but are the basis of all higher cognition and thought (Diamond, 2002). In some sense, ELLs represent a midpoint on a continuum between monolingualism and bilingualism, so it might be expected that the consequences of their language experience also fall between the endpoints. In some studies, for example, children with unbalanced proficiency in their two languages (although they were not ELLs) showed cognitive benefits that were less dramatic than those found for more balanced bilinguals but nonetheless were different from the performance of monolinguals (Bialystok, 1988; Bialystok & Majumder, 1998). In a study by Mezzacappa (2004), in which he compared the executive control development of children ages 4–7 years from various disadvantaged groups for which poorer development in these abilities is well established, he surprisingly found that Hispanic children outperformed children in the other groups, a difference he suggested might reflect their bilingual background. In contrast, the study by Carlson and Meltzoff included a group of early second-language learners, and their performance on the executive control tasks was no different from that of monolinguals.

In addition to the relative balance in proficiency between the two languages, the relation between the two languages is also crucial in determining the linguistic and cognitive outcomes of bilingualism. In a series of studies we showed that bilingual children were more advanced than monolinguals in understanding the symbolic relation between notation and meaning—that is, how print refers to language (Bialystok, 1997). This is one of the most crucial insights that children must grasp to become independent readers. However, a study that compared Chinese–English bilinguals with children for whom both languages were written alphabetically showed that there was initial confusion for the Chinese-speaking children, most likely because of the significant differences between the rules of the writing system (Bialystok, Shenfield, & Codd, 2000). Mono-lingual children who were learning either English or Chinese performed comparably on this task (Bialystok & Luk, 2007). Therefore, unbalanced proficiency in two languages or even balanced proficiency in two lan-guages with a particular relation to each other has pervasive effects on children's development. For this reason, educators need to know about children's proficiency in other languages and understand as well the relation between the language used at home and the system taught in school.

Educational practice is most concerned with children's competence in the language of schooling, so it is clear that the challenge for ELLs in the school system is primarily to deal with their proficiency in Eng-lish. However, as we have shown, children's development and academic achievement, in fact, depends on their entire linguistic profile. Therefore, our discussion of children's progress in acquiring literacy skills focuses on the effect of bilingualism in the broad sense in which it is taken to mean children's exposure to multiple languages at home, and not only on their level of English competence or their official status as ELLs.

Linguistic Basis of Learning to Read

The relationship between oral language development and literacy acqui-sition is complex: There is no simple line connecting children's evolving competence with speech to the qualitative leap to reading. One dimen-sion of this complexity is that various levels of language proficiency con-tribute to different aspects of literacy acquisition. Children's progression toward independent and competent reading is dependent on their pro-ficiency in all aspects of language—phonological ability, knowledge of morphemes (the smallest units of meaning in a language), syntax, vocab-ulary, and even discourse. These aspects of oral language proficiency have been studied to varying degrees in both monolingual and bilingual speakers, and in important ways, the impact of bilingualism on each is different (Lesaux, Rupp, & Siegel, 2007; Speece, Ritchey, Cooper, Roth, & Schatschneider, 2004).

A kind of "overseer" of all these aspects of language proficiency is *metalinguistic awareness*. Because the ability to manipulate language as a tool in an abstract way is a linguistic achievement that is rooted in domain-general cognitive development, there is an intricate relation between children's evolving linguistic and cognitive abilities. It is also a requirement for using language symbolically to meet the goals of literacy. Not only is metalinguistic awareness a prerequisite for literacy, but it is also a product of it, creating a self-propelling system of increasingly complex symbolic usage. Since reading in an alphabetic system requires associating a written symbol with a unit of sound, it is obvious that awareness of the sound system of the language—that is, phonological awareness—is the most important of these metalinguistic insights.

The predictive power of phonological awareness for the acquisition of literacy in a language that is written in an alphabetic system is beyond dispute. But the centrality of the phonological insight for literacy is broader than just making the associative links between sounds and letters. Surprisingly, phonological awareness has also been documented as important for children learning to read in Chinese, a language for which sound–symbol correspondences have no apparent role (Ho & Bryant, 1997). Subsequent research has clarified differences in the development of phonological awareness and its role in early literacy for children learning either English or Chinese by pointing to differences in the level of phonological awareness and the way it impacts reading in each of these languages (McBride-Chang, Bialystok, Chong, & Li, 2004), but its essential importance throughout varieties of literacy acquisition has been substantiated. (See Newman, Chapter 5, this volume.)

The centrality of phonological awareness for reading, especially in alphabetic languages, makes it a crucial area in which to determine whether there are developmental differences between monolingual and bilingual children. Although a number of studies has attempted to clarify this possibility, the results have been mixed. Some studies reported bilingual advantages in phonological awareness at about 5 years old (Bruck & Genesee, 1995; Campbell & Sais, 1995), but these advantages tended to disappear by 6 years old, when children were exposed to reading instruction (Bruck & Genesee, 1995). Some studies that claimed to be demonstrating an advantage in phonological awareness used tasks that only marginally assessed those insights (Yelland, Polland, & Mercuri, 1993). In a series of studies investigating various aspects of children's ability to manipulate individual sounds to follow a rule, we found only marginal evidence for bilingual superiority in this skill (Bialystok, Majumder, & Martin, 2003).

Like metalinguistic awareness in general, phonological awareness is rooted not only in children's knowledge of language but also in their cognitive ability to access and manipulate aspects of linguistic representation. It is this interface of language and cognitive ability that might be most important for reading. In a study of English–Cantonese bilinguals learning to read in both languages, we showed that the general cognitive underpinnings of phonological awareness transferred across languages, but that children needed to learn and become aware of the language-specific features individually (Luk & Bialystok, 2008). An extension of this idea was shown in a study of 6-year-old children's phonological awareness and decoding in English (Bialystok, Luk, & Kwan, 2005). The children were monolingual, Spanish–English bilingual, Hebrew–English bilingual, or Chinese–English bilingual. Like English, Spanish and Hebrew are alphabetic systems because the written notations represent sounds; unlike English, Chinese is a character-based system in which the written notations represent morphemes (Coulmas, 1989). Children profited from similarity and could transfer what they had learned from one alphabetic system to another, but distinct systems that offered no basis for transfer between an alphabetic system and the character-based system of Chinese were learned individually by children at no cost to the developing system being taught in school.

By second grade, children's reading begins to rely on morphological awareness in addition to phonemic awareness. Morphology involves *roots* and *affixes*, the smallest units of meaning in a language. Being aware that *able* can go on the end of many verbs, for example, means that a child can read a word such as *doable* and understand the word's meaning despite never having heard the word aurally. Casalis and Louis-Alexandre (2000) examined monolingual children from kindergarten to second grade and found a close relationship between phonological analysis and morphological analysis in learning to read French. The authors found that children relied more on phonological analysis in the first grade, but on a combination of phonological and morphological analysis by the second grade. Carlisle and Fleming (2003) examined derivational morphological analysis (e.g., *sing* [verb] + -*er* [suffix] yields *singer* [noun]) and found that it contributed to monolingual third graders' reading comprehension. As in phonological awareness, there is also evidence for cross-linguistic transfer of morphological skills among bilinguals (Wang, Cheng, & Chen, 2006), but no evidence for an absolute advantage in morphological awareness in bilinguals.

One way in which morphological analysis differs from phonological analysis is in its representation of meaning. Whereas letters are arbitrary symbols, morphemes carry independent meaning that not only tend to have similar pronunciations across words (supporting decoding) but also tend to have the same meaning across words (supporting reading comprehension). Since literacy is an integration of top-down and bottom-up processing, morphology plays a unique role in facilitating both. From a top-down perspective, higher levels of language processing are typically more relevant to comprehension and lower levels are more critical for decoding. When morphemes combine to form words, the emphasis increasingly shifts to reading comprehension (Kuo & Anderson, 2006). Clearly the more words a child knows, the more easily it will be to recognize them in written form, assuming that a certain level of automatized decoding is in place.

Like other aspects of grammar, such as morphology, syntax is likely to play more of a role in older readers than in beginning readers (Oakhill, Cain, & Bryant, 2003). At higher levels of reading, the integration of word knowledge, decoding, and morphology all converge on syntax. It is through syntax that children can infer meanings of new morphemes by their syntactic placement and of new vocabulary words by their semantic and syntactic context. In this way, there is a complex integration of linguistic systems that supports reading as children move out of the decoding phase (Oakhill et al., 2003; Storch & Whitehurst, 2002). Indeed, syntactic knowledge has been associated with reading success in monolinguals (Bowey, 1986; Muter, Hulme, Snowling, & Stevenson, 2004). Although this relationship has not been investigated among ELL and bilingual children to date, one study found that syntactic ability was only related to monolingual readers' success and not to that of English as a second language (ESL) children (Jongejan, Verhoeven, & Siegel, 2007). Although children who are just learning English (either ESL or ELL) would undoubtedly have poorer command of grammatical structure than native speakers, there is no evidence that bilinguals who are learning English along with another language have any compromised knowledge of grammar. The *awareness* of grammar, however, is a different matter. Early research showed that aspects of metalinguistic awareness, such as grammatical sensitivity (Galambos & Goldin-Meadow, 1990) and word awareness (Bialystok, 1987), were acquired more precociously by bilingual children than by monolinguals. These insights may facilitate the higher-level processes of extracting meaning from text as children learn to read.

One of the strongest predictors of reading comprehension is semantic knowledge, particularly vocabulary size (Roth, Speece, & Cooper, 2002). This relationship is self-evident in that the more words a child knows, the more likely he or she will be able to understand complex texts that contain such words. Because children with poor vocabularies have demonstrated poor reading comprehension, ELLs and bilingual children may be at a disadvantage in reading comprehension as a result of their lower English proficiency. Indeed, Proctor, Carlo, August, and Snow (2005) found that lower vocabulary scores were related to lower reading comprehension performance among ELLs in grade 4. However, the question of whether or not bilinguals' low vocabularies will contribute to a similar relationship is not yet known. We are currently examining this question by investigating the relationship between formal language proficiency in English and reading comprehension skills in young bilingual readers. It may be that bilinguals have learned enough academic vocabulary in English from their years of English schooling to ensure that their reading comprehension is not compromised, despite lower formal proficiency.

Aspects of oral language beyond the formal linguistic categories of phonology, morphology, syntax, and semantics also play a role in literacy acquisition. For example, academic discourse skills such as narrating, defining, and explaining incorporate many literate features of language, despite the fact that they occur in an oral form. Such features include decontextualized language (i.e., talking about things that are not physically present, or things that are abstract), less frequent or more abstract vocabulary, and more complex syntax (Snow, 1983; Snow & Dickinson, 1991). Some researchers have found a relationship between these types of discourse abilities and reading comprehension among monolinguals (e.g., Griffin, Hemphill, Camp, & Wolf, 2004) and bilinguals (e.g., Chang, 2006), whereas others have not (e.g., Roth, Speece, & Cooper, 2002). In the case of ELLs and bilinguals, academic discourse skills are typically acquired in the context of English schooling and may therefore not be compromised by lower formal proficiency. That is, despite lower vocabularies in general, ELLs and bilinguals may acquire specific academic discourse skills as a result of learning them in English within the classroom. This dissociation between proficiency and discourse production was found in our recent work in academic discourse in kindergarten (Peets, Lahmann, & Bialystok, 2008), a finding that has implications for both schooling and assessment. The dissociation suggests that children's skills may be underestimated by standardized tests alone. Moreover, if children are using discourse forms effectively, then these forms become a context through which not only important curricular material is acquired, but also through which the more formal linguistic forms may be practiced and learned.

Cognition and the Acquisition of Literacy

It is apparent that the acquisition of literacy rests on children's linguistic development; it is less obvious that cognitive processing is also instrumental in this singular achievement. The most crucial difference between the linguistic and cognitive abilities that underlie literacy for bilingual children is that development of the former are tied to the language-specific factors described earlier, but development of the latter are domain general and are available to all children who are bilingual, irrespective of the specific pairs of languages they speak. The primary cognitive outcome for bilingual children is an enhanced development of executive control.

A growing body of research has demonstrated that bilingual children develop executive control more precociously than monolingual children (reviewed in Bialystok, 2001). The degree of advantage enjoyed by bilingual children appears to be calibrated to their level of experience with two languages. Early research showed that children who had more balanced proficiency in their two languages demonstrated greater benefits in a sentence judgment task requiring executive control than did children with less experience in one of their languages (Bialystok, 1988; Bialystok & Majumder, 1998); unbalanced children, in turn, outperformed monolinguals, indicating a continuous relation between bilingual experience and cognitive outcomes. On nonverbal tasks assessing executive control, both Carlson and Meltzoff (2008) and Mezzacappa (2004) reported significant advantages for children who could be designated as ELL on the basis of their socioeconomic status and home language environment. Thus, these advantages in cognitive control emerge simply from the experience of using two languages, with greater benefits as the experience increases. Importantly, executive control has a central role to play in the acquisition of literacy.

Perhaps the main component of executive control is working memory, the ability to hold information in mind while it is being processed or manipulated. Working memory is involved in all stages of reading: constructing the word from the constituent sounds, integrating the words into sentences, and extracting the intended meaning from all those processes. In simple memory tasks in which children were asked to hold information in mind and repeat it back unaltered, as in assessments of digit span, there was no evidence for any difference between monolingual and bilingual children (Bialystok & Feng, in press). However, the hallmark of working memory is the additional requirement to perform some transformation on that information, and it is that feature of working memory that makes it part of the executive control system and not simply the memory system. Therefore, to the extent that a working memory task requires manipulation and control, then bilinguals should show better performance than monolinguals because of their more advanced development of executive control. Crucially, the role of memory in reading fits exactly with the profile for working memory in that constant processing is required on the information that is the current focus of attention. Hence, differences in these working memory processes that can be traced to language experience would have consequences for children's efforts in learning to read.

A task that systematically manipulated the degree of executive control involved in a nonverbal spatial working memory task changed the recall instructions from simple recall to recall that had to conform to a specified pattern (Feng, Diamond, & Bialystok, 2007). As the pattern became more complicated, more executive control was required to perform the task. Two studies compared 6-year-old children who were monolingual English speakers or bilingual children who spoke a non-English language at home and English at school and in the community. All the children performed similarly in simple retrieval conditions, but as the demands for executive control increased, the bilinguals began to outperform the monolinguals. Thus, the subtle demands for working memory that are embedded in reading are handled more efficiently by bilingual children than by comparable monolinguals.

Another cognitive ability required by reading is the need to selectively focus attention on a complex display (i.e., the text) and to monitor that attention to construct meaning. A task used in the adult literature investigating control processes in memory retrieval is known as "release from proactive interference (PI)." Participants read a list of words belonging to a single semantic category, such as animals, recall them, and then immediately hear another list from the same category. Three such lists are presented, and the ability to recall the words declines as the interference builds up from the previous list—"Was *elephant* on the list I just heard or was that two lists ago?" The fourth list consists of words from a different semantic category, and the typical result is that memory performance is restored to that of the first list because there is now no interference. The responsibility for monitoring to avoid these intrusions is part of the executive control system. The relevant finding, therefore, would be to compare the extent to which intrusions from previous lists affect the performance of monolinguals and bilinguals. If the greater executive control of bilinguals extends to a verbal monitoring task of this type, then they should produce fewer intrusions. This is exactly what was found in a study of monolingual and bilingual 7-year-olds (Bialystok & Feng, 2009), in spite of lower language proficiency in the bilingual children, as indicated by performance on a test of receptive vocabulary.

These studies illustrate the role of the executive control system in skills that are relevant for children's early acquisition of literacy. The superiority of bilingual children in developing these cognitive skills places them in a privileged position for the challenges involved in becoming independent readers.

BEST PRACTICES

In this chapter we have discussed the important connections that exist between oral language ability, cognition, and the acquisition of literacy. We have identified the formal proficiency limitations associated with acquiring literacy as a bilingual or ELL child, while highlighting other compensatory abilities, such as metalinguistic awareness and improved executive functions. Thus, because the bilingual or ELL child brings both disadvantages and advantages to the task of reading, one area of pedagogical focus should be the development of high levels of oral language skills. It is evident that oral language skills are a strong predictor of learning to read in monolingual children, but it is equally apparent, from the results of the studies reviewed here, that developing oral language skills in bilingual children is a particularly important instructional focus. Teaching should target both literacy-specific language skills as well as basic conversational fluency, including vocabulary. In preparing children to become skilled readers, we must ensure that they have a strong foundation in oral language and emergent literacy skills. That is, the oral language precursors to reading must form a solid linguistic foundation before the task of decoding or comprehending is to be achieved. Specifically, ensuring that children are exposed to a wide range of academic discourse types with less common vocabulary is essential. The relevant precursors to literacy include both language-specific and general cognitive abilities, and literacy practices must nurture the development of all of them.

For children who are bilingual and especially for those learning to read in both their languages, the role of cross-linguistic transfer must be considered whenever possible. Heritage language experiences may include being told or read stories and having printed materials (products, newspapers, books, grocery lists) in the home. Incorporating this knowledge into early childhood education would be, in many cases, continuing home practices, and in other cases, introducing this type of day-to-day emergent literacy during preschool. If children are encouraged to make "pretend lists" and "read" magazines as part of their preschool curriculum of play and experiential learning, then they will acquire this essential foundation for subsequent English literacy acquisition. In this sense, the language in which the symbolic activity is carried out is less important than the introduction to the idea of literacy and text, so taking advantage of other languages and other types of text that are familiar from the home can enhance this learning experience for some children. In a similar way, ELL children may bring early literacy in their heritage language to schooling in English. As we have seen, the extent to which aspects of a home language can transfer to educational experiences in the school language depends on the relation between the two languages, and some awareness of these unique relationships would be beneficial for teachers. Teachers could ask children about their literacy experience, children could bring in samples of books or journals to share, enriching the learning experience for all the children. This dialogue promotes cultural sensitivity and facilitates a process of creating links between language and literacy across different languages for the child.

From the perspective of the sound system and its connection with decoding, teaching sound–symbol correspondence and sound awareness in emergent literacy activities is essential, just as it is for monolingual children. What may differ among bilinguals and ELLs is the extent to which they are familiar with both the English sound system and the alphabetic writing system. Therefore, enriched activities to support this awareness should be adopted in the classroom and made explicit in ways that monolingual children may not require. That is, a monolingual child will have more home exposure to the sound system of English and may likely have more English literacy experience, for example, in terms of more English storybooks at home. Therefore this type of learning may need to be made more explicit for those children who do not share the same linguistic background as that used in the school system, to ensure that they are on more of an equal footing with monolinguals in their development of sounds and sound–symbol correspondence.

Although bilingual children may have deficits in grammar based on general proficiency lags, their superior metalinguistic awareness compensates in preparing them for interpreting the complex syntax of literate language. And although monolinguals' oral language skills in English may be more implicit, bilinguals may benefit from explicit teaching in reading strategies at the level of grammar. Incorporating morphological and syntactic analysis activities allows children to break down complex structures into smaller, more interpretable, parts. In turn, this process of analysis would support both decoding (e.g., recognizing familiar morphemes) and comprehension (e.g., understanding familiar morphemes and interpreting clause relations and conjunctions). This type of pedagogical approach would address the English language disadvantages by making use of bilingual cognitive and metalinguistic advantages. These advantages could be exploited at the critical pedagogical shift from the third grade to the fourth and fifth, in which a shift from "learning to read" and "reading to learn" (Chall, 1983) occurs. The move from decoding to reading comprehension is a difficult transition that relies upon a wide variety of cognitive and linguistic resources. By teaching metalinguistic skills at the levels of morphology and syntax at this time, as well as laying a solid foundation in academic discourse in the years leading up to this critical stage, we prepare ELL and bilingual children better for the complex tasks of reading to learn, or reading comprehension.

There may also be some transfer of structures at the discourse level, particularly in the case of narrative, but other structures could be taught explicitly as well. For example, bilingual and ELL children could be exposed to more oral forms that are associated with literacy success (e.g., narratives, definitions, formal explanations) to increase their exposure beyond that of their monolingual peers as well as to provide formal lessons in discourse structure to enable them to interpret written English text more easily. We know from cross-linguistic studies of discourse that not all languages use the same macro structures (Hickman, 2004), yet these structures have relationships with academic success and the language of schooling (Griffin et al., 2004). Introducing children to those forms that are critical for school success will enable them to work with varying levels of proficiency in achieving academically appropriate modes of communication, both oral and written.

SUMMARY OF MAIN IDEAS

The evidence is now overwhelming that the language experience of children from the time they are born has a significant effect on the organization of their cognitive and linguistic systems and influences their development and school achievement. Teachers need to pay attention to the home language backgrounds of children because these language experiences have significant consequences, in particular for their impact on children's acquisition of literacy in the language of schooling.

In this chapter we highlight several ways in which the relevant language and cognitive abilities of bilingual children may be different from those of monolinguals and describe how these differences—some manifest as advantages and others as disadvantages—impact on children's efforts in learning to read in the language of school. In our holistic approach, our view is that schooling should build on all aspects of the child's competencies, including those that were developed in a different language. In some cases, the language and cognitive skills transfer easily across languages, facilitating the learning experience, but even if the transfer is less direct, the child's learning experience is more productive if it builds on what is already known.

Our suggestions are aimed at the problem of how to maximize the learning experience for ELL and bilingual children in classrooms where they are attempting to acquire literacy in a language that is not the primary language of the home. However, the consequence of such procedures is that not only will those children have a smoother transition into the language of schooling, but the monolingual children in the classroom will have a glimpse at the larger world that includes languages and cultures beyond their own. Not a bad outcome, all around!

IMPLICATIONS FOR RESEARCH, PRACTICE, AND POLICY

Evidence that bilingual children come to school with different cognitive and linguistic skills than monolinguals needs to be considered at every point in research, educational practice, and policy. Language assessments are standard procedure in schools, and important decisions are made on the basis of these performance results. However, bilingual children are likely to underperform on formal assessments of language proficiency, such as vocabulary or grammatical knowledge, even though there is no detriment to their overall achievement. For example, in spite of lower vocabulary scores than monolinguals, bilinguals show more advanced ability in decoding, even when the writing system used in the two languages is completely different (Bialystok et al., 2005). Therefore, educational assessment must be based on a detailed understanding of the child's language background, and it must interpret results in terms of those experiences.

A primary concern for research in literacy is the need to clarify the difference between ELLs and bilinguals. What is the population being studied? Is there an assumption of a deficit model in research for both groups? We need to think in terms of compensatory abilities, such as executive functioning and *using* language effectively for specific purposes, as opposed to notions of reduced ability or lower proficiency alone. We also must carry out more research aimed at identifying differences in literacy development as a function of the specific details of children's language experience, including the relation between the language pairs as well as the relation between the child's proficiency in the two languages.

The implications of such differences extend to instruction where teachers need to decide how to consider the backgrounds of children who speak another language. Do ELL children require the same considerations as bilingual children? Is one mode of literacy instruction appropriate for monolingual, ELL, and bilingual children? Some research suggests that this is the case (Lesaux et al., 2007), but little research has been undertaken thus far, and proficiency issues are clearly putting many ELL children at risk for reading difficulty (Proctor et al., 2005). It may be that these three groups should be considered separately, with individual models of instruction that rely on different emphases according to unique developmental patterns and strengths within each group.

The issue of reading failure or difficulty among ELL and bilingual children is particularly relevant in the case of possible learning disability. A salient role for assessment is to identify children who have special needs or are at risk of failing because of specific challenges. The instruments used for these diagnostic assessments tend to include a large segment of verbal ability and are standardized on a population without regard for language experience. Two potential implications of these assessments are relevant for bilingual children. First, language-specific disorders that are identified on the basis of performance on tasks measuring linguistic processing may erroneously include bilingual or ELL children if appropriate language background information is not included in the assessment. In contrast, identification of children with attention-deficit/hyperactivity disorder (ADHD) may miss children who are bilingual because of their advantageous performance in the executive control tasks that are used to determine the existence of that condition. Therefore, because language and cognitive abilities are organized and developed differently in children with multiple language experiences, these children may be misclassified on the basis of results of standardized tests.

Once it has been established whether or not ELL and bilingual children indeed face unique challenges that inhibit reading acquisition, then interventions that are based on a sound knowledge of language and literacy development are essential. These interventions can take the form of formal instruction as well as increased exposure (as compared to the exposure typical for monolingual children) to school-related language and reading materials. This formal instruction and increased exposure must begin very early on, starting with emergent literacy and extending through all relevant levels of language, as discussed above. For ELL children who have already begun literacy development in a heritage language, the bridge to English must be made in a way that connects these two experiences. An emphasis on both bilingual and biliterate education is clearly an issue of policy, and it is only through research-based evidence that a case can be made to increase funding and curriculum development toward these goals.

ACKNOWLEDGMENT

Preparation of this chapter was supported by Grant No. R01HD052523 from the National Institutes of Health to Ellen Bialystok.

REFERENCES

Bialystok, E. (1987). Words as things: Development of word concept by bilingual children. *Studies in Second Language Acquisition, 9,* 133–140.

Bialystok, E. (1988). Levels of bilingualism and levels of linguistic awareness. *Developmental Psychology, 24,* 560–567.

Bialystok, E. (1997). Effects of bilingualism and biliteracy on children's emerging concepts of print. *Developmental Psychology, 33,* 429–440.

Bialystok, E. (2001). *Bilingualism in development: Language, literacy, and cognition.* New York: Cambridge University Press.

Bialystok, E., & Feng, X. (2009). Language proficiency and executive control in proactive interference: Evidence from monolingual and bilingual children and adults. *Brain and Language, 109,* 93–100.

Bialystok, E., & Feng, X. (in press). Language proficiency and its implications for monolingual and bilingual children. In A. Durgunoglu (Ed.), *Language and literacy development for language learners.* New York: Guilford Press.

Bialystok, E., Feng, X., & Diamond, A. (2009). *Do bilingual children show an advantage in working memory?* Manuscript submitted for publication.

Bialystok, E., & Luk, G. (2007). The universality of symbolic representation for reading in Asian and alphabetic languages. *Bilingualism: Language and Cognition, 10,* 121–129.

Bialystok, E., Luk, G., & Kwan, E. (2005). Bilingualism, biliteracy, and learning to read: Interactions among languages and writing systems. *Scientific Studies of Reading, 9,* 43–61.

Bialystok, E., & Majumder, S. (1998). The relationship between bilingualism and the development of cognitive processes in problem-solving. *Applied Psycholinguistics, 19,* 69–85.

Bialystok, E., Majumder, S., & Martin, M. M. (2003). Developing phonological awareness: Is there a bilingual advantage? *Applied Psycholinguistics, 24,* 27–44.

Bialystok, E., Shenfield, T., & Codd, J. (2000). Languages, scripts, and the environment: Factors in developing concepts of print. *Developmental Psychology, 36,* 66–76.

Bowey, J. A. (1986). Syntactic awareness in relation to reading skill and ongoing reading comprehension monitoring. *Journal of Experimental Child Psychology, 41,* 282–299.

Bruck, M., & Genesee, F. (1995). Phonological awareness in young second language learners. *Journal of Child Language, 22,* 307–324.

Campbell, R., & Sais, E. (1995). Accelerated metalinguistic (phonological) awareness in bilingual children. *British Journal of Developmental Psychology, 13,* 61–68.

Carlisle, J. F., & Fleming, J. (2003). Lexical processing of morphologically complex words in the elementary years. *Scientific Studies of Reading, 7,* 239–253.

Carlson, S. M., & Meltzoff, A. N. (2008). Bilingual experience and executive functioning in young children. *Developmental Science, 11,* 282–298.

Casalis, S., & Louis-Alexandre, M. (2000). Morphological analysis, phonological analysis, and learning to read French: A longitudinal study. *Reading and Writing, 12,* 303–335.

Chall, J. S. (1983). *Stages of reading development.* New York: McGraw-Hill.

Chang, C. (2006). Linking early narrative skill to later language and reading ability in Mandarin-speaking children: A longitudinal study over eight years. *Narrative Inquiry, 16,* 275–293.

Coulmas, F. (1989). *The writing systems of the world.* Oxford, UK: Blackwell.

Diamond, A. (2002). Normal development of prefrontal cortex from birth to young adulthood: Cognitive functions, anatomy, and biochemistry. In D. Stuss & R. Knight (Eds.), *Principles of frontal lobe function* (pp. 466–503). New York: Oxford University Press.

Feng, X., Diamond, A., & Bialystok, E. (2007, March–April). *Manipulating information in working memory: An advantage for bilinguals.* Poster presented at the bienniel meeting of the Society for Research in Child Development, Boston.

Galambos, S. J., & Goldin-Meadow, S. (1990). The effects of learning two languages on levels of metalinguistic awareness. *Cognition, 34,* 1–56.

Griffin, T. M., Hemphill, L., Camp, L., & Wolf, D. P. (2004). Oral discourse in the preschool years and later literacy skills. *First Language, 24,* 123–147.

Hickman, M. (2004). Coherence, cohesion, and context: Some comparative perspectives in narrative development. In S. Stromquist & L. Verhoeven (Eds.), *Relating events in narrative* (pp. 281–306). Mahwah, NJ: Erlbaum.

Ho, S., & Bryant, P. (1997). Phonological skills are important in learning to read Chinese. *Developmental Psychology, 33,* 946–951.

Jongejan, W., Verhoeven, L., & Siegel, L. S. (2007). Predictors of reading and spelling abilities in first- and second-language learners. *Journal of Educational Psychology, 99,* 835–851.

Kuo, L., & Anderson, R. C. (2006). Morphological awareness and learning to read: A cross-linguistic perspective. *Educational Psychologist, 4,* 161–180.

Lesaux, N. K., Rupp, A. A., & Siegel, L. S. (2007). Growth in reading skills of children from diverse linguistic backgrounds: Findings from a 5–year longitudinal study. *Journal of Educational Psychology, 99,* 821–834.

Luk, G., & Bialystok, E (2008). Common and distinct cognitive bases for reading in English–Cantonese bilinguals. *Applied Psycholinguistics, 29,* 269–289.

McBride-Chang, C., Bialystok, E., Chong, K. K. Y., & Li, Y. (2004). Levels of phonological awareness in three cultures. *Journal of Experimental Child Psychology, 89,* 93–111.

Mezzacappa, E. (2004). Alerting, orienting, and executive attention: Developmental properties and sociodemographic correlates in an epidemiological sample of young, urban children. *Child Development, 75,* 1373–1386.

Muter, V., Hulme, C., Snowling, M. J., & Stevenson, J. (2004). Phonemes, rimes, vocabulary, and grammatical skills as foundations of early reading development: Evidence from a longitudinal study. *Developmental Psychology, 40,* 665–681.

Oakhill, J. V., Cain, K., & Bryant, P. E. (2003). The dissociation of word reading and text comprehension: Evidence from component skills. *Language and Cognitive Processes, 18,* 443–468.

Oller, D. K., & Eilers, R. E. (Eds.). (2002). *Language and literacy in bilingual children.* Clevedon, UK: Multilingual Matters.

Peets, K. F., Lahmann, C., & Bialystok, E. (2008, November). *Bilingual children's narratives in English.* Poster presented at the Boston University conference on language development, Boston.

Proctor, P. C., Carlo, M., August, D., & Snow, C. (2005). Native Spanish-speaking children reading in English: Toward a model of comprehension. *Journal of Educational Psychology, 97,* 246–256.

Roth, F. P., Speece, D. L., & Cooper, D. H. (2002). A longitudinal analysis of the connection between oral language and reading. *Journal of Educational Research, 95,* 259–272.

Snow, C. E. (1983). Literacy and language: Relationships during the preschool years. *Harvard Educational Review, 53,* 165–189.

Snow, C. E., & Dickinson, D. K. (1991). Social sources of narrative skills at home and at school. *First Language, 10,* 87–103.

Speece, D. L., Ritchey, K. D., Cooper, D. H., Roth, F. P., & Schatschneider, C. (2004). Growth in early reading skills from kindergarten to third grade. *Contemporary Educational Psychology, 29,* 312–332.

Storch, S. A., & Whitehurst, D. J. (2002). Oral language and code-related precursors to reading: Evidence from a longitudinal structural model. *Developmental Psychology, 38,* 934–947.

Wang, M., Cheng, C., & Chen, S. (2006). Contribution of morphological awareness to Chinese–English biliteracy acquisition. *Journal of Educational Psychology, 98,* 542–553.

Yelland, G. W., Pollard, J., & Mercuri, A. (1993). The metalinguistic benefits of limited contact with a second language. *Applied Psycholinguistics, 14,* 423–444.

7

Learning English
as a Second Language

María Estela Brisk

FOCUS POINTS

- Successful teachers recognize and respect variation in the cultural and educational backgrounds of students and their families.

- Successful teachers utilize the cultural and linguistic diversity among English language learners in their classroom to engage them, thereby enriching and expanding the learning environment for all students.

- Language teaching must be an integral part of teaching "content," even in secondary schools. Teaching aspects of language appropriate for a particular content area facilitates understanding and use of academic language by English language learners.

CHAPTER PURPOSE

Over 20% of the students attending public schools in the United States speak a language other than English at home (U.S. Bureau of Statistics, 2008).

> During the 1990s growth in the number of children of immigrants was substantially faster in secondary than elementary schools (72 versus 39%). This pattern was paralleled by a faster increase in the number of LEP [limited English proficient] students in secondary schools. (Capps et al., 2005, p. 12)

Only 12.5% of the teachers working with these students have received any preparation or can communicate in the language of the students (National Center for Education Statistics, 2002). Thus, classrooms that include an English-speaking teacher working with a combination of native speakers of English and speakers of other languages pose a challenging situation. The presence of bilingual learners may overwhelm teachers, particularly if they have not had experience functioning in other languages and cultures, or with populations very different from their own. In turn, it is difficult for students to learn content through a language that they have not mastered because they have to simultaneously focus on content and language (Gibbons, 2003). Schools need to take action to build bridges among the monolingual teacher and native English-speaking students and the bilingual learners, creating nurturing classroom environments to maximize learning for all students. Such classrooms not only help speakers of languages other than English but also students who speak varieties of English different from that used in schools.

In a nurturing classroom:

- The teacher knows the students and their families.
- Classroom climate and organization support second-language (L2) development.
- Language is integrated into the curriculum and instruction.

The purpose of this chapter is to review research and propose practices that support the three principles listed above. These principles apply to any classroom serving bilingual learners, but they are especially addressed to teachers who teach only in English.

REVIEW OF RESEARCH AND THEORY

Students and Their Families

A teacher's knowledge and understanding (or lack thereof) of students and their families impact L2 acquisition. Students' level of heritage language literacy, previous education, cultural background, and sense of identity influence their acquisition of the L2. Their parents' language use, literacy, and education levels may impact teachers' perceptions of students' potential. In turn, parents' notions of L2 acquisition and cultural values result in different levels of support and home policies toward L2 learning and bilingualism as well as different attitudes toward school practices.

Students' Language, Literacy, and Educational Backgrounds

Bilingual or multilingual students' literacy knowledge can vary greatly. They may be in the initial stages of literacy either because they are just entering school or because they have not had a chance to attend school. Often politics or economics in the country of origin curtail the chances of steadily attending school. For these students, especially if they come at the high school level, adjustment to school is extremely difficult (García, 1999). School curriculum and instruction are not planned with these students' needs in mind. In addition, for these students to be identified as having low levels of literacy shatters their own sense of identity as capable individuals who have overcome a great deal of hardship and risk in their lives. Other students come to school with strong literacy backgrounds in their heritage language. They have benefited from consistent schooling in their country of origin. These students quickly adapt and are able to excel in some areas, allowing them to develop their identity as good students (Hersi, 2007).

Age interacts with level of education. Older students with a good educational background can learn English relatively quickly and successfully. Their knowledge of content allows them to focus on the new language. Younger students, on the other hand, need to learn the language and many new concepts simultaneously. The main advantage for younger students is the ability to acquire native-like pronunciation (Genesee, Paradis, & Crago, 2004). Older students with limited schooling have the hardest time because they need to learn both content and language while overcoming the discomfort of being behind their same-age classmates. In addition, students' understanding of the way a classroom functions facilitates communication even when the students have not mastered the language of instruction. Students who have been in school understand what they are expected to do, when they are expected to respond to a teacher, or when they need to carry out a particular task. Even when the norms in the school systems they come from differ, students have some sense that they need to figure out what they are expected to do. Children who have never been in school have a much harder time understanding what they need to do. Neither their background knowledge nor their limited language proficiency helps (Kleifgen & Saville-Troike, 1992).

Immigrant students come to school with knowledge of one or more languages, including some English, depending on the country of origin and previous experiences. However, 76% of bilingual elementary-age students and 56% of middle- and secondary-age students are actually born in the United States (Capps et al., 2005) but live in homes and even neighborhoods that regularly use another language. Thus, their language experience and development differ from students who hear and use only English. These students are often fluent in oral English; however, their experience with English comes mainly from interacting with other children. These students need the additional language input provided by adults, as well as the language needed to function in school settings.

Students' Cultural Backgrounds

Students' cultures influence their background knowledge and behavior in school. Background knowledge, in turn, impacts L2 comprehension and use. Kleifgen and Saville-Troike (1992) found that recent arrivals with minimal knowledge of English could communicate using their background knowledge. In turn, background knowledge may not be helpful when there are cultural differences that lead to varying interpretations of a lesson's content. Culture also impacts students' ways of interacting in class. For example, in a high school math class, where students were encouraged to work in groups, Muslim girls from Sudan would not allow boys in their groups unless they were related to one of the girls. Responses to teachers, as well as expectations of what and how teachers should teach and organize their classrooms, influence students' behavior and ways of communicating (Brisk, Burgos, & Hamerla, 2004).

Students' Identity

Multilingual students may enact different identities with respect to their language and cultural affiliation. Some students develop an integrated identity by which they maintain their heritage language and affiliation to their family and ethnic group and at the same time embrace the host language and culture. Others develop a transnational identity, seeing themselves connected not only to their heritage language and culture but also to the country of origin (Glick-Schiller, Basch, & Szanton-Blanc, 1992). Yet other students reject either their heritage language and culture or the host language and culture (Brisk, 2006). This sense of identity often changes as students mature. An integrated or transnational identity is more favorable for L2 acquisition because students do not give up their heritage background to embrace the new culture and language (Taylor, 1987).

It is important for teachers to become aware of students' sense of identity not only as bilingual individuals but also as competent learners. Feeling competent, regardless of level of English proficiency, will allow students "to become successful participants in school (academic) communities" (Hawkins, 2004, p. 18).

Students' Families

Teachers must also know the families, their language and literacy practices, the language goals they have for their children, and their cultural values. Bilingual parents are better suited to support the development of English in their children because they can use the heritage language to clarify meaning with them.

A number of parents are not fluent in English. However, lack of proficiency in English does not mean that the family does not support education or learning the language. Huss-Keeler (1997) reports on how surprised a teacher was when she visited a family of one of her Pakistani students. Contrary to her image of a disinterested family, she encountered a rich and caring home environment. Equally important is not to make assumptions with respect to home language knowledge and use regardless of whether a child has been identified as an English language learner. For example, a child identified as a Spanish speaker by the teacher also spoke Urdu and was learning to read and write in Arabic (Horan, 2007).

Families have different goals for their children's language learning. All families want their children to learn English. Some also want them to develop the heritage language, while others fear that their native language will get in the way of learning English. There is no need for parents to fear that their children will not learn English because children are usually quick to embrace the society's predominant language (Caldas & Caron-Caldas 2002).

Differences in cultural values can influence parents' support for school activities and approaches to teaching. For example, Vietnamese parents do not view favorably requirements that their children write personal stories or read fictional narratives—two classroom practices commonly used in initial language and literacy development. For them schooling is supposed to be for learning content and not sharing personal information. Parents are often against the reading of fiction that reflects particular moral values. They prefer to keep the teaching of moral values in the family (Dien, 2004). Therefore, some teacher–family interactions may be problematic and require sensitivity to the family's concerns while at the same time necessitating an explanation of the teacher's goals for instruction.

Classroom Climate and Organization for Optimal Language Development

To encourage L2 development, classroom environments need to be welcoming of students from different cultures. They also need to be organized to encourage language use and to maximize comprehension of instruction and expectations.

Recognition of Students' Languages, Cultures, and Talents

A welcoming classroom values students' "funds of knowledge," including their language, culture, and individual talents. A classroom context that respects all students' languages and cultures is conducive to L2 acquisition. When newcomers feel that English speakers appreciate their language and cultural background, they are more willing to learn the language and culture of those who surround them in school. Showing respect for students' languages and dialects means allowing their use in classrooms. Choice of language is defined by context (Gibbons, 2003). There are situations wherein it is perfectly appropriate to use the heritage language, whereas others call for communication in English. Some teachers fear that students, especially older students, will use heritage languages to exclude other students or to disrespect teachers. As long as the teacher creates an atmosphere of respect, use of native languages will not turn into a discipline problem.

Teachers themselves should attempt to use or learn the basics of students' native languages. If teachers are not very fluent in their attempts, they can have a laugh at themselves, helping students feel comfortable about their own attempts to learn a new language. A teacher, using her high school Spanish, read aloud the Spanish part of a bilingual book, much to a new arrival's amusement. The student immediately attempted to read the English side.

Respect for language also implies respect for the language variety or dialect the students use. Students need to learn that different situations call for different choices of language, given their audience, topic, or whether the language is oral or written. These three factors combine to define the "register" of the language (Derewianka, 1991). Children solving a problem in class may use their everyday dialect; however, when reporting to the class as a whole they should be encouraged to use the variety of English used in schools to learn and share knowledge. Similarly, they may write "C U" for "see you" in an e-mail to a friend, but they would be expected to write the full words in a version to be published in the high school magazine.

Evidence of respect for and interest in varying student cultures is found in school values and curriculum. Values from home and community should be understood and reinforced in school. In turn, parents and community should reinforce school expectations (Clayton, Barnhardt, & Brisk, 2008). Incorporating students' culture in the curriculum means not only teaching them about their cultural heritage but also using their cultural knowledge to introduce new concepts and language to facilitate comprehension and language acquisition. For example, a fourth-grade teacher sensed that her Dominican students did not understand the discussion on competing loyalties of the colonials in the late 18th century. They thought that if they were Americans, they should not feel loyalty to England. As soon as she questioned them about whether they felt they were Americans or Dominicans, they identified with the dilemmas of the colonials. Focusing on the students' cultures does not come at the exclusion of other cultures, including the American culture. L2 learners want and need to learn new things, but they also appreciate when classroom content acknowledges their background and the topics that are important to them.

In an environment where L2 learners are constantly challenged by having to perform in their weaker language, students need to develop an identity as experts who can productively participate in the classroom community. Teachers need to find out about students as individuals to locate their expertise. For example, a fourth-grade girl from Mexico was a beginner in English but she was an accomplished violinist. The teacher found out by chance and asked her to perform, turning her into an instant star in the class (Cary, 2000).

Strategies That Encourage Classroom Engagement

Teachers can use a variety of strategies to support language use, facilitate comprehension, and help L2 students engage in learning. Use of thematic units, using nonlinguistic ways of conveying meaning, using oral and written forms of the L2 to support each other, organizing the students in a variety of groupings, and finding students' expertise are a few proven strategies that work (Echevarria, Vogt, & Short, 2004).

Thematic units help students' comprehend the content and enlarge their vocabulary development. Once students understand the topic of the unit, they can concentrate on learning the content and language. In addition, new vocabulary related to the topic should be used multiple times and in different contexts, increasing the chances of learning it (Carlo et al., 2004).

Oral language is difficult to follow when students are not fluent or are still getting used to a new speaker. Supporting what is being said with objects or pictures helps students get an idea of the topic. Unlike written language, oral language disappears as it is being used, and students cannot go back to check something they did not understand. Having key concepts and directions in writing and pointing to them while speaking allows students to go back and check. In turn, rehearsing orally gives the students the opportunity to organize their thoughts and try the language. Writing what they have said helps them acquire what they learned orally.

Types of grouping have different impact on language development. Whole-class organization allows for the teacher to model academic language and for students to try it. Pair work and small groups encourage talk, but it is more natural for students to use a less formal, everyday type of language. Since L2 students are usually reluctant to speak in whole-class settings (Brock, 2007), teachers need to scaffold the experience by offering academic vocabulary as they speak and by allowing students to prepare and rehearse what they will say during small-group work (Gibbons, 2003).

Integrating Language with Curriculum and Instruction

Mainstream teachers in elementary schools see their role as teaching both literacy and content, whereas in secondary schools they see themselves only as teachers of content. However, an essential aspect of teaching literacy and content is teaching language. This is true even in secondary schools, since, as noted earlier, some students still need language instruction. Bernhardt (1991) found that successful reading in the L2 requires not only background knowledge and knowledge of literacy, but knowledge of the second language. In addition, Hyland (2007) argues that

> teachers of *writing* clearly need to be teachers of *language*, as it is an
> ability to exercise appropriate linguistic choices in the ways they treat
> and organise their topics for particular readers which helps students to
> give their ideas authority. (p. 151; original emphasis)

Teaching language means teaching the discourse or written text organization, vocabulary, grammar, pronunciation, and spelling required in a variety of situations with a variety of audiences. In addition, it means teaching the technical language of content-area subjects.

When teaching content, teachers "hope that language occurs" (Gersten & Baker, 2000, p. 70). For L2 learners teaching language "cannot be left to chance, especially in settings where there are few opportunities out of school for the language of the classroom to be 'picked up'" (Cleghorn, Mtetwa, Dube, & Munetsi, 1998, p. 474). Unfortunately, "many teachers are unprepared to make the linguistic expectations of schooling explicit to students" (Schleppegrell, 2004, p. 3).

In addition, students new to English are eager to fit in; for them, oral language development is a priority because they see fluency in English as the conduit to becoming full members of the class community (Koga, 2009). They need to acquire not only the oral academic language to perform in classroom interaction but also social language needed to communicate with classmates.

Teaching content in students' L2 is challenging at two levels. The first level is students' ability to grasp the content in a language they may not yet have mastered. The second level is teaching students the academic language commonly used in that discipline to allow students to be more precise in their meanings and to share in the culture of the discipline.

BEST PRACTICES

There are many books suggesting multiple strategies to work with bilingual learners (e.g., Brisk & Harrington, 2007; Echevarria et al., 2004). Following are some suggestions that will help teachers create an environment wherein bilingual learners thrive and learn the L2, functioning successfully in the American classroom. The teaching of language has been addressed more extensively because it is essential, and it is often addressed only in rather vague terms.

Home Questionnaires

Teachers should send a simple questionnaire home with all students, inquiring about the language used at home to get a true picture of the home linguistic context. One teacher reported that after sending questionnaires home and obtaining the results, her students were more willing to share about their language and cultural backgrounds. Previously they were reluctant to discuss or even acknowledge those backgrounds. She felt that the whole classroom atmosphere changed. Now this teacher regularly sends a questionnaire home at the beginning of the school year.

In one school the fourth-grade math teacher turned the questionnaire into a math project. The students created a simple questionnaire asking about the country of origin and language(s) of the family. Then they requested that all classroom teachers distribute them. They documented the results in a bar graph, showing that there were 20 different language groups in the school. The staff was surprised to realize the variety of languages present at the school (Brisk, 2006).

Situational Context Lessons

Situational context (SC) lessons draw on the background, concerns, and interests of the students to create units of study. These types of lessons work particularly well with reading, language arts, and social studies curricular objectives. Students study a topic, connect it to self, and propose solutions. SC lessons assist teachers in getting to know their students in more depth. They also provide an opportunity to integrate the students' culture, sometimes including language, and life experiences into the curriculum (Brisk et al., 2004).

These lessons can be adapted to any grade level. For example, first graders studied different writing systems. English speakers found it interesting, and speakers of other languages actively engaged in sharing their languages' writing systems. One Korean parent came to school and shared additional aspects of their culture. All students received a copy of their name spelled in a different writing system. A middle school class in an urban school was particularly concerned about violence. The students discussed their concerns and experiences, heard from a police officer, and concluded with a presentation to the whole school about how to address violence in the neighborhood surrounding their school (Brisk & Harrington, 2007). The girls' soccer team in a suburban high school studied the impact of media on girls with their coach. They discussed the contents and influences of magazines and other media on self and became determined to be more critical in the future.

An important aspect of SC lessons is the use of multicultural literature sources. Such books facilitate the discussion and understanding of related issues. For example, a teacher was having a hard time helping her fifth graders to understand the notion that foreign relations with countries impacts how immigrants are treated in the United States. However, as soon as they read *Baseball Saved Them*, her students quickly related to the issue and were able to discuss the experiences of their own ethnic group. This book is about a Japanese child in an internment camp during World War II (Brisk et al., 2004)

Contextualized Language Use and Instruction

Teaching language in context allows teachers to provide instruction in academic English while respecting students' languages, including varieties of English. Gibbons (2002) proposes creating different contexts in the classroom that move through what she calls a "mode continuum" from informal conversational language, to more formal oral presentations, to children's writing, to published texts. Students initially work in groups on a task. They typically use informal conversational language. The teacher asks them to share their work with the whole class, scaffolding the use of academic English, including the technical terms of the lesson's content area. A written product follows, wherein features of written language are encouraged. At different points of the unit students are exposed to published books that provide examples of academic written language.

Giving the different forms of language legitimacy in the appropriate contexts is the best way to show respect for students' uses of language while encouraging the acquisition of academic English. Within this approach, teachers can encourage use of students' heritage language. For example, while working in the small groups, speakers of the same language can use it to solve the problem and facilitate understanding. Newcomers can initially write in their own language. Students literate in their heritage language can read about the topic of the lesson in that language. Teachers can secure the support of families, community members, or college students who are doing their practice teaching at the school and are fluent in the language to read or work with the students.

Teach Language All the Time and in Explicit Ways

To support L2 learners' engagement in education, all teachers need to teach language. Content-area teachers are best suited to teach the academic English needed to function in that content area. Following is an overview of the various aspects of language and specific difficulties encountered by L2 learners. Components of language included are discourse and text structure, vocabulary, grammar, pronunciation, spelling, and mechanics (see Table 7.1). To facilitate language teaching, teachers should choose a limited number of aspects connected with the lesson content. For example, for a social studies lesson, a second-grade teacher planned to teach students report writing by focusing on the structural organization of reports, the use of present tense, and capitalization because of the number of proper names used in social studies.

Discourse and Text Structure

Oral narrative styles differ across cultures. McCabe and Bliss (2003) studied the oral narratives of European North American children, as well as children from four other cultural backgrounds. Their research showed that the narrative styles differed in a number of aspects. For example, some of the children they studied used associated topics rather than focusing on one topic, were not concerned with sequencing, and used a great deal of conjunctions. It is important that teachers recognize that this narrative style is not evidence that the students are confused or disorganized in their presentation but rather it is the way they have been socialized to speak. It is important to accept this talk to avoid silencing the children while scaffolding American styles of narrating. The "Wax Museum of Personalities" is one way a teacher helped her students develop skills in oral narratives, following the expected structure in the American culture. Students chose a famous person, took the identity of the person, wrote a short narrative about his or her life with support from the teacher and classmates, rehearsed their "speech," and presented it when the museum was open to the public—that is, to other children in the school.

Similarly, in written language, text organization differs across cultures. For example, in American English persuasive pieces start with a thesis statement, followed by arguments supported by evidence, and conclude by reiterating the thesis. The arguments can be solely in favor of the thesis, or the writer can present arguments that both support and oppose the thesis. American Indians believe that persuasion must always present both points of view and let the audience decide (Conklin & Lourie, 1983). Japanese use softer arguments for persuasion than Americans, whereas Arabic speakers accept exaggeration (Connor, 2002; Hinkel, 2002). Teachers can provide students with graphic organizers that illustrate the text structure of particular genres to help students organize their writing.

Vocabulary

Learning vocabulary is a crucial aspect of L2 development. English-speaking students may know between 50 and 80 thousand words by the time they reach high school (Anderson & Nagy, 1992; Graves, 2006; Menyuk, 1999). L2 learners have a massive task ahead of them. They need to acquire both everyday vocabulary and vocabulary needed for specific content areas. There are many sources of difficulty when learning vocabulary, such as acoustic similarity (*some day* vs. *Sunday*), part of speech (He is so *greed* [greedy]), homophones (*whole* vs. *hole*), and others (for more detailed information, see Birch, 2002; Menyuk & Brisk, 2005; see also Bedore, Peña, & Boerger, Chapter 4, this volume). In some cases, students may know an English word but may not know the specific meaning in the American context. For example, students may interpret a reference to "Boston Tea Party" literally, unaware of the historical significance. Figurative language, including metaphors, similes, personification, hyperbole, and idioms, is another extremely difficult aspect of language to acquire. The most difficult is idioms because they need to be learned as a chunk, and the meaning is not always obvious from the phrase—for example, "raining cats and dogs." Irujo (1986) found that it took many years for L2 learners to master idioms.

Teaching vocabulary means more than just presenting lots of words and their definitions. It also means teaching vocabulary *in depth*, including the pronunciation and spelling, word formation, part of speech, synonyms and antonyms, and multiple meanings (Proctor, Uccelli, Dalton, & Snow, 2009). Carlo and colleagues (2004) proposed a model for teaching vocabulary in depth whereby target vocabulary is presented in the context of meaningful text in both English and the native language. The words are later presented in several contexts to show the variation in meaning. In addition, students are taught semantic features such as word associations, antonyms, and synonyms, word morphology, and cognates. Words taught are periodically reviewed. Thematic instruction is another way to provide opportunities for using words in multiple contexts.

Content-area teachers need to teach the technical vocabulary as well as the concepts of their discipline. One successful science program used everyday language to introduce the scientific concepts. After the students had an understanding of the science, teachers then introduced the scientific vocabulary. For example, photosynthesis was explained using "light" for photons, "clean air that humans breathe in" for oxygen, and so on. Researchers found that students who were first taught concepts using common expressions and later taught the academic language demonstrated improved conceptual and linguistic understanding of science (Brown & Ryoo, 2008).

Grammar

Teaching grammar is essential "to create clear, well-structured, unambiguous sentences" (Derewianka, 1999, p. 3). L2 learners often cannot express complex thoughts because of their inability to construct complex sentences showing complicated relationships (Barratt-Pugh & Rohl, 2001). Some of the more ubiquitous problems in English are inappropriate prepositions, omission or overuse of articles, omission of the *s* in third-person singular, and past tense and plural formation, to name a few (see Genesee et al., 2004, for a complete list). Teachers should provide a list of these issues to enable L2 learners to monitor their language, especially in writing.

At the clause level, difficulties arise mainly with constructions such as the possessive, questions, and negation: For example, "He became a governor of the New Spain of Mexico" or "I no want to go." Word order in clauses may be influenced by the heritage language's word order. For example, a Portuguese speaker commonly says, "I wonder where is your office" (Swan & Smith, 2001, p. 122) because in Portuguese the verb goes after the question word in indirect speech.

Combining clauses into longer sentences is complicated especially with respect to anaphoric relations and verb tenses. For example, a third grader wrote: "When I was at the nurses room they was't there. When I don't now where's the class room is somebody find me." There is no antecedent for *they* in her account, and in the second sentence she switches to present even though her whole story is in the past.

Spelling and Conventions

English spelling and conventions of the writing system are difficult for L2 learners. Unlike many of the languages they speak that tend to have shallow orthography, English has a deep orthography. In shallow orthographies, letters represent specific sounds with a great degree of regularity. For example, in Spanish the sound /f/, as in *Frank*, is always spelled with an <f>. In English it can be spelled as <f> (*Frank*), <ph> (*phase*), or <gh> (*rough*). English spelling depends both on phonology as well as morphology. Students can sound out the word *rat* and guess the spelling based on the sounds. However, the second <c> in *electric, electricity*, and *electrician* has three different sounds, yet the spelling does not change because the root of the word is kept when making the new word. In addition, L2 learners use their native language knowledge to spell words. For example, a Vietnamese student wrote *xu* for *shoe*. In Vietnamese the sound /sh/ is spelled <x>, and the vowel sound in *shoe* is spelled <u>. Conventions such as capitalization and punctuation in other languages are also often different from English. L2 learners need to be explicitly taught the new rules (see Newman, Chapter 5, this volume, especially Appendix 5.1, for more on language differences).

A good strategy to help students with issues of grammar, spelling, and conventions is the reformulation approach. In this approach, a native speaker of English rewrites a learner's piece, preserving all the learner's ideas, but making it sound as native-like as possible. It is best to apply this approach to pieces that are organized and have a message that is clear. This approach, which lends itself to small-group work or conferencing, facilitates L2 by calling attention to issues of vocabulary, grammatical structure, and spelling. The most important aspect is the discussion about language because through such exchanges, learning occurs (Brisk & Harrington, 2007; Swain & Lapkin (2002).

Pronunciation

L2 learners need to understand and master individual sounds—that is, vowels, consonants, and consonant clusters—as well as the prosody of the new language, including rate, intonation, stress, and vowel length. The English vowel system is particularly problematic for L2 learners because it has so many more sounds than most languages. Whereas English has 12 vowel sounds, most languages have 3–5 vowels. This complexity may lead English language learners to pronounce *ship* like *sheep* and *full* like *fool*. One of the most difficult consonant sounds is the initial sound in *thin,* which Quebecois pronounce as *tin* and Germans as *sin* (see Swan & Smith, 2001, for a thorough consideration of sources of difficulties by a variety of language speakers). A number of strategies are recommended to facilitate the acquisition of individual sounds; for example, by presenting minimal pairs (*ship–sheep*) in meaningful contexts, explaining difficult sounds (e.g., put tongue between teeth for *think*), answering comprehension questions that require discrimination of sounds, and encouraging a free production of sounds in communicative activities (González-Bueno, 2001).

Derwing and Rossiter (2003) found that prosodic aspects of pronunciation, such as rate, intonation, stress, and vowel length, were the types of errors that native speakers most frequently named as barriers to understanding the speech of L2 learners. When L2 learners were instructed in prosody, they were not only better understood by native speakers, but their speech also included more sentences than did the speech of those learners who were trained solely in the pronunciation of difficult phonemes. The learners who received instruction on individual phonemes pronounced individual words better, but their speech was less fluent and understandable. Given the importance of prosody in the intelligibility of L2 learners' speech, researchers and practitioners recommend global instruction of pronunciation, including word and sentence stress, intonation and rhythm, projection, and speech rate. Materials such as *Jazz Chants* by Graham (1978) and *Sounds Great* by Beisbier (1995) were successfully used to train L2 learners (Derwing & Rossiter, 2003).

As noted earlier, age has an impact on the ease and accuracy of pronunciation. Children acquiring English before the age of 7 have a greater chance to acquire native-like pronunciation (Genesee et al., 2004), especially if they acquire it in an English-speaking environment. After that, individuals vary in their ability to improve their pronunciation.

SUMMARY OF MAIN IDEAS

This chapter suggests that to create nurturing English-medium classes, teachers need to (1) get to know their students and their families, (2) foster a classroom climate and organize instruction for optimal L2 development, and (3) incorporate L2 instruction throughout the curriculum. In addition, specific strategies to implement these principles were outlined (see Table 7.1).

IMPLICATIONS FOR RESEARCH, PRACTICE, AND POLICY

As this chapter demonstrates, there are many ways for teachers to educate bilingual learners in English-medium classes. The suggestions are not always easy to implement. They require teachers to lose the fear of connecting with students and parents who are not fluent in English; to change deep-rooted attitudes toward dialects and languages other than standard English; to venture into unfamiliar cultures; and to acquire a conscious knowledge of the English language in order to be able to teach it to students. Clayton (2008) found that mainstream teachers had a more stressful job than bilingual education teachers because the use of the heritage languages as well as English facilitates teaching and learning. However, Clayton also showed that there are successful teachers in the mainstream who help bilingual students get an education.

Teachers should slowly implement the suggestions in this chapter in order to experience success and gain confidence. For example, for the first few months of the year teachers might focus on getting to know the students and their families, perhaps also choosing one aspect of language to include in their class objectives. They can aim at covering all the ideas

TABLE 7.1. The Nurturing Classroom: Theory and Practice

Principles	Theory	Practice
The teacher knows the students and their families.	Students • Heritage language literacy level • Educational background • Oral language proficiency • Cultural background Identity Families • Level of education, language, and literacy • Language learning goals and cultural values	• Family questionnaires • Situational context lessons • Contextualized uses of language • Teach language explicitly and all the time.
Classroom climate and organization are geared for optimal language development.	• Heritage language and home dialect are safe to use in the classroom. • Heritage cultures are part of the curriculum. • Students' expertise is highlighted. • Classroom strategies support language use and comprehension.	
Language is integrated into the curriculum and instruction.	• Language instruction is included in the teaching of reading, writing, and content areas. • Second-language teaching requires specificity.	

noted in this chapter over a few years, making their own adaptations and bringing additional ideas.

The suggestions in this chapter assume immersion in English-medium classes, the most common policy in U.S. schools. However, there are other ways of obtaining an education when one's native language is not English. Some schools, both in the United States and elsewhere in the world, have chosen to deliver instruction in more than one language. Some of these schools serve children whose parents work for international organizations such as the European Community (EC) or the United Nations (UN). Others serve immigrant or native populations that speak a variety of languages.

European Schools (ES)—public schools for the children of European Union (EU) officials—serve, on average, nine language groups. In addition to children of EU officials, ES promote enrollment of children from the country where the school is located, including language minority immigrants. These schools achieve multilingualism and multiculturalism by gradually transitioning the instruction from the pupil's heritage language (L1), to the second language (L2), a third language (L3), and sometimes even a fourth language. In ES, all pupils follow the same curriculum, and students who fall behind are continuously supported through pullout classes and after-school programs (Housen, 2002; Muller & Beardsmore, 2004).

The United Nations International School (UNIS; *www.unis.org/academic_programs/curriculum/index.aspx*) in New York serves K–12 children of UN workers, representing 115 countries. The main language of instruction is English. In addition, all students study French or Spanish as an L2 and in the seventh grade, all students begin the study of a third language. There is instruction in students' mother tongues either in school or after-school programs.

In the United States some schools that include immigrant students adapt a variety of strategies to include languages other than English. For example, a high school in Massachusetts with Spanish-, Haitian-, and Cape Verdean–speaking students provides instruction in the native language and sheltered English immersion classes. Some students are also integrated into mainstream classes. Newly arrived students with interrupted formal schooling, whose reading ability is much below grade level for their age, attend the literacy strand. This is an intensive, self-contained, all-day course of study featuring literacy, ESL, science, and mathematics (Rennie Center for Education Research & Policy, 2007).

The International Network of Public Schools serves high school immigrants who have been in the United States for 4 years or less. Unlike other programs, these schools serve the students by organizing project-based heterogeneous groups. Students are mixed by age, grade, academic ability, linguistic proficiency, native language, and prior schooling. To promote heritage language development, occasionally these project-based groups are organized by common language (Internationals Network of Public Schools, *www.internationalsnps.org*).

Some schools, like two-way schools, develop skills in the two languages spoken by the majority of the students. Often these schools include speakers of languages other than those used for instruction, as in the Aloha Huber Park Spanish/English two-way program. Russian, Korean, and Japanese students also attend this program, becoming multilingual (Beaverton School District, *www.beaverton.k12.or.us*).

Even when schools and teachers use only English as the medium of instruction and work hard to help bilingual students achieve proficiency in English, they should keep in mind that bilingualism is possible and desirable, as the examples of these programs demonstrate. (See also Bialystok & Peets, Chapter 6, this volume.) In present times, when connections across the world are becoming the norm, knowledge of other languages is an asset. Moreover, bilingual learners "can no longer be thought of as a group apart from the mainstream in today's culturally and linguistically diverse classrooms, they *are* the mainstream" (Gibbons, 2003, p. 13).

REFERENCES

Anderson, R. C., & Nagy, W. (1992). The vocabulary conundrum. *American Educator, 16*(4), 14–18, 44–47.

Barratt-Pugh, C., & Rohl, M. (2001). Learning in two languages: A bilingual program in Western Australia. *The Reading Teacher, 54*(7), 664–676.

Beisbier, B. (1995). *Sounds great: Intermediate pronunciation and speaking* (Book 2). Boston: Heinle & Heinle.

Bernhardt, E. B. (1991). A psycholinguistic perspective on second language literacy. *AILA Review, 8*, 31–44.

Birch, B. M. (2002). *English L2 reading: Getting to the bottom.* Mahwah, NJ: Erlbaum.

Brisk, M. E. (2006). *Bilingual education: From compensatory to quality schooling* (2nd ed.). Mahwah, NJ: Erlbaum.

Brisk, M. E., Burgos, A., & Hamerla, S. R. (2004). *Situational context of education: A window into the world of bilingual learners.* Mahwah, NJ: Erlbaum.

Brisk, M. E., & Harrington, M. M. (2007). *Literacy and bilingualism: A handbook for ALL teachers* (2nd ed.). Mahwah, NJ: Erlbaum.

Brock, C. H. (2007). Exploring an English language learner's literacy learning opportunities: A collaborative case study analysis. *Urban Education, 42*(5), 470–501.

Brown, B., & Ryoo, K. (2008). Teaching science as a language: A "content-first" approach to science teaching. *Journal of Research in Science Teaching, 45*, 525–664.

Caldas, S., & Caron-Caldas, S. (2002). A sociolinguistic analysis of the language preferences of adolescent bilinguals: Sifting allegiances and developing identities. *Applied Linguistics, 23*, 490–514.

Capps, R., Fix, M. E., Murray, J., Ost, J., Passel, J. S., & Herwantoro, S. (2005). *The new demography of America's schools: Immigration and the No Child Left Behind Act.* Retrieved October 15, 2008, from *www.ncela.gwu.edu/stats/2_nation.htm.*

Carlo, M., August, D., McLaughlin, B., Snow, C., Dressler, C., Lippman, D., et al. (2004). Closing the gap: Addressing the vocabulary needs of English-language learners in bilingual and mainstream classrooms. *Reading Research Quarterly, 39,* 188–215.

Cary, S. (2000). *Working with second language learners: Answers to teachers' top ten questions.* Portsmouth, NH: Heinemann.

Clayton, C. (2008). *Whatever it takes: Exemplary teachers of English language learners.* Unpublished doctoral dissertation, Boston College.

Clayton, C., Barnhardt, R., & Brisk, M. E. (2008). Language, culture, and identity. In M. E. Brisk (Ed.), *Language, culture, and community in teacher education* (pp. 21–45). New York: Erlbaum.

Cleghorn, A., Mtetwa, D., Dube, R., & Munetsi, C. (1998). Classroom language use in multilingual settings: Mathematics lessons from Quebec and Zimbabwe. *International Journal of Qualitative Studies in Education, 11*(3), 463–477.

Conklin, N. F., & Lourie, M. A. (1983). *A host of tongues: Language communities in the United States.* New York: Free Press.

Connor, U. (2002). New directions in contrastive rhetoric. *TESOL Quarterly, 36*(4), 493–510.

Derewianka, B. (1991). *Exploring how texts work.* Newtown, Australia: Primary English Teaching Association.

Derewianka, B. (1999). *A grammar companion for primary teachers.* Newtown, Australia: Primary English Teaching Association.

Derwing, T. M., & Rossiter, M. J. (2003). The effects of pronunciation instruction on the accuracy, fluency, and complexity of L2 accented speech. *Applied Language Learning, 13,* 1–17.

Dien, T. T. (2004). Language and literacy in Vietnamese American communities. In B. Pérez (Ed.), *Sociocultural contexts of language and literacy* (pp. 137–179). Mahwah, NJ: Erlbaum.

Echevarria, J., Vogt, M., & Short, D. J. (2004). *Making content comprehensible for English learners: The SIOP model* (2nd ed.). Boston: Pearson Education.

Garcia, O. (1999). Educating Latino high school students with little formal schooling. In C. J. Faltis & P. Wolfe (Eds.), *So much to say: Adolescents, bilingualism, and ESL in the secondary school* (pp. 61–82). New York: Teachers College.

Genesee, F., Paradis, J., & Crago, M. B. (2004). *Dual language development and disorders: A handbook on bilingualism and second language learning.* Baltimore: Brookes.

Gersten, R., & Baker, S. (2000). The professional knowledge base on instructional practices that support cognitive growth for English-language learners. In R. Gersten, E. Schiller, & S. Vaughn (Eds.), *Contemporary special education research syntheses of the knowledge base on critical instructional issues* (pp. 31–81). Mahwah, NJ: Erlbaum.

Gibbons, P. (2002). *Scaffolding language, scaffolding learning: Teaching second language learners in the mainstream classrooms.* Portsmouth, NH: Heinemann.

Gibbons, P. (2003). Mediating language learning: Teacher interactions with ESL students in a content-based classroom. *TESOL Quarterly, 37,* 247–273.

Glick-Schiller, N., Basch, L., & Szanton-Blanc, C. (1992). Transnationalism: A new analytic framework for understanding migration. In N. Glick-Schiller, L. Basch, & C. Szanton-Blanc (Eds.), *Towards a transnational perspective on migration: Race, class, ethnicity and nationalism* (pp. 1–24). New York: New York Academy of Sciences.

González-Bueno, M. (2001). Pronunciation teaching component in SL/FL education programs: Training teachers to teach pronunciation. *Applied Language Learning, 12*, 133–146.

Graham, C. (1978). *Jazz chants: Rhythms of American English for students of English as a second language.* New York: Oxford University Press.

Gravelle, M. (2000). *Planning for bilingual learners: An inclusive curriculum.* Sterling, VA: Trentham Books.

Graves, M. (2006). *The vocabulary book: Learning and instruction.* New York: Teacher's College Press.

Hawkins, M. R. (2004). Researching English language and literacy development in schools. *Educational Researcher, 33*(3), 14–25.

Hersi, A. A. (2007). Between hope and hostility: Understanding the experiences of African immigrant students in an urban high school. *Boston College Dissertations and Theses* (UMI No. AAI3283882). Retrieved October 10, 2008, from *escholarship.bc.edu/dissertations.*

Hinkel, E. (2002). *Second language writers' text.* Mahwah, NJ: Erlbaum.

Horan, D. A. (2007). *Teaching elementary writing: Teachers' practices and beliefs in the New England states.* Unpublished doctoral dissertation, Boston College.

Housen, A. (2002). Processes and outcomes in the European schools model of multilingual education. *Bilingual Research Journal, 26*, 45–64.

Huss-Keeler, R. L. (1997). Teacher perception of ethnic and linguistic minority parental involvement and its relationship to children's language and literacy learning: A case study. *Teaching and Teacher Education, 12*(2), 171–182.

Hyland, K. (2007). Genre pedagogy: Language, literacy and L2 writing instruction. *Journal of Second Language Writing, 16*(3), 148–164.

Irujo, S. (1986). Don't put your leg in your mouth: Transfer in the acquisition of idioms in a second language. *TESOL Quarterly, 20*(2), 287–304.

Kleifgen, J. A., & Saville-Troike, M. (1992). Achieving coherence in multilingual interaction. *Discourse Processes, 15*(2), 183–206.

Koga, N. (2009). *Understanding the U.S. Kaigaishijos' second language learning experiences in elementary mainstream classrooms.* Unpublished doctoral dissertation, Boston College.

McCabe, A., & Bliss, L. S. (2003). *Patterns of narrative discourse: A multicultural, life span approach.* Boston: Allyn & Bacon.

Menyuk, P. (1999). *Reading and linguistic development.* Cambridge, MA: Brookline Books.

Menyuk, P., & Brisk, M. E. (2005). *Language development and education: Children with varying language experience.* Hampshire, UK: Palgrave MacMillan.

Muller, A., & Beardsmore, H. B. (2004). Multilingual interaction in plurilingual classes in European school practice. *Bilingual Education and Bilingualism,* 7(1), 24–42.

National Center for Education Statistics. (2002). *Schools and staffing survey, 1999–2000: Overview of the data for public, private, public charter, and bureau of Indian affairs elementary and secondary schools.* Washington, DC: Author. Retrieved December 2, 2008, from *nces.ed.gov/pubs2002/2002313. pdf*

Proctor, C. P., Uccelli, P., Dalton, B., & Snow, C. E. (2009). Understanding depth of vocabulary online with bilingual and monolingual children. *Reading and Writing Quarterly, 25*(4), 311–333.

Rennie Center for Education Research and Policy. (2007). *Seeking effective policies and practices for English language learners.* Cambridge, MA: Author.

Schleppegrell, M. J. (2004). *The language of schooling: A functional linguistics perspective.* Mahwah, NJ: Erlbaum.

Swain, M., & Lapkin, S. (2002) Talking it through: Two French immersion learners' response to reformulation. *International Journal of Educational Research, 37,* 285–304.

Swan, M., & Smith, B. (2001). *Learner English: A teacher's guide to interference and other problems.* Cambridge, UK: Cambridge University Press.

Taylor, D. M. (1987). Social psychological barriers to effective childhood bilingualism. In P. Hornel, M. Palij, & D. Aaronson (Eds.), *Childhood bilingualism: Aspects of linguistic, cognitive and social development* (pp. 183–195). Hillsdale, NJ: Erlbaum.

U.S. Bureau of Statistics. (2008). *School enrollment in the United States: 2006.* Washington, DC: Author. Retrieved December 3, 2008, from *www.census. gov/prod/2008pubs/p20–559.pdf.*

PART III

ASSESSMENT AND INTERACTION

Working with Children and Families

$\underline{8}$

Communicative Repertoires and English Language Learners

Betsy Rymes

FOCUS POINTS

- For the speaker of any language(s), "correctness" is a construction that functions secondarily to communicative goals.

- Rather than being "correct" or "incorrect," a speaker's multiple *communicative repertoires* emerge and/or recede according to use and context.

- Speakers accommodate to the communicative repertoires of their interlocutors, although the directionality of accommodation—who accommodates to whom—varies.

- What has come to be labeled *language* is just one aspect of a much broader and communicatively relevant category, *communicative repertoire.*

- Building metasociolinguistic awareness of communicative repertoires is a life-long process that is facilitated by travel across social boundaries.

CHAPTER PURPOSE

Walk into any U.S. public school in a major metropolitan area. Look around. Listen. Stroll down the hall. Step into a classroom. What do you see? What do you hear? Chances are you see and hear countless different ways of communicating, many of which are only minimally understood by you. Imagine you are a language teacher in this context. What are

177

your responsibilities here? How could you possibly be the "expert"? In this chapter I argue that by developing understandings of communicative repertoires in their teaching context, teachers can become experts in helping all students, especially English language learners, navigate this complex communicative terrain. This chapter describes how the concept of *communicative repertoire* can be useful as a lens for understanding and analyzing interaction in classrooms. It also illustrates why an understanding of how students develop and become aware of their own communicative repertoire—rather than how students develop correctness in any homogeneous standard target language—is a relevant goal and application of the analysis of classroom discourse.

REVIEW OF RESEARCH AND THEORY

A *communicative repertoire* is the collection of ways that individuals use language and literacy and other means of communication (e.g., gestures, dress, posture, accessories) to function effectively in the multiple communities in which they participate. Individuals' communicative repertoires are inevitably more developed in one social realm and more limited in another. Like a pianist who may have an expansive "classical repertoire" but a limited repertoire of "folk songs" or "jazz," an individual speaker may have a well-developed "academic" repertoire, but a very limited "football fan" or "blind date" repertoire. A 2-year-old may have a vast repertoire that is functionally communicative with her mother, but she may not be considered a viable communication partner in many other contexts—a university seminar, for example. Nevertheless, even a 2-year-old is developing distinct repertoires for different social contexts and will have a different repertoire for speaking with her mother than she uses at day care or with her older brothers.

Unlike the term *register,* as used in other chapters in this volume, *repertoire* (as traditionally used by Gumperz [1964] in the phrase *verbal repertoire* and as I am using it here) explicitly includes the use of multilingualism. In this respect, an individual's communicative repertoire not only includes different ways of using language across situations, but also may include different ways of using multiple languages across situations. For example, broadly speaking, an individual student may use Spanish at home, a combination of Spanish and English with school friends, and English, exclusively, in English literature class. Layered into this use of multilingualism are the different "Englishes" and "Spanishes" that the individual negotiates in each setting; the Spanish and English used with friends will differ from both the Spanish used at home and the English used in class. Each setting requires a different repertoire that includes both different languages and different functional variations of those languages.

Human development across the lifespan consists in large part of the growing awareness and accumulation of such communicative repertoires and the effects they have (Bruner, 1983). This is true for babies, as they take increasingly active roles in the various communicative realms in which they participate; it is also true for every living being that moves in and out of different social settings with varying communicative expectations. Tom Wolfe entertainingly captures this in his novel of collegiate life, *I Am Charlotte Simmons* (2004). In this fictional world, all characters struggle to find their voice in the prestigious environs of "Dupont University." In the following passage, Charlotte, a scholarship girl from Southern Appalachia, wrestles with how to write home to her parents about her initial experiences as a freshman:

> Dear Momma and Daddy,
>   I'll admit my eyes blurred with mist when I saw you drive off in the old pickup.
>   *The old pickup? ... my eyes blurred with mist? ...* What on earth did she think she was writing? ... She rocked forward with another trill of low-grade guilt to confront her letter home...*the old pickup.* Daddy is totally dependent on the poor, miserable old truck, and I'm treating it like it's something quaint. *Eyes blurred with mist...* Yuk! She could just imagine Momma and Daddy reading *that.* The "pretty writing." (p. 158)

Charlotte labels her academic/literary repertoire "pretty writing" and recognizes that this part of her repertoire has a very different functionality in her home community than it does in a community of academics. Indeed her own "coming of age" is a process of coming to terms with her rapidly expanding communicative repertoires and their effective uses. For her, the journey through "Dupont University" is one that exposes her to a vast range of new communicative repertoires. Her challenge is to understand them and to be able to use them to her advantage—and to transcend the loneliness that she initially feels, trapped in a communicative repertoire that she shares neither with her new acquaintances at Dupont nor her family back home.

Charlotte Simmons's interior monologue about "pretty writing" encapsulates a struggle that countless students have about the way in which they speak and the language choices that they make across academic, family, and other social contexts. Charlotte Simmons's fictional insights resonate with the experiences of nonfictional personalities who have come from humble origins but gone on to excel in the most elite institutions of higher learning. For example, the *New York Times* describes Supreme Court Justice Clarence Thomas, and then-nominee to the Supreme Court Sonia Sotomayor, as questioning the adequacy of their own repertoires when they began to attend prestigious universities: They both worried "what others would think when they opened their mouth" (p. 1):

> Ms. Sotomayor had grown up in the Bronx speaking Spanish; Mr. Thomas's relatives in Pin Point, Ga., mixed English with Gullah, a language of the coastal South. Both attended Catholic school, where they were drilled by nuns in grammar and other subjects. But at college, they realized they still sounded unpolished. (Kantor & Gonzalez, 2009, pp. 1, 21)

As this narrative of these highly successful people indicates, Thomas and Sotomayor were aware that part of their success would depend on the ways in which they managed their own speaking.

This awareness of communicative repertoire and its effects is also echoed in the ways that high school students talk about their feelings regarding their own language habits. Speakers of multiple languages, in particular, encounter this tussle among repertoires. Consider, for example, the words of Seba, a ninth-grade girl originally from Morocco, now an "English language learner" attending a Philadelphia-area high school, musing about what her multiple languages mean to her.

> "I definitely think Arabic is the most popular language that I speak 'cause everybody—every person loves to speak Arabic because they think is—everyone speaks Arabic. They say—like, any kind of person likes to speak Arabic because it's popular. Anywhere you go, people say, 'Oh, hey' in Arabic. I'm like, everybody knows that. So, I think Arabic is the one language I love to keep going on.
>
> "And I used to take Spanish when I was in my home country. And, I used to take a lot of classes. I used to learn a lot of languages, but I didn't keep going on them. So when I came here, my mom—she does speak Spanish—she tried to push me, but I'm like, no, I have to learn English, so I forgot about Spanish. I forgot a little about French. But I'm holding on to Arabic. Yeah. It's the only language that I can talk with my mom.

"All the words we say in home are like half Arabic, half English, half French, half—all the languages, they're like mixed together."

Seba, like the fictional Charlotte Simmons, seems to be trying to account for the ways of speaking that attach her to home. In the United States she says, "I have to learn English, so I forgot about Spanish." Still she is clearly part of a social milieu, even in the United States, in which "every person loves to speak Arabic." Arabic, she says is "the most popular language." As a ninth grader in a Philadelphia-area high school, English is clearly important, but other languages also continue to play an important role in her life: Arabic is, she says, "the only language that I can talk with my mom." She also describes her language at home, with her mother, as a mixture of many languages. Her repertoires cannot simply be demarcated by the standard names or linguistic distinctions between "English" or "Arabic." She recognizes that "the words we say at home" are not simply textbook versions of language, but a more complicated repertoire of "half Arabic, half English, half French, half—all the languages, they're like mixed together."

These three, wide-ranging examples illustrate five critical issues in the analysis of communicative repertoires:

1. *"Correctness" is a construction that functions secondarily to communicative goals.* Charlotte Simmons is not worrying how "correct" her language is in her letter home. She is attempting to modulate it to be appropriate to the community of speakers she is addressing (her small-town parents back home). Similarly, Seba does not care about linguistic purity at home, but rather calls on "all the languages ... mixed together." In many situations speaking textbook-like English would be communicatively disastrous.

2. *One's repertoires emerge and/or recede according to use and context.* Charlotte Simmons rekindles her "home" register in the letter to her parents, but finds it a struggle to use this language while steeped in her new academic context. Seba similarly describes how she "used to learn a lot of languages" but finds that now she is mainly just "holding on to Arabic" (and English) in the United States.

3. *Accommodation to the communicative repertoires of one's interlocutors is inevitable, though the directionality of accommodation—or, who accommodates to whom—varies.* Charlotte Simmons, out of respect and deference to her parents, accommodates to their expectations and communicative habits (rather than expecting them to accommodate to her

"pretty writing"); the Supreme Court Justices accommodate to the higher education repertoire in which they want to fully participate (rather than asserting the validity of their own Spanish- or Gullah-influenced speech in that context); in radical contrast, Seba sees all of her languages as allowing her to accommodate to the communicative needs of her mother (rather than accommodating to an ideology of linguistic purity or a sense of English as an official language).

4. *What has come to be labeled "language" is just one aspect of a much broader and communicatively relevant category, "communicative repertoire."* All language users deploy different ways of speaking to different types of people or in different social situations. While Charlotte Simmons is discussing different ways of using the "same language" ("English"), Seba is discussing different languages that she labels "Arabic," "Spanish," "French," and "English." What's useful in each of these cases is not the labeling of distinct "languages," but the recognition that, in varied contexts, different communicative repertoires account for communicative success.

5. *Building metasociolinguistic awareness of communicative repertoires is a lifelong process that is facilitated by travel across social boundaries.* Charlotte Simmons seems to be painfully aware of the contrast between her "pretty language" and her parents' expectations of a letter from her. Clarence Thomas and Sonia Sotomayor recognize the effects their varied repertoires had in shaping their impressions at elite colleges. Seba displays awareness that her multiple languages function differently in the United States than they did in Morocco. Each of these examples illustrates how traversing social boundaries can create metasociolinguistic awareness, illuminating the different functionality of their repertoires. Gaining this kind of metasociolinguistic awareness of multiple repertoires and the role one's own repertoire plays in communicative success (or failure) is a primary goal of pursuing classroom discourse analysis. The remainder of the chapter addresses how each of these features of "communicative repertoire" is illuminated through the analysis of classroom communication.

Communicative Repertoires in the Classroom

Rethinking Correctness

Spend a few minutes in any classroom discussion and it becomes clear that being "correct" and speaking in a "polished" manner is, for many students, not a top priority. In fact, sometimes students—even when they know "correct" answers or "polished" ways of speaking—find it socially problematic to use that repertoire. To return briefly to Tom Wolfe's fictional "Dupont University," for example, a "giant" basketball player, JoJo, who covertly wants to be an intellectual, finds himself trapped into performing ignorance when he starts to give a thoughtful response to a question about *Madame Bovary*. When the professor asks the class why Madame Bovary's husband performed a risky, but potentially heroic, operation, JoJo begins: " 'He did it,' said the Giant, 'because his wife had all these ambitions ... ' " (Wolfe, 2004, p. 108). Immediately, JoJo's teammates in the class sense that this answer may be (horror!) accurate, and they begin to sarcastically give each other fist bumps and exclaim, " 'Hey, JoJo, read the book,' " and " ' ... we got us another *scholar*.... ' " After the professor settles the commotion and encourages JoJo to continue, with a " 'Mr. Johanssen? As you were saying,' " Mr. Johannsen (i.e., JoJo) faces a choice. Which of his repertoires will he use here? The "Mr. Johanssen" repertoire or the "JoJo" repertoire? He responds: " 'Oh yeah. He did the operation because ... his wife wanted some money to buy some stuff' " (Wolfe, 2004, pp. 108–109). Clearly, he has chosen his " JoJo" repertoire, affiliated with his basketball peers, and disaffiliated from his aspiring scholarly self. Being "correct" in this classroom wasn't the difficult job for "JoJo"; rather, the difficult part about giving the right answer was that it called on a repertoire that would lead him to be completely cut off from (and humiliated by) his basketball peers.

In real classrooms, just as in Tom Wolfe's fictional university, finding voice in ways that are recognized by the teacher as "correct" while still maintaining face among peers can be a complicated negotiation. Often, students draw on an entirely different repertoire in their peer-to-peer communication, while a teacher attempts to continue with his own lesson, as in the following high school discussion of "current events" (Gutiérrez, Rymes, & Larson, 1995, pp. 462–263).

> Teacher: What did the Supreme Court decision in *Brown versus the Board of Education* have to do with?
>
> Student: James Brown?
>
> Student: Richard Brown?
>
> Student: Shut up.
>
> Student: You shut up.
>
> Student: James Brown?
>
> Student: Al Green.
>
> Teacher: (*attempting to call on someone*) Ye:::s?

Here, clearly, James Brown and Al Green are elements of a communicative repertoire in which some of these high school students revel, but to which their teacher is not attuned (or is, perhaps, deliberately ignoring). But even this brief example illustrates that some students are more fluent in the "James Brown" repertoire than others. When another student attempts to join in the banter with "Richard Brown" (certainly not recognizable as a musical icon like James Brown or Al Green), that student receives a swift "Shut up," which is countered with an inelegant "You shut up." Clearly, this student is lacking facility in a newly emergent repertoire. When another student comes up with "Al Green," he steers the repartee back into the "James Brown" repertoire. Now, the teacher tries to resuscitate the teacher repertoire with a characteristic, long-drawn out, "ye:::s" in an attempt to call on a student and bolster the teacher-fronted turn-taking pattern that characterizes a traditional school-talk repertoire. He receives little response. As the teacher-centered discussion proceeds, the students continue their riff on James Brown, building a student-centered classroom "underlife" (Goffman, 1974).

The "James Brown" repertoire emerges above largely because students share a common, mass-mediated inventory of references that can swiftly establish a new repertoire as common communicative currency among them. Just as the high school students use a reference to popular culture to create their own communicative realm tangential to the teacher's, the elementary school children in the following example use the reference to a Pokémon character, "Chancey," to accomplish the same interactional function. While the teacher is drawing on a teacher repertoire to draw students into sounding out, then pronouncing, a word on a card in the Phonics Game, the students make another connection. Their side play about "Chansey the Pokémon" is indented to make the foray into the students' Pokémon repertoire visible in the transcript (Rymes & Pash, 2001, p. 329):

> Teacher: -C- -H- says?
>
> David: Can.
>
> Rene: an- chan-
>
> Teacher: Chan- -C- -Y-
>
> (*two-second pause*)
>
> Rene: Chances.
>
> Teacher: Cha:n:c:y.
>
> Rene: Chancy.
>
> Rene: Ohp (*looking at David and smiling*) Pokémon.

David: It's a Pokémon.

Teacher: And you have to tell me why the *a* is short.

In this example at least two clear communicative repertoires are in play. One is the teacher–student academic display repertoire in which the she patiently coaxes correct answers out of Rene. But as soon as the word *Chancy* is articulated fully, Rene and David launch another repertoire, that of Pokémon fans. Just as the name *Brown* occasioned student repertoire vamping on "James Brown," here *Chancy* gets taken up as *Chansey*, a Pokémon, another mass-mediated icon that provides common ground among the students and, simultaneously, a departure from the teacher's repertoire.

As these examples illustrate, clearly "correctness" on the teacher's terms is not always what students are working to achieve. A more useful way of describing the action in the above examples is a careful negotiation of repertoires. In JoJo's case, his performance of being *not* correct covered for his "knowing." In the cases of the James Brown and Chansey examples, being correct was redefined on student terms as awareness of mass-mediated icons. But, in all these cases, are students learning any more in the teacher repertoire than they are on their own? In the Chansey example, these students are English language learners (ELLs) in a pullout program. And, over the course of the semester, their digressions from the phonics game, although technically "off task," produced far more extended talk in English than their careful sounding out of game cards with the teacher.

Although extended talk about a Pokémon may not strike a teacher as "learning," I would disagree. In this context, in which teachers are struggling to get students both talking and reading in English, raised awareness of this popular-culture-based student repertoire of English could be a starting point for more talk in and about the English language. This is the new perspective a focus on communicative repertoire opens up: Departures from the classroom repertoire and the expectations of correctness within it, need not be departures from language learning.

Inversely, *a performance* of correctness can function as a cover for *not* knowing. This phenomena has been described variably as "passing" (Goffman, 1959), "studenting" (Knobel, 1999), or "procedural display" (Bloome, Puro, & Theodorou, 1989). Learning the repertoire for passing as correct has been noted particularly among ELLs who learn to use contextualization cues (Gumperz, 1982); rather than having a literal understanding of the content, they home in on "right answers" (Rymes & Pash, 2001) to pass as fluent in English (Monzó & Rueda, 2009).

For example, in the excerpt below, taken from a small-book discussion among second graders, in which she is the only ELL, Rene quickly chimes in with the "right" answer on the heels of his classmates. This is representative of Rene's tendency to deftly use his peers' responses to formulate his own identity as competent (here, the square brackets indicate overlapping talk):

TEACHER: What do all the men have on their heads?
TIFFANY: Ha[ts
RENE: [Hats

In other cases, Rene reads a teacher's intonation or phrasing of a question to arrive at the "correct" answer. As in conversation, sometimes one just needs to know what one's interlocutor wants to hear:

TEACHER: What is ↑wrong with ↓that? Is there anything wrong with that?
SARA: No.
DAVID: No.
RENE: No.

As Monzó and Rueda (2009) point out, this kind of passing as fluent in English can become especially common in English-only contexts, in which alternative communicative repertoires are quashed. Such passing practices, like the more overtly disruptive practices of playing dumb or building a student-centered underlife, may keep students from direct engagement with what is deemed correct in the teacher's mind. Monzó and Rueda insightfully add, however, that even in cases of passing, deft use of this seemingly superficial repertoire may be a way to carefully preserve one's social identity as competent, while more privately learning what needs to be learned. Whether students are using their range of repertoires to affiliate with peers, to distance themselves from the teacher, or to hide certain gaps in other repertoires, a close look at all these interactional phenomena highlights delicate maneuvers deployed each day to both preserve dignity and to negotiate status in widely varying communities—including the academic community.

Emerging and Receding Repertoires

Instead of focusing on correctness, looking at communicative repertoires entails a new approach to pedagogy. We can begin to understand this shift in pedagogical strategy by noticing how communicative repertoires emerge and recede in classroom talk and by monitoring the results. For example, many years ago, while doing research at an alternative school in Los Angeles, in which many students had been in jail and were currently on parole, I noticed which teachers and students often ended up in discussions about jail. Sometimes these discussions went smoothly, sometimes they led to conflict, sometimes they led to a dead end, even when the same teacher was involved. Upon a closer look at the communicative repertoires involved, it seemed that when the teacher's repertoire emerged as dominant, discussions faltered. In one such case, after students had begun a discussion of their own jail time, the teacher, Tim, had begun to tell about his experience being arrested and put in jail for "driving while black." This attempt at empathy led to an abrupt end to student sharing when he uttered something apparently unique to his own repertoire as a moral summing up of his own experience:

> TIM: They put me in jail for 5 days.
> FELIPE: For what?
> GRACE: (*Coughs twice.*)
> JOE: Five days—that ain't nothing—5 days.
> GRACE: Oh, yeah.
> JOE: I was locked up for 2 [months.
> FELIPE: (*to Tim*) Where at?
> TIM: [It was a long time for me::
> **I decided that that was not proper.**

After Tim used *not proper* to assess his own experience in jail, students' questions about his experiences slowed and then stopped. It seems clear that students would never describe their own experiences as *not proper*. Indeed, they had been using very different terms to describe their experiences. Whereas Tim says, "They put me in jail," Joe was "locked up." What Tim admits was a "long time" for him, the students claim, "ain't nothing." Still, even this exchange of repertoires ceases after the teacher's talk takes on what seems to be a naive, moralizing tone. When he goes on to coax a lesson learned out of the group, the pace of the discussion comes to a halt, and after a long pause, students simply seem to be trying to give him what he wants to hear.

> TIM: What wh- wh what do people hope to gain by putting you in jail?
> FELIPE: (*1.0 second pause—sigh*) Teach him a lesson or something.

TIM: Okay. Teach him a lesson.

In this conversation, then, when student and teacher repertoires emerged as distinct, dialogue faltered. However, in another jail discussion, this teacher seemed to assimilate to his students' repertoire. In the discussion excerpted below, several girls had been talking about how many good-looking men there are in jail, when suddenly Keneisha, who has just returned from a brief jail visit, makes a statement about her own experience there:

KENEISHA: I ain't never wanna go back.
TIM: (*0.8 second pause*) I hear ya.

In this conversation at the same school, but with different students and several weeks later, instead of reacting to a student story about jail with moralizing adult lexicon, Tim leaned back in his chair and uttered the casually empathic, "I hear ya." After this emergent matching of repertoires, the discussion flowed. Ultimately, the students in the second group ended up agreeing with the teacher's perspective that going to jail is "not proper," though they never used that diction to express it. In this way, the teacher, by modulating his repertoire, earned "rights to advise" these students (for further analysis of these contrasting examples, see Rymes, 1996).

In the first jail discussion, Tim's repertoire emerged as a stark contrast to the students'. But in the second, his repertoire was modulated as he voiced empathy with Keneisha. This opportunity for the expression of like-mindedness seemed to emerge as a matter of chance. But awareness of circulating repertoires and their effects can build once it is acknowledged as a valuable activity. Recognizing the ebb and flow of teacher and student repertoires across contexts makes it possible to do more than simply focus on a correct "standard," or the "proper" thing to do, and to focus instead on moving across discourse boundaries so that human connection and relevant learning can occur.

Accommodating Repertoires Different from Our Own

Recognizing new repertoires needn't mean we conform to student repertoires or expect them to learn ours. Certainly, as many have argued, there is a power code that buys access to school success, and denying students access to this code can become an unintentional form of negative discrimination (e.g., Delpit, 1996). I do not disagree with this perspective. The repertoires perspective I am advocating does not deny that students need to learn a local "power code" in order to have access to economic opportunity. However, there are many nonpower codes that are value-added features of an individual's communicative ability if such ways of speaking are understood for their functional relevance: Speaking Spanish, for example, can be framed as a deficit or an asset. Many businesses would be eager to hire a "Spanish–English bilingual," but would hesitate if this person were instead labeled a "non-native speaker." I am arguing that learning about repertoires in one's classroom can help raise consciousness of the value-added repertoires that are already circulating and to frame them as such.

Recognizing the value of circulating repertoires in one's classroom not only legitimizes otherwised potentially vilified ways of speaking, it also makes classroom dialogue more fulfilling for everyone. Just as a fulfilling conversation involves much more than giving ones' interlocutors pat answers or what we think they want, classroom talk need not involve students giving the teacher what they think he or she wants to hear—or for that matter, a teacher trying to sound just like his or her students! In any sustained dialogue, conversationalists begin to take on characteristics of each other's communicative repertoires. Similarly, over the course of a year, participants in a classroom community will probably begin to take on aspects of one another's repertoires. Sometimes, this does involve giving the teacher what he or she wants (as when students try to pass as English fluent); in others, it may involve giving in to peer pressure (as when JoJo plays "dumb"). As Tim, the teacher above illustrates, in the best cases, an individual carefully modulates his or her repertoire to achieve dialogue with others. No one is "giving in," but both are gaining by occupying a third position in which collaboration across repertoires is possible.

As Sonia Nieto (1999) writes, "accommodation" must be bidirectional. Students accommodate to school routines and repertoires, but teachers accommodate to students' repertoires as well. Not surprisingly, schools that do well show evidence of both kinds of accommodation: Students learn repertoires of school success; teachers learn that students' native repertoires are valuable (e.g., Lucas, Henze, & Donato, 1990; Sheets, 1995). When students' native communicative repertoires are recognized, they begin to see themselves as academically capable—that is, as capable of expanding their repertoires. These studies also illustrate that successful schools do not necessarily need new curricula or radical restructuring, but a change in culture and attitude.

"Communicative Repertoire" Rather Than "Language": Awareness of Classroom Discourse

Makoni and Pennycook (2007) point out that the term *language* itself is a construction, one that has become historically reified but that rarely is something of use to actual speakers. However, speaking analytically, if we are not analyzing "language" in classrooms, where do we start? With "communicative repertoire." But, how do we recognize distinct repertoires without demarking boundaries linguisticially? We use locally defined boundaries as discerned in classroom talk. This can involve different kinds of words (*Chancy* vs. *Chansey*; *ambitions* vs. *stuff*) or names (*JoJo* vs. *Mr. Johansen*), different ways of speaking ("that was not proper" vs. "I hear ya"; "put me in jail" vs. "got locked up"), gestures (fist bumps vs. a pleased nod; sitting up straight vs. slouching), turn-taking habits (hands raised vs. massively overlapping talk)—and sometimes these repertoires will include multiple "languages" as well.

In the roughest sense, we know contrasting repertoires when we hear and see them. Additionally, work in sociolinguistics and classroom discourse over the last 30 years has illuminated more refined tools to define and recognize communicative repertoires. For example, we now know about different narrative styles (Au, 1980; Michaels, 1981), turn-taking patterns (Erickson, 1996; Mehan, 1985), participation frameworks (Goffman, 1974; Philips, 1984), and the role of passing and underlife in institutions (Goffman, 1959). But what may be more important than looking at these finite structural distinctions or generalized institutional epiphenomena is learning to recognize the distinct communicative repertoires in our classrooms and to explore them. The goal of any language teacher is to augment *everyone's* awareness of the communicative repertoires in play in one's environment and how those repertoires can be deployed with facility and elegance—and to useful ends. A starting point in working to achieve this awareness is to have students document the characteristics of their own repertoires. Start with the categories suggested in Figure 8.1. Add more as they emerge (and new categories inevitably will).

By analyzing discourse in their classroom and school, teachers and students can begin to notice the range of repertoires and their functional value. "Discourse notebooks," in which teachers and students record and discuss language variation as they hear it, can be a good starting place. Each page in the discourse notebook can use the same kinds of categories illustrated in Figure 8.1, with additional local categories being added as needed. Discussions of the discourse notebooks are likely to lead to

Names/Nicknames: What different names do students/teachers have?

Popular Culture References: Which pop cultural icons are alluded to?

Gestures: What are some characteristic gestures of students and teachers?

Turn-Taking Habits: Is highly overlapping speech common and expected? Are long pauses more the norm?

Ways of Telling Stories: What characteristic ways of telling stories do students and teachers have?

Languages in Play: What languages are in use? By whom?

Pronunciation of Certain Words: Are different languages pronounced differently by different people? Which are used/not used?

FIGURE 8.1. Categories for classroom communicative repertoire comparison.

important metasociolinguistic insights and directions for further investigation.

Discourse notebooks may not seem feasible for primary school students. However, teachers can still ask students to begin noticing how they use language in different ways depending on the different contexts. A kindergarten teacher, for example, can ask her students to take note of "greetings." A homework assignment to notice "what your family says to you when you come home from school in the afternoon" could lead to a conversation the next day about greetings in different homes, greetings at school, or greetings among friends.

Gaining Metasociolinguistic Awareness: Analyzing Classroom Discourse

A critical goal of classroom discourse analysis, then, is to develop students' awareness of their communicative repertoires and the functionality of those repertoires across contexts. As Canagaraja (2007) has emphasized, "We have to develop the sensitivity to decode differences in dialects as students engage with a range of speakers and communities. What would help in this venture is the focus on developing a metalinguistic awareness" (p. 238). Given that so much of successful language use involves social context, this chapter suggests a broader goal: meta*socio*linguistic awareness. To achieve the goal of increased metasociolinguistic awareness, the new critical territory revealed by the everyday practice of classroom discourse analysis should be emphasized. When the goal is the achievement of greater metasociolinguistic awareness, the *process* of doing classroom discourse analysis can be as important as the findings. Doing classroom discourse analysis potentially develops new habits of metadiscursive reflection in teachers and students—habits that are crucial in a contemporary multilingual, ever-globalizing educational context.

To gain more finely grained metasociolinguistic awareness, teachers/researchers can supplement informal discourse notebooks with more systematic classroom discourse analysis. Conducting this type of analysis is an ideal way to understand the range of repertoires circulating in a classroom and how they are distributed across different classroom events. So, just as Gumperz (1964) began to explore verbal repertoire by noticing how individuals used multiple languages differently and deliberately on different social occasions, a classroom discourse analyst studies the relationship between classroom *events* and *language use* within them.

An x-ray view of classroom discourse studies might reveal the following basic steps:

1. Identify distinct classroom events.
2. Characterize the language within those events.
3. Identify variations in the language within those events.

Initially, classic classroom discourse studies focused primarily on Steps 1 and 2, above, describing normative expectations for classroom talk. For example, Hugh Mehan's (1985) study identified teacher-fronted classroom events (Step 1) and the ubiquitous "initiation–response–evaluation" turn-taking pattern within them (Step 2). This research also characterized the typical kind of questions (known answer) and answers (brief and swiftly offered) that are most functional within this event.

Other early studies, however, also were intent on identifying individual variations within distinct classroom speech events (Step 3, above). Sarah Michaels (1981), for example, identified the "sharing time" classroom event (Step 1) and characterized typical, successful storytelling turns within that event (Step 2). She found that successful stories were centered on a single topic (e.g., making sand candles) and that the teacher was able to ask follow-up questions with facility. But Michaels also identified unsuccessful storytelling turns and began to investigate why those stories were not working (Step 3). She found that the African American children in the class were bringing a distinctly different communicative repertoire to sharing time, in which sharing involved chaining together a series of personal events that included many family members, memories, and details.

Other studies, rather than comparing individuals within a speech event, have compared language across speech events and how the language expectations within those events affect student verbal behavior. Susan Philips (1984), for example, documented distinct participation frameworks within classrooms on the Warm Springs Indian Reservation and characterized the different turn-taking patterns within each of those events. Then she investigated participation patterns within each of those distinct events. She found that Indian students remained silent during teacher-fronted events, but were highly involved in collaborative group work. By raising awareness of how students participated differently in different events, she illuminated elements of the Indian students' communicative repertoire that were unrecognized by many educators and thus not available as resources on which to build further learning activities. Philips's study suggested that simple shifts in classroom arrangements for speech events could have radical effects on the educational experiences of Indians on the Warm Springs Reservation.

Inspired by these studies, teachers have begun to conduct similar studies in their own classrooms. Teacher researchers have been especially drawn to the comparative framework exemplified by Michaels's work, comparing student repertoires within a single event. Steve Griffin (2004), for example, used Michaels's methods to study sharing time in his elementary school classroom, investigating the troubling, non-normative, and increasingly disruptive participation of one student. Eventually, his own transcript analysis led him to change his sharing-time procedures, largely because he was able to describe the type of radical new story his one troubling student was contributing. Soon after, all the students wanted to experiment with this storytelling style, and sharing time took on a lively new quality, with everyone in the classroom expanding their communicative repertoire.

Although it is increasingly common for teachers to do discourse analysis, like Steve Griffin, when classroom discourse analysis emerged as a methodology, it was mainly the work of university researchers who schlepped around with mountains of recording equipment and spent hours back at the lab transcribing and analyzing. Hugh Mehan and his colleagues even referred to themselves as the "schleppers" back in the 1980s. Fortunately, recording equipment is now light, compact, and relatively inexpensive. There's nothing to stop teachers from clicking the "record" button and seeing what they discover. As a result, the initial methodological challenge for a teacher–researcher is largely conceptual: to identify those events worthy of recording and then carefully investigate that language once it is recorded. Following the tried-and-true steps taken in discourse analyses can be an initial jumping-off point for a novice classroom discourse analyst:

1. Spend some time identifying the different speech events in the classroom. Identify either a focal event or relevant comparative events.

2. Record the focal event and begin to characterize the language in that event. To do so, you will not need to transcribe the talk fully. Start by listening to the tape and, using the categories listed in Figure 8.1 as an initial guide, identify instances of talk that make this event distinctive. For example, listen for multilingualism and its effects; listen for the use of names and nicknames; listen for greetings, brand names, praise, or politeness tokens. Begin to characterize this event's normative language patterns. Transcribe those instances of talk that are most relevant to this characterization.

3. Look for variation in language use within that event or across comparison events. You may want to investigate the participation of one "disruptive" student, as Griffin did. Alternatively, like Philips, you may want to investigate how certain students participate differently across different events.

Once you have recorded an event, transcribed sections of it, and begun to see the repertoires in play, you will be hooked. And, as you begin to see how language use differs across events, you discover a vast range of communicative repertoires. This discovery can be empowering for a teacher and for students. As you become more metasociolinguistically facile, you will be able to more clearly identify the kinds of language use in your classroom, and to more clearly articulate for students the kinds of language you hope they will be able to produce in different situations.

BEST PRACTICES

Given the above descriptions, or *communicative repertoires*, consider these suggestions:

1. Teachers must recognize and honor the validity of each individual student's *communicative repertoire*.
2. Teachers must develop ways of assisting (scaffolding) their students in their attempts to master the conventional *communicative repertoire* required by all schooling situations.

3. A beginning point for this process is the development of *metaso-ciolinguistic awareness* for both students and teachers. Students and teachers can embark on this project through informal discourse notebooks and more formal systematic classroom discourse analysis.

In my experience, the process of analysis and discussion itself will change how students view and value their own immensely diverse communicative resources and will help them to see the functional value of adding new repertoires that may be necessary for school success.

SUMMARY OF MAIN IDEAS

Teaching, and language teaching in particular, has traditionally focused on language as a code, with the task of the teacher to get that code transferred into the heads of students. This perspective assumes that language carries meaning apart from social context—or, conversely, that the skills we teach when we teach a language are transferable to any context. Years of research indicate, however, that language is highly context dependent. There is no one "native speaker norm." Therefore, our task as language teachers is far more complex than simply transferring vocabulary and grammar into our students. Instead, successful language teaching involves familiarizing students with their own multiple communicative repertoires and equipping them with new ones.

IMPLICATIONS FOR RESEARCH, PRACTICE, AND POLICY

As described here, investigating communicative repertoires in the language classroom can be a way of implementing what Kumaravadivelu (2001) has called "postmethods" pedagogy. Why *post methods*? Teaching methods, especially in the language classroom, presuppose a static, acontextual entity called *language* that must somehow be transmitted into students' heads. Even a method such as the "communicative approach" sees communication as a means to a different end: correct, native-like language use. What I am proposing is awareness of communicative repertoires as the end in itself. This would not be achieved by role plays or by invoking imaginary repertoires of "native speakers," but through a collective empirical investigation of circulating repertoires and their everyday uses and misuses.

Through this kind of work, as administrators, teachers, policymakers, and providers of professional development, we can help students learn how they can use their repertoires to, as Canagaraja puts it, "shuttle between communities, and not to think of only joining *a* community" (2007, p. 238). Such a goal is absolutely essential to become "culturally relevant teachers" (Ladson Billings, 2001), to "create pride in cultural and linguistic differences" (Monzó & Rueda, 2009, p. 38), and for teachers and students, more generally, to develop as culturally effective human beings.

ACKNOWLEDGMENT

Some sections of this chapter appeared originally in Rymes (2010).

REFERENCES

Au, K. H. (1980). On participation structures in reading lessons. *Anthropology and Education Quarterly, 11*, 91–115.

Bloome, D., Puro, P., & Theodorou, E. (1989). Procedural display and classroom lessons. *Curriculum Inquiry, 19*(3), 265–291.

Bruner, J. (1983). *Child's talk: Learning to use language.* New York:Norton.

Canagarajah, S. (2007). After disinvention: Possibilites for communication, community, and competence. In S. Makoni & A. Pennycook (Eds.), *Disinventing and reconstituting languages* (pp. 233–239). Clevedon, UK: Multilingual Matters.

Delpit, L. (1996). *Other people's children: Cultural conflict in the classroom.* New York: New Press.

Erickson, F. (1996). Going for the zone: The social and cognitive ecology of teacher–student interaction in classroom conversations. In D. Hicks (Ed.), *Discourse, learning, and schooling* (pp. 29–62). Cambridge, UK: Cambridge University Press.

Goffman, E. (1959). *The presentation of self in everyday life.* New York: Anchor Books.

Goffman, E. (1974). *Frame analysis: An essay on the organization of experience.* Boston: Northeastern University Press.

Griffin, S. (2004). I need people: Storytelling in a second-grade classroom. In C. Ballenger (Ed.), *Regarding children's words: Teacher research on language and literacy* (pp. 22–30). New York: Teachers College Press.

Gumperz, J. (1964). Linguistic and social interaction in two communities. *American Anthropologist, 66*(6, Part 2), 137–154.

Gutiérrez, K., Rymes, B., & Larson, J. (1995). James Brown vs. *Brown v. the Board of Education*: Script, counterscript, and underlife in the classroom. *Harvard Educational Review, 65*(3), 445–471.

Kantor, J., & Gonzalez, D. (2009, June 7). For Sotomayor and Thomas, paths fork at race and identity. *New York Times*, pp. 1, 21.

Knobel, M. (1999). *Everyday literacies: Students, discourse and social practice.* New York: Peter Lang.

Kumaravadivelu, B. (2001). Toward a postmethod pedagogy. *TESOL Quarterly, 35,* 537–560.

Ladson-Billings, G. (2001). *Crossing over to Canaan: The journey of new teachers in diverse classrooms.* San Francisco: Jossey-Bass.

Lucas, T., Henze, R., & Donato, R. (1990). Promoting the success of Latino language minority students: An exploratory study of six high schools. *Harvard Educational Review, 60*(3), 315–340.

Makoni, S., & Pennycook, A. (Eds.). (2007). *Disinventing and reconstituting languages.* Clevedon, UK: Multilingual Matters.

Mehan, H. (1985). The structure of classroom discourse. In T. A. van Dijk (Ed.), *Handbook of discourse analysis: Vol. 3. Discourse and dialogue* (pp. 119–131). London: Academic Press.

Michaels, S. (1981). Sharing time: Children's narrative styles and differential access to literacy. *Language in Society, 10,* 423–442.

Monzó, L., & Rueda, R. (2009). Passing for English fluent: Latino immigrant children masking language proficiency. *Anthropology and Education Quarterly, 40*(1), 20–40.

Nieto, S. (1999). *The light in their eyes: Creating multicultural learning communities.* New York: Teachers College Press.

Philips, S. U. (1984). *The invisible culture.* New York: Longman.

Rymes, B. (1996). Rights to advise: Advice as an emergent phenomenon in student–teacher talk. *Linguistics and Education, 8*(4), 409–437.

Rymes, B. (2004). Contrasting zones of comfortable competence: Popularr culture in a phonics lesson. *Linguistics and Education, 14,* 321–335.

Rymes, B. (2010). Sociolinguistics and classroom discourse analysis. In N. Hornberg & S. McKay (Eds.), *Sociolinguistics and language teaching* (2nd ed.). New York: Cambridge University Press.

Rymes, B., & Pash, D. (2001). Questioning identity: The case of one second language learner. *Anthropology and Education Quarterly, 32*(3), 276–300.

Sheets, R. H. (1995). From remedial to gifted: Effects of culturally centered pedagogy. *Theory into Practice, 34*(3), 186–193.

Wolfe, T. (2004). *I am Charlotte Simmons.* New York: Picador.

9

Difficulty, Delay, or Disorder

*What Makes English Hard
for English Language Learners?*

Carol Westby
Deborah Hwa-Froelich

FOCUS POINTS

- There is no evidence that English is any more difficult for young children to learn than other languages, that bilingual education delays English language learners' development of English proficiency, or that there is a critical period beyond which language learning is particularly difficult.

- A dynamic systems theory of language learning maintains that multiple factors within the environment and within the child account for children's language learning. These environmental and individual factors interact in differing ways in different children.

- It is difficult to distinguish between language delay and language disorder in English language learners because grammar, vocabulary, and discourse characteristics that are often used to identify language disorders in monolingual children are frequently also characteristic of stages in second-language learning.

- Rather than evaluating children's present language skills, processing-based assessments evaluate how children approach language learning and are useful for identifying language disorders in English language learners.

• If language learning is dependent on a variety of environmental and individual factors that are unique to each person, then intervention programs to promote language proficiency must consider these multiple factors.

CHAPTER PURPOSE

This chapter addresses issues related to differentiating language learning disorders, language learning delays, and language learning difficulties in English language learners (ELLs). The following possibilities are considered in explaining the complexity of understanding, evaluating, and promoting English language proficiency in ELLs. The purpose of this chapter is to explore factors that may explain why so many ELL students fail to acquire English at the proficiency level sufficient for academic success. There are three possibilities:

1. *Difficulty:* ELLs have difficulty learning English because (1) some aspects of the English language make it difficult to learn, or (2) there are environmental factors that place additional stress on them. For example, it is well known that poverty influences children's learning of vocabulary, syntactic complexity, a range of language functions, and motivation for learning (Snow, Porche, Tabors, & Harris, 2007).

2. *Delay:* ELLs are simply delayed in acquiring English; that is, they are learning their second language (L2) at a reasonable pace, but the amount and quality of their language is like that of younger children whose first language (L1) is English. Their language is delayed compared to their L1 peers because they have not had as much time to learn English. Although they might have the language necessary for conversational interactions, they are delayed in acquiring the academic language essential for their grade because they have not had sufficient exposure to this type of language.

3. *Disorder:* Some ELLs may have intrinsic language disorders—specific neurologically based language impairments that negatively affect their ability to learn any language easily and well.

Few studies have documented ELL children's developing oral language skills, yet oral language skills underlie academic success (Catts, Fey, Zhang, & Tomblin, 1999; Miller et al., 2006; Swanson, Rosston, Gerber, & Solari, 2008). Without adequate oral language skills, ELL students will experience academic difficulties. Limited English skills and limited content knowledge are major contributors to the poor academic performance of ELL students (Proctor, Carlo, August, & Snow, 2005). For each ELL student, educators and speech–language pathologists (SLPs) need to determine if the limited English language skills are due to language difficulties, delays, or disorders so that they can provide the most appropriate interventions to promote academic language proficiency.

REVIEW OF RESEARCH AND THEORY

A variety of factors has been proposed to explain the difficulties ELLs have learning English.

Is English Particularly Difficult to Learn?

Reading English is more difficult than reading a number of other written languages (Ellis et al., 2004). English has a complex, opaque orthography that requires students to use two separate systems to decode print: a phonological processing system for phonologically regular words (e.g., *hat*, *bat*, *rat*, *cat*), and a lexical processing system for irregular words (e.g., *yacht*, *choir*, *light*) (Romani, DiBetta, Stouknida, & Olson, 2008). Children reading more transparent orthographies such as Finish or Korean become fluent readers far sooner than children reading English, due to its fairly opaque orthography.

With respect to oral English, for young children there is no indication that English is more difficult as an L2 than any other language, regardless of how different it is from their L1. Wong Fillmore (1983) found that Spanish and Chinese preschool children exhibited similar rates and patterns of oral English development. For older students and adults, L1 appears to have some influence on the way they approach L2 learning. Dulay and Burt (1974) found that Chinese L1 children showed the same acquisition sequence in terms of which morphemes (i.e., meaning units) they acquired early and late as Spanish L1 children, but they had lower mean accuracy scores for use of the morphemes that mark number and verb tense.

For adults who are learning an L2, the greater the difference between their L1 and the L2, the more time they require to achieve some degree of proficiency (National Virtual Translation Center, 2006). In the United States 79% of ELL students speak Spanish as an L1 (Center for Public Education, 2007), a language that has some similarities to English, so it is unlikely that large numbers of ELL students exhibit delays or limited proficiency in English due to its complexity or differences from their L1.

Bilingual Education and Exposure to English

An attitude promoted by the U.S. government is that bilingual education negatively impacts ELLs' acquisition of English. This belief is based on three myths:

1. The more time students spend in an L2 context, the quicker they learn the language.
2. Children learn L2s quickly and easily.
3. There is a critical time period for learning an L2.

Intensity of Experience

Although it intuitively makes sense that students who have more exposure to the target L2 would acquire the L2 more quickly than students who have less exposure, surprisingly this is not the case. Overall, research is consistent in showing that ELLs who receive some type of specialized bilingual program (transitional early- or late-exit bilingual or two-way immersion) catch up to, and in some studies surpass, the achievement levels of their ELL peers and English-only peers who were educated in English-only classrooms (Thomas & Collier, 2002). ELLs who participated in programs that provided extended instruction through the students' L1 (i.e., two-way immersion and late-exit programs) outperformed students who received short-term instruction through their L1 (transitional early-exit programs). Bilingual proficiency and biliteracy are positively related to academic achievement in both languages. For example, bilingual Hispanic students have demonstrated higher academic achievement scores than their monolingual English-speaking Hispanic peers (Lindholm-Leary, 2001).

Children's Language Learning

Bilingual education opponents advocate English immersion (submersion) programs because they believe that language learning is very easy for young children and that preschool and early-elementary schoolchildren acquire the target L2 very quickly when they are surrounded by it. Wong Fillmore (1983) reported, however, that of 48 kindergarten children who spoke Spanish or Cantonese as an L1, only 5 had reasonable English fluency after 2 years of exposure. A study of ELL children ages 4½–7 in Edmonton, Canada also revealed that they did not learn an L2 as rapidly as expected (Genesee, Paradis, & Crago, 2004). After 1½ years of school in L2, less that 50% of the ELL children were as accurate as their native-speaking peers on common English morphemes and had vocabulary scores at a low–normal range. Furthermore, the children exhibited an extremely wide variation in their grammar and vocabulary scores, and there was no correlation between months of exposure to English and grammar and vocabulary scores.

Critical Period Assumption

According to the critical period hypothesis, L2 language learning becomes more difficult in adolescence because of neurobiological changes. The evidence for a biological basis for a critical language learning period has been challenged in recent years, however (Bruer, 2008; Collier, 1987). Bruer (2008) suggests that older students and adults may have difficulty acquiring an L2 not because a critical period for language learning has closed but because repeated exposure to the L1 reduces their flexibility, thus making it difficult for them to tune into L2 phonology. Other researchers (Flege, 1999; Geert, 2007) argue that differences in apparent ease or difficulty of L2 acquisition at different ages may reflect psychological and social factors rather than biological ones.

Research by Mayberry and Lock (2003) indicates that there is probably not a critical period for L2 language learning, but there is a critical period for L1 learning. Both deaf adults who learned American Sign Language (ASL) before age 3 and hearing adults who acquired an L1 other than English from birth and began learning English as their L2 between ages 6 and 13 performed at near-native levels on grammatical judgment and sentence comprehension tasks in a subsequently learned L2. In contrast, deaf adults who did not learn their first language until after age 6 performed poorly on several of the syntactic structures.

Mayberry's research may have implications for ELL students. Students who have developed a strong L1 are more likely to acquire proficiency in L2 than students who did not develop a strong L1 at early years. Collier (1987) analyzed how long it took immigrant students in the United States to become proficient in English for content subjects when schooled only in English. She found that students who were 8–12 years old on arrival were the first to reach norms for native speakers (50th percentile on a standardized test) on all content-area tests, doing so within 4–5 years. Students who were 5–7 years old on arrival fell significantly behind the older children in academic achievement, requiring 4–8 years to reach the 50th percentile. Arrivals at ages 12–15 experienced the greatest difficulty reaching age and grade norms, requiring 6–8 years. The 8- to 12-year-olds had the advantage of strong oral and written skills in their first language, and they were able to bring their understanding of language to L2 learning. The oldest group of students had good L2 learning rates, but because they had to quickly acquire a more complex form of English than the 8- to 12-year-olds and had far fewer years in which to do so, their proficiency at final assessment was lower than the other two groups. Collier's findings support Mayberry's conclusions: Students who had a strong L1 when they began L2 learning developed higher proficiency levels than those students who had longer exposure to an L2, but had lower L1 proficiency when their L2 was introduced.

How Is Language Learned?

Are some ELL children introduced and expected to learn an L2 before they have been adequately exposed to an L1? Is simple exposure to a language sufficient, or must language be explicitly directed to the child, and must the child be active in communication?

Dynamic Systems Theory

A number of researchers in L2 learning have embraced dynamic systems theory. In 2007 and 2008 entire issues of *Bilingualism: Language and Cognition* and *The Modern Language Journal* were devoted to a dynamic systems theory approach to understanding multilingualism. A dynamic systems approach to L2 acquisition recognizes the crucial role of the interaction of multiple environmental and individual variables at different levels of communication (word, sentence, discourse) and in different languages (De Bot, Lowie, & Verspoor, 2007). Environmental factors can include values and beliefs about communication; expectations about who talks to whom about what and how; and the style, structures, and functions of the language that is used. Individual variables can include factors that motivate an individual to communicate, temperament, present language skills, working memory skills, and learning strategies/preferences. By employing a dynamic systems approach to L2 learning, educators and SLPs consider both the students' unique language-processing skills and the multiple home and school environmental factors that facilitate or inhibit their language learning.

Communication Styles

Adult–child and sibling interactions strongly influence children's language development. Children learn not only the vocabulary and syntax of their language, they also learn who talks to whom, the reasons one talks, what is talked about, and how one organizes what one talks about. Children from Western middle-class backgrounds learn a communication style that generally matches the communication styles of teachers. They learn to use language not only to get their needs and the needs of others met, but also to share past experiences and talk about ideas in books. Children from these backgrounds arrive at school with larger vocabularies, more complex syntax, and the ability to use language to predict, reason, and project into the thoughts and feelings of others (Hart & Risley, 1995; Tabors, Snow, & Dickinson, 2001). They enter school with not only a conversational language proficiency, but they are also on their way to developing the academic language proficiency required in U.S. schools. ELL children from low socioeconomic backgrounds or from families who have not been exposed to Western education have to develop English not only to meet their daily needs but for performing in school. They have to develop some structures and functions in English that are not used in their L1, and they have only the few hours that they are in school to do so. Two-thirds of ELLs are from low-income families, and 48% of ELLs in pre-K through fifth grade have parents who did not finish high school (Capps et al., 2005). Consequently, they are likely to have less exposure to academic language in their L1.

Language Influence of Schooling

School as well as home environments influence ELLs' language development. Carhill, Suarez-Orozco, and Paez (2008) investigated the academic language proficiency of adolescent first-generation ELL students. Although time in the United States is positively correlated with students' English language proficiency—those who have been here longer tend to demonstrate higher levels of proficiency relative to their English-speaking peers—several other factors were more predictive of students' proficiency. ELL students who were in schools with overall higher poverty rates and minority representation had lower English proficiency scores than ELL students in schools with lower poverty rates and more integrated student populations. ELL students who were in schools in which English monolingual students had higher English proficiency scores also achieved higher English proficiency scores.

What Type of Language Is Being Assessed?

All persons typically find conversational language easier than academic language. Primary purposes of conversational language are to get needs met and to share personal experiences through narrative discourse. Syntactic patterns are simple (active sentences with subject–verb–object construction); vocabulary is familiar and concrete and few connective words are used (primarily *and*, *then*, *so*). In contrast, academic language has a wider variety of functions and discourse structures, more varied and abstract vocabulary, and more complex syntactic patterns. (Some characteristics of academic language are shown in Table 9.1). Language impairment in oral conversational language predicts language impairment in academic language. Adequate oral conversational language, however, does not ensure development of proficient academic language. Even monolingual children who do not exhibit obvious language impairments in their oral conversational language may experience language impairment in academic language.

Academic English

The majority of ELL children develop conversational English proficiency, but many fail to develop the academic English proficiency necessary for school success. They develop sufficient vocabulary and skill in morphology and syntax in an L2 to make their needs known, share familiar experiences, and repeat and paraphrase information. They can successfully order a hamburger and fries, chat with friends at lunch, and talk about a recent experience (e.g., a family gathering, a favorite movie or computer game). They do not, however, develop the academic language used to describe complex ideas, higher-order thinking processes, and abstract concepts (e.g., the American Revolution, Civil Rights movement, force/gravity/photosynthesis). After nearly 7 years in the United States only 19 adolescents (7.4%) of the 274 students in a study by Carhill and colleagues (2008) scored at or above the normed mean for English-speaking same-age peers on a test evaluating proficiency in academic English. On average, these students demonstrated academic English proficiency scores equivalent to the second percentile of native English-speaking peers.

Some Reasons Why Academic Language Proficiency Lags

ELL students usually receive little time in supportive services before being enrolled in general education classes. There is a push to reclassify ELL

TABLE 9.1. Characteristics of Academic Language

Functions

- To describe complex concepts—for example, relationships between characters, causes and effects of events
- To describe higher-order thinking processes—for example, analyzing, evaluation, synthesizing, persuading, predicting, explaining, comparing
- To describe abstraction (relationships that cannot be pointed out or illustrated)—for example, "On the other hand, the two scientists had differing views on the topic of evolution."

Vocabulary

- Connective words—for example, *if ... then, because, therefore, although, as a consequence, as a result, similarly, in contrast, whereas, ultimately*
- Nominalization: Verbs are turned into nouns; condenses lengthy explanations into a few words—for example, "The *condemnation* of dissenting *perspectives* led to *revolution*."
- Multiple meanings for words—for example, *innocent* can have three distinct meanings: not guilty; naïve or inexperienced; harmless
- Qualifiers—for example, *perhaps, usually, generally, relatively, theoretically, likely, presumably*

Grammar

- Passive voice (subject may not be present)—for example, "The radius is then plugged into the formula for the area of the circle."
- Dependent clauses—for example:
  - Adverbial: *Although several precautions were taken*, the key was lost.
  - Adjectival (relative): The colonists, *who felt that they did not have representation*, dumped the tea into Boston Harbor.
  - Noun: *Where the rebels were going* was unknown.

Discourse

- Different organizational structures for narrative, procedure, explanation, compare–contrast, cause–effect, persuasion

children as quickly as possible. A number of the tests used, however, focus on proficiency in oral interactive language skills, not the type of language skills required for academic success (Saunders & O'Brien, 2006).

Because ELL students often sound fluent in conversational language, deficits in academic language go unrecognized. In a supportive environment, it takes approximately 2–3 years to achieve proficiency in conversational language and 5–7 years to achieve proficiency in academic language (Cummins, 1984). Many ELL students fail to develop academic language because they have not received adequate instruction and experiences in its use. Other ELL students, however, fail to develop academic language because they do indeed have intrinsic language impairments that were not manifested with conversational language. Parents from most cultures will recognize a 5-year-old who makes few attempts to communicate or who is unintelligible or is producing poorly structured sentences. Parents spend more time in conversational language with their children than they do in academic language. Thus it is more likely for parents to observe errors in conversational language. In contrast, academic language success is based on comprehension of, or the ability to draw inferences from, literate discourse or text. These skills are not easily assessed by parents or even by teachers in a classroom setting. Large numbers of ELLs exhibit difficulty in acquiring academic language in English, possibly because they lack academic language in their L1 and/or because they have had limited exposure to and limited explicit instruction in L2 academic language. Consequently, ELL students with true intrinsic language impairments who have difficulty acquiring the forms and content of academic language may be overlooked.

Process-Based Assessment Measures of Language

Assessment of possible language impairment is particularly difficult in bilingual children. Child language specialists have suggested that it is not likely that children have a language impairment in L2 if they do not have a language impairment in L1. However, because ELL children in the United States often begin to lose their L1 as soon as they are exposed to an L2, it is not easy to determine if they have a true impairment in L1 (Anderson, 1999). Furthermore, morphosyntactic errors—such as omission of plural and possessive -s or past tense -ed morphemes and vocabulary weaknesses in ELLs learning an L2—often look similar to those made by younger L1 English learners and by L1 English learners with language impairments (Genesee et al., 2004). Therefore, it is challenging to discriminate children whose errors are typical for an L2 learner from children whose errors are indicative of a language-learning problem.

Researchers have proposed a variety of process-based assessments as a way to identify ELL children who are likely to have language impairments. Process-based assessment approaches attempt to (1) minimize the linguistic knowledge necessary to complete tasks, (2) evaluate underlying processing factors (such as processing speed or working memory), or (3) evaluate the ease with which children learn language-like tasks (known as *learnability*).

Minimizing Linguistic Information

Several studies have shown that English-speaking children with language impairment are slower than their neurotypical peers on a range of nonlinguistic auditory and visual tasks and make more errors on working memory tasks (Leonard et al., 2007). Similar studies with ELL students have had mixed results. Kohnert and Windsor (2004) investigated the nonlinguistic performance of linguistically diverse learners. They measured how quickly English-only speakers with language impairments, typically developing English-only speakers, and typically developing bilingual Spanish–English speakers were able to differentiate high and low tones and blue and red circles. English-only children with language impairment took significantly longer to respond than English-only typically developing children. Although typically developing bilingual children generally responded more rapidly than children with language impairment, they were not significantly more rapid. Thus, ELLs' performance on nonlinguistic tasks may appear similar to children with language impairment.

Evaluating Underlying Processing Factors

Tasks requiring children to listen to, retrieve, and repeat novel words or nonwords of varying syllabic lengths have been used to measure verbal working memory. Nonword repetition tasks have been shown to differentiate typically developing children from children with language impairment in several languages (e.g., English [Dollaghan & Campbell, 1998]; Cantonese [Stokes, Wong, Fletcher, & Leonard, 2006]; Spanish [Girbau & Schwartz, 2007]). Children are asked to repeat words with an increasing number of syllables (e.g., *flin*, *zoller*, *conscenbral*). As the number of syllables in the nonsense words increases, children with language impairment exhibit significantly more difficulty than neurotypical children. Unlike standardized language tests, nonword repetition has been shown to be unaffected by socioeconomic level (Engel, Santos, & Gathercole, 2008); therefore, nonword repetition tasks appear to have potential for identifying ELLs with language impairment, but at this time it is only a research methodology.

These studies have all used syllable structures that obey the phonotactic rules of the child's native language—that is, stimuli used L1 phonemes in sequences common to the L1 language (e.g., in English, nonwords such as *blin* and *fiptopal* follow English sound sequences, but *ngep* or *zpemrth* do not). How should these tasks be developed for ELL students? Should the nonsense words use syllable structures from the students' L1 or from English? How might L1 language attrition or degree of

L2 proficiency influence performance? Children might successfully repeat syllables that have a familiar structure (i.e., are phonologically possible in their language) but have more difficulty repeating syllables that do not have a familiar structure (i.e., are not phonologically likely in their L1).

Difficulty on processing and working memory tasks could explain why children might have difficulty in language learning. Slow or incomplete phonological processing could lead to protracted development of language because new words or structures would have to be encountered more often than usual to be adequately processed and incorporated into the child's language systems. Limitations in working memory could also result in syntactic difficulties. Children with working memory limitations may find it difficult to consider both the nonsyntactic, content information and the syntactic information when processing sentences. As a result they may choose an incorrect verb form (Leonard et al., 2007).

Evaluating Learnability

Fast mapping and dynamic assessment approaches have also been suggested as a way to determine those ELL children who may have language impairments. These measures investigate an individual child's ability to learn a language.

Fast mapping refers to children's ability to learn novel vocabulary after one or two exposures in a play activity or in a video presentation (Dollaghan, 1985). In nonbilingual studies, significant differences were found between the performance of children who were typically developing and those who had specific language impairment. Roseberry and Connell (1991) used a fast-mapping approach to teach an invented grammatical morpheme to Spanish-speaking children. (The invented morpheme was a suffix, pronounced as an unstressed vowel that was given the meaning of "part of." Thus, *booka* was taught to mean *part of a book*). Spanish-speaking children with language impairment had significantly more difficulty learning the morpheme than neurotypical Spanish-speaking children.

In dynamic assessment, adults teach the cognitive–linguistic strategies the children need to perform the tasks. They note not only whether the child learns the task, but also the learning processes and strategies the child uses during the teaching. The concept of dynamic assessment is typically an aspect of the response-to-intervention (RTI) model that is being used under No Child Left Behind (NCLB) and the Individuals with Disabilities Education Act (IDEA). The purpose of an RTI approach is to determine the nature or reason for a child's learning difficulties: Has the child lacked exposure to the content or to appropriate instruction, or does the child have intrinsic processing problems that make learning difficult? During intervention, the adult monitors the child's response to the intervention and adapts or modifies instruction as needed. If the child continues to exhibit difficulty in mastering the tasks even with this targeted instruction, it is possible that he or she may have an intrinsic learning impairment. Under NCLB, there is less of a need to diagnose a child with a language impairment in order to receive appropriate services. Thus, ELLs who are not mastering the classroom curriculum at the level of their peers can receive additional support without being classified as children in need of special education.

Dynamic assessment procedures have been used to evaluate vocabulary and narrative learnability for ELL children (Miller et al., 2006; Peña & Quinn, 1992). When using dynamic assessment, the examiner provides a mediated learning experience (MLE) for the child—explicitly explaining the goal of the task, why it is important, how to proceed with the task, and how this information may be used in other contexts (Miller, Gillam, & Peña, 2001). For example:

- *Goal:* "Today we're going to learn how to use the words *if . . . then* and *because* to connect ideas in sentences."
- *Why important:* "Using these words helps us understand why something happens or under what circumstances something may happen. For example: 'The colonists dumped the tea in Boston Harbor *because* they thought the British taxes were unfair. *If* Paul Revere had not warned the colonists that the British were coming, *then* more people would have been hurt.'"
- *Use in other contexts:* "You can use these words to explain to a friend why you feel as you do or why you want to do something or don't want to do something. People will often listen to our ideas more if we give them reasons—for example, 'I wanna go to the fair because I heard that Pink is having a show at the coliseum.'"

By differentiating ELLs who are typical L2 learners from those who have particular language-learning difficulties, educators are positioned to provide more appropriate and effective interventions to promote L2 development. The process-based approaches, which evaluate children's speed of processing and working memory and assess the ease with which they learn new information, have the potential to enable educators to make this differentiation. Information from process-based assessments can support the provision of services in school using an RTI framework.

At this time, however, these approaches have primarily been used in research contexts. Consequently, standard protocols and normative data that could be used to make this differentiation are not available. Educators and SLPs must rely on their observations and experiences when interpreting children's performance on process-based assessment.

BEST PRACTICES

Demographic and research data clearly demonstrate that large numbers of ELL students do not have the English language proficiency essential for success in the 21st century. Regardless of the reason for this limited proficiency (difficulty, delay, or disorder), students need to receive an educational program that promotes their language development. NCLB requires that any child who is not making adequate progress receive additional support services.

Francis, Rivera, Lesaux, Kieffer, and Rivera (2006) have provided research-based guidelines for academic instruction interventions for ELL students. They focus on the development of academic language, stressing particularly the use of direct, explicit instruction in phonological awareness/phonics, vocabulary development, and strategies and knowledge that promote comprehension of narrative and expository texts. These guidelines also emphasize that ELLs need significant opportunities to engage in structured academic talk. There is no evidence that bilingual approaches have negative effects on academic achievement, and in most cases bilingual instruction has positive effects (Francis, Lesaux, & August, 2006). Consequently, where possible, bilingual programs that continue to develop L1 along with L2 should be promoted. In both languages, programs should emphasize language skills implicated in higher-order cognitive processes and in language for literacy and academic purposes. There is evidence that there can be transfer of language skills from L1 to L2, particularly if educators provide explicit instruction that promotes such transfer (Carlo, 2009).

How Should Language Be Taught?

According to a dynamic systems theory of language learning, multiple factors—both endogenous (within the child) and exogenous (within the environment)—contribute to a child's language development. Child psychologists Nelson and Arkenberg (2008) believe that a dynamic systems perspective provides a framework for understanding the multiple cooperating variables that promote development. They are interested in accelerating skill acquisition in children who have language delays and disorders. They have used the term *dynamic tricky mix* to explain their view of how language/literacy emerges in both neurotypical children and children with language impairments. Nelson and Arkenberg consider the learning process to be a dynamic tricky mix because the mix of components differs for each child and is not static—it changes with the environmental inputs, as well as the children's changing development, and their responses to the environment and learning. Intervention with children involves keeping track of the complexity of dynamic factors influencing their language/literacy performance and providing ways of boosting their depth of engagement so that their learning emerges.

The LEARN Framework

Nelson and Arkenberg suggest that it is possible to dramatically accelerate children's language/literacy learning when educators and SLPs collaborate to identify a convergence of endogenous and exogenous conditions that promote learning. They proposed the LEARN acronym as a way of organizing these conditions (*launchers* + *enhancers* + *adjustment* + *readiness* + *networks* = *LEARN*). The content of these conditions is also consistent with current best practices in language learning intervention. If the conditions are mixed in appropriate ways, ELLs and children with language impairment should find that their processing speeds and working memory limitations may constitute less of a burden.

Launching Conditions

Children become more involved in tasks and better remember tasks if they are motivated to participate and challenged appropriately (Guthrie & Humenick, 2004). Educational activities should be purposeful and meaningful. For example, history may include individual research into the children's familial, ethnic, or racial history to make links between state, national, or international events.

Enhancing Conditions

Enhancing conditions are the interaction strategies that adults use to facilitate students' learning and the metacognitive strategies that students use to guide their own learning. Language is socially constructed and dependent on the scaffolding support of others, which promotes shared meaning. The use of instructional conversation (IC) is one way to support students' development of academic language (Saunders & Goldenberg, 1999). ICs are theme-based discussion lessons geared toward creating opportunities for students' conceptual and linguistic development.

The teacher can use questions that differ in level of abstraction. Rather than focusing on questions that orient students to the perceptual and concrete (e.g., questions that ask for labels, repetition, or descriptions of physical appearance of objects or events), they can focus on questions that foster more complex and abstract language, for example:

- Questions that require students to reorder perception by asking for predictions of events and thoughts and feelings or for descriptions of similarities and differences not based on physical characteristics (e.g., How were Martin Luther King, Jr. and Gandhi alike?).
- Questions that require explanations and justifications for how or why (e.g., Why are scientists worried about global warming?).

Higher-level questions require more academic language. By incorporating different levels of questions, the teacher encourages expression of students' ideas, builds upon information students provide and experiences they have had, and guides students to increasingly sophisticated levels of language and understanding. ICs provide opportunities for students to use academic language and to be supported as they do so. Academic conversations that instruct and stimulate thinking might be particularly important for ELL students, many of whom receive insufficient opportunities for conceptual and linguistic development at both home and school.

Direct, intense, explicit teaching through mediated learning experiences (MLEs) (discussed earlier) can also promote students' metacognitive awareness of the learning process and how to monitor and regulate their own learning.

Adjustment Conditions

Adjustment conditions are of two types: (1) the adjustments educators make to lessons based upon their observation and evaluation of children's response to activities, and (2) the adjustments children make as a result of their attitudes toward the task and their ability to do it. Because children are not at the same language developmental levels, teachers need to identify students' varying language levels and needs and determine the degree of support and practice that individual children require. For example, when using ICs, teachers consider how much time they should devote to accessing students' prior knowledge and building background knowledge and the types of questions to pose. Children themselves make adjustments to how they approach their learning activities. Children who are motivated to learn the material for the sake of learning or because they enjoy the learning activities are likely to persist as tasks become more challenging. In contrast, children who think they are not capable of completing a task are less likely to persist as it becomes more challenging (Elliot, 1999).

Readiness Conditions

The term *readiness conditions* refers to what children bring to the instructional situation. Educators should evaluate children's readiness for learning. This includes not only an evaluation of their present processing and language/literacy skills, but also an awareness of how their cultural, familial, and environmental circumstances may influence their learning. Such data about students provide educators with information regarding what content they should teach and how they might best teach it.

Network Conditions

Knowledge is best remembered and used when it is linked to/networked with other knowledge. This linkage is essential for developing the neural networks necessary for representational thought. Theme-based units provide opportunities to integrate ideas from multiple educational domains. Rather than doing isolated lessons, educators can assist students in discovering relationships among curricular content. For example, a unit can be developed around the 2008 Caldecott award-winning book, *The Invention of Hugo Cabret* (Selznick, 2007). Hugo is an orphan who lives in the walls of a Paris train station at the turn of the 20th century, where he tends to the clocks and steals what he needs to survive. Hugo's recently deceased father, a clockmaker, worked in a museum where he discovered an automaton—a robot-like figure seated at a desk, pen in hand, as if ready to deliver a message. After his father's death, Hugo becomes obsessed with getting the automaton to function. This book provides opportunities to discuss not only the story itself (literature/reading comprehension) and the history of early movies (social studies), but also to explain scientific principles (the cams, levers, and gears that make clocks and automatons work) and procedures for constructing a paper automaton. Lessons of this type are also multisensory. Students read the story, view the pictures in the book, and watch old movies, such as *A Trip to the Moon* (mentioned in the book), on YouTube; and they build an automaton. Multisensory activities involve parallel processing, which aid in the development of neural networks.

SUMMARY OF MAIN IDEAS

Large numbers of ELL students fail to develop academic English language proficiency. Some common beliefs about what contributes to this difficulty are unsubstantiated myths. In actuality:

- Young children do not easily develop an L2 just by being submersed in it.
- ELL students' difficulty in developing English proficiency is not a result of the structure of English or of insufficient exposure to English in bilingual programs.
- Bilingual education does not negatively affect English language acquisition, and in the majority of cases, bilingual education results in improved academic language proficiency in both L1 and L2. Children with a stronger L1 base learn an L2 to higher proficiency levels.

Children who enter school with less experience in academic language in their L1 are at greater risk for failing to develop adequate academic language proficiency in their L2. In the United States, low socioeconomic levels and low parental education levels are particularly associated with reduced academic language skills (Engel et al., 2008; Hart & Risley, 1995; Locke, Ginsberg, & Peers, 2002). Children from these environments enter school with less exposure to academic language in either L1 or L2. If they are enrolled in schools with high-minority and high-poverty populations, their likelihood of developing academic English proficiency is further reduced. Differentiating between language delays and language disorders in ELL students is extremely difficult, particularly with formal standardized tests. Process-based and dynamic assessment procedures that evaluate students' learnability and modifiability have the potential for differentiating language delays from disorders. A dynamic systems framework can be used to explore the factors that influence language learning and to frame instructional intervention programs that could accelerate students' acquisition of academic English language proficiency.

IMPLICATIONS FOR RESEARCH, PRACTICE, AND POLICY

In all countries, poverty is a major factor contributing to the degree to which ELL students achieve proficiency in an L2. For unknown reasons, however, in the United States poverty has more of an influence on low L2 proficiency than in other industrialized countries. Because such a high percentage of ELL students in the United States are from low socioeconomic backgrounds, poverty is probably the major factor contributing to ELL students' failure to achieve high levels of L2 proficiency. Further research is needed to understand the multiple ways that poverty influences language learning and academic performance and what types of political, social, and educational interventions can reduce these effects.

Researchers have shown that children from low socioeconomic backgrounds enter school with reduced vocabularies and reduced syntactic complexity compared to their same-age peers from more advantaged environments. Clearly, educators need to jump-start the language learning of many ELLs and promote their acquisition of more complex academic language. A dynamic systems approach provides a framework or rationale for the activities that should be part of a language curriculum, but to use this framework effectively, educators need an explicit understanding of the language and the interactional strategies that promote language learning in the classroom.

Programs That Build Academic Language

Unfortunately, many teachers have an insufficient grasp of spoken and written language structure and would have difficulty teaching language and literacy explicitly to children who struggle. Some teacher education programs have been developed to train teachers on the nature of language and strategies for working with ELL students. Three programs are briefly described. The ultimate goal of these programs is to develop students' academic language proficiency.

ICs (Sanders & Goldenberg, 1999), discussed earlier, provide students with the opportunity to hear and develop academic language through meaningful discussions of academic content that is linked to their prior experiences.

The sheltered instruction observation protocol (SIOP; Echevarria, Vogt, & Short, 2008) is a comprehensive model that helps teachers plan and deliver lessons that allow English learners to acquire academic knowledge as they develop English language proficiency. Based on a variety of best practices with ELLs, SIOP has eight interrelated components: lesson preparation, building background, comprehensible input, strategies, interaction, practice/application, lesson delivery, and review/evaluation. Teachers use a set of observation protocols to monitor their implementation of each component.

The focus of the Cognitive Academic Language Learning Approach (CALLA; Chamot & O'Malley, 1994) is the development of academic language functions (e.g., informing, comparing, analyzing, inferring, persuading, synthesizing) and strategies that students can use across all academic content to monitor and self-regulate their own learning. Using these strategies independently can be difficult for ELLs if they are attempting to develop L2 vocabulary and syntactic patterns at the same time. Consequently, although the CALLA can be used across all grades, the evidence suggests that it works better with middle and high school students who have more knowledge of English vocabulary and structure.

All three of these approaches have some research documenting efficacy, but further research is needed to document the degree to which they increase students' language and literacy proficiency. Moreover, effective teaching of ELL students would require an understanding of just how they learn an L2, but there is a lack of studies documenting ELLs' development of oral English conversational and academic language (Saunders & O'Brien, 2006). Oral language proficiency is widely used to determine program placement and advancement for ELL students, but the focus of these assessments is more on conversational proficiency rather than academic proficiency. Oral English language development, especially academic-oriented proficiency, is a neglected field of research.

RTI for ELLs

Finally, the RTI intervention approach has the potential to be quite beneficial to ELL students. Using an RTI approach, general educators collaborating with SLPs, bilingual educators, and special educators can provide any ELL student who is not making adequate progress with appropriate small-group and individualized support without qualifying the student for special education services. Within these small-group and individualized lessons, educators and SLPs can employ evidenced-based mediated learning experiences over a period of time and observe and document students' progress in response to the intervention. Those students who require intensive support or who exhibit very slow development (compared to other students with similar initial skills and backgrounds) may need to be further evaluated for intrinsic language learning impairment.

This process should reduce the over- or underidentification of ELL students for special education, yet enable all students to receive the educational support they require to be successful.

REFERENCES

Anderson, R. (1999). Impact of first language loss on grammar in a bilingual child. *Communication Disorders Quarterly, 21*(1), 4–16.

Bruer, J. T. (2008). Critical periods in second language-learning: Distinguishing phenomena from explanations. In M. Mody & E. R. Silliman (Eds.), *Brain, behavior, and learning in language and reading disorders* (pp. 72–96). New York: Guilford Press.

Capps, R., Fix, M., Murray, J., Ost, J., Passel, J., & Herwantoro, S. (2005). *The New demography of America's schools: Immigration and the No Child Left Behind Act*. Washington, DC: The Urban Institute. Retrieved November 28, 2008, from *www.urban.org/publications/311230.htm*.

Carhill, A., Suarez-Orozco, C., & Paez, M. (2008). Explaining English language proficiency among adolescent immigrant students. *American Educational Research Journal, 45*(4), 1155–1179.

Carlo, M. S. (2009). Cross-language transfer of phonological, orthographic, and semantic knowledge. In L. M. Morrow, R. Rueda, & D. Lapp (Eds.), *Handbook of research on literacy and diversity* (pp. 277–291). New York: Guilford Press.

Catts, H. W., Fey, M. E., Zhang, X., & Tomblin, J. B. (1999). Language basis of reading and reading disabilities. *Scientific Studies of Reading, 3*(4), 331–362.

Center for Public Education. (2007). *Preparing English language learners for academic success*. Retrieved March 16, 2009, from *www.centerforpubliceducation.org/site/c.kjJXJ5MPIwE/b.3531983/k.A79C/Preparing_language_learners_for_academic_success.htm#b2*.

Chamot, A. U., & O'Malley, J. M. (1994). *The CALLA handbook: Implementing the cognitive academic language learning approach*. Reading, MA: Addison Wesley.

Collier, V. P. (1987). Age and rate of acquisition of second language for academic purposes. *TESOL Quarterly, 21*, 617–641.

Cummins, J. (1984). *Bilingualism and special education*. San Diego, CA: College-Hill.

De Bot, K., Lowie, W., & Verspoor, M. (2007). A dynamic systems theory approach to second language acquisition. *Bilingualism: Language and Cognition, 10*(1), 7–21.

Dollaghan, C. (1985). Child meets word: Fast mapping in preschool children. *Journal of Speech and Hearing Research, 28*, 449–454.

Dollaghan, C., & Campbell, T. (1998). Nonword repetition and child language impairment. *Journal of Speech, Language, and Hearing Research, 41*, 1136–1146.

Dulay, H., & Burt, M. (1974). Natural sequences in child second language acquisition. *Language Learning, 24,* 37–53.

Echevarria, J., Vogt, M., & Short, D. J. (2008). *Making content comprehensible for English learners: The SIOP model.* Boston: Pearson.

Elliot, A. J. (1999). Approach and avoidance motivation and achievement goals. *Educational Psychologist, 34,* 169–189.

Engel, P. M. J., Santos, F. H., & Gathercole, S. E. (2008). Are working memory measures free of socioeconomic influence. *Journal of Speech, Language, and Hearing Research, 51,* 1580–1587.

Flege, J. (1999). Age of learning and second language speech. In D. Birdsong (Ed.), *Second language acquisition and the critical period hypothesis* (pp. 101–131). Mahwah, NJ: Erlbaum.

Francis, D. J., Lesaux, N. K., & August, D. L. (2006). Language of instruction for language minority learners. In D. L. August & T. Shanahan (Eds.), *Developing literacy in a second language: Report of the National Literacy Panel* (pp. 365–414). Mahwah, NJ: Erlbaum.

Francis, D. J., Rivera, M., Lesaux, N., Kieffer, M., & Rivera, H. (2006). *Practical guidelines for the education of English language learners: Research-based recommendations for instruction and academic interventions.* Houston, TX: Center on Instruction. Retrieved January 10, 2007, from *http://www.centeroninstruction.org/resources.cfm?category=ell&subcategory=research&grade_start=0&grade_end=12.*

Geert, P. V. (2007). Dynamic systems in second language learning: Some general methodological reflections. *Bilingualism: Language and Cognition, 10,* 47–49.

Genesee, F., Paradis, J., & Crago, M. (2004). *Dual language development and disorders: A handbook on bilingualism and second language learning.* Baltimore: Brookes.

Girbau, D., & Schwartz, R. G. (2007). Non-word repetition in Spanish-speaking children with specific language impairment (SLI). *International Journal of Language and Communication Disorders, 42,* 59–75.

Guthrie, J. T., & Humenick, N. M. (2004). Motivating students to read. In P. McCardle & V. Chhabra (Eds.), *The voice of evidence in reading research* (pp. 329–354). Mahwah, NJ: Erlbaum.

Hart, B., & Risley, T. R. (1995). *Meaningful differences in the everyday experience of young children.* Baltimore: Brookes.

Kohnert, K., & Windsor, J. (2004). The search for common ground: Part II. Nonlinguistic performance by linguistically diverse learners. *Journal of Speech, Language, and Hearing Research, 47,* 891–903.

Leonard, L. B., Ellis Weismer, S., Miller, C. A., Francis, D. J., Tomblin, J. B., & Kail, R. V. (2007). Speed of processing, working memory and language impairment in children. *Journal of Speech, Language, and Hearing Research, 50,* 408–428.

Lindholm-Leary, K. J. (2001). *Dual language education.* Avon, UK: Multilingual Matters.

Locke, A., Ginsberg, J., & Peers, I. (2002). Development and disadvantage: Implications for the early years and beyond. *International Journal of Language and Communication Disorders, 37*(1), 3–15.

Mayberry, R. I., & Lock, E. (2003). Age constraints on first versus second language acquisition: Evidence for linguistic plasticity and epigenesis. *Brain and Language, 87,* 369–384.

Miller, J. F., Heilmann, J., Nockerts, A., Iglesias, A., Fabiano, L., & Francis, D. J. (2006). Oral language and reading in bilingual children. *Learning Disabilities Research and Practice, 21*(1), 30–43.

Miller, L., Gillam, R. B., & Peña, E. D. (2001). *Dynamic assessment and intervention: Improving children's narrative abilities.* Austin, TX: PRO-ED.

National Virtual Translation Center. (2006). *Language learning difficulty for English speakers.* Retrieved November, 25, 2008, from *www.nvtc.gov/lotw/months/november/learningExpectations.html.*

Nelson, K., & Arkenberg, M. E. (2008). Language and reading development reflects dynamic mixes of learning conditions. In M. Mody & E. R. Silliman (Eds.), *Brain, behavior, and learning in language and reading disorders* (pp. 315–348). New York: Guilford Press.

No Child Left Behind Act of 2001, Pub. L. No. 107-110, 115.

Peña, E. D., & Quinn, R. (1992). The application of dynamic methods to language assessment: A nonbiased procedure. *Journal of Special Education, 26,* 269–281.

Proctor, C. P., Carlo, M., August, D., & Snow, C. (2005). Native Spanish-speaking children reading in English: Toward a model of comprehension. *Journal of Educational Psychology, 97,* 246–256.

Romani, C., DiBetta, A. M., Stouknida, E., & Olson, A. (2008). Lexical and non-lexical processing in developmental dyslexia: A case for different resources and different impairments. *Cognitive Neuropsychology, 25,* 798–830.

Roseberry, C. A., & Connell, P. J. (1991). The use of an invented language rule in the differentiation of normal and language-impaired Spanish-speaking children. *Journal of Speech, Language, and Hearing Research, 34,* 596–603.

Saunders, W. M., & Goldenberg, C. (1999). Effects of instructional conversations and literature logs on limited- and fluent-English-proficient students' story comprehension and thematic understanding. *Elementary School Journal, 99*(4), 277–301.

Saunders, W. M., & O'Brien, G. (2006). Oral language. In F. Genesee, K. Lindholm-Leary, W. M. Saunders, & D. Christian (Eds.), *Educating English language learners: A synthesis of research evidence* (pp. 14–63). New York: Cambridge University Press.

Selznick, B. (2007). *The invention of Hugo Cabret.* New York: Scholastic.

Snow, C. E., Porche, M. V., Tabors, P. O., & Harris, S. R. (2007). *Is literacy enough? Pathways to academic success for adolescents.* Baltimore: Brookes.

Stokes, S. F., Wong, A. M.-Y., Fletcher, P., & Leonard, L. B. (2006). Nonword repetition and sentence repetition as clinical markers of specific language impairment: The case of Cantonese. *Journal of Speech, Language, and Hearing Research, 49,* 219–236.

Swanson, L., Rosston, H., Gerber, M., & Solari, E. (2008). Influence of oral language and phonological awareness on children's bilingual reading. *Journal of School Psychology, 46*(4), 413–429.

Tabors, P. O., Snow, C. E., & Dickinson, D. K. (2001). Homes and schools together: Supporting language and literacy development. In D. K. Dickinson & P. O. Tabors (Eds.), *Beginning literacy with language: Young children at home and school* (pp. 313–334). Baltimore: Brookes.

Thomas, W. P., & Collier, V. P. (2002). *A national study of school effectiveness for language minority students' long-term academic achievement.* Santa Cruz, CA: Center for Research on Education, Diversity, and Excellence.

Wong Fillmore, L. (1983). The language learner as an individual: Implications of research on individual differences for the ESL teacher. In M. Clarke & J. Handscombe (Eds.), *On TESOL '82: Pacific perspectives on language learning and teaching* (pp. 157–173). Washington, DC: Teachers of English to Speakers of Other Languages.

10

Implications for Assessment and Instruction

Alison L. Bailey

FOCUS POINTS

- Different kinds of language assessment should be designed to cover the variety of purposes they serve in school.

- Continued weaknesses in the technical quality of assessments impact state systems of English language learner language assessment as a whole.

- The dearth of information on the empirical basis of academic language for assessment development continues to have consequences for the validity and effectiveness of assessment not only in the area of language assessment but in content-area assessment as well.

- Operational definitions of social and academic language, based on authentic usage in school, are already impacting new language assessments.

- Formative assessment is poised to play a major role in linking assessment to instruction.

CHAPTER PURPOSE

We hear a lot about assessment overrunning class time and taking away the teacher's ability to cover content, but not all assessment need be viewed this way. Indeed *formative assessment of the language development of English language learners (ELLs) should take place all the time,*

222

every minute of every day, by every teacher who teaches these students reading, mathematics, science, and American history. Without continual up-to-date information on a student's language needs and abilities, teachers will not be able to teach either language or content material effectively. Teaching with a dual emphasis on content instruction and assessment, including language and literacy assessment, can help form critically needed knowledge about students' learning so that teachers can best instruct them. While particularly true for teachers of English as a second language (ESL), it can become important for any teacher at a time when students can exit ELL programming without the requisite proficiency to successfully participate in all aspects of their U.S. schooling experience. This premature dismissal from ELL programming can be due to a mismatch between the lower language demands of English language proficiency tests and the more challenging language demands of classroom texts, teacher talk, and academic achievement tests. An English language proficiency test may "say" a student is ready to learn in an environment without additional support for English, but teachers need to know if this is a valid description of their own students and what they can do if it is not.

The main purpose of this chapter is to provide a detailed overview of current language assessment practices with ELL students. The chapter exemplifies concerns found in every part of the ELL language assessment system—from a family's initial encounter with a home language survey, to the neglect of classroom-level assessment of student learning along the way, to a student's final exit from ELL programming and an absence of language support monitoring beyond this point.

The chapter also focuses on strategies that promote language teaching and learning. Assessment and instruction are often treated as separate endeavors by educators and researchers. However, this chapter demonstrates that assessment and instruction can be brought closer together. Throughout the chapter there is an emphasis on where the field of education can work to improve the system of English language and literacy assessment for ELL students.

REVIEW OF RESEARCH AND THEORY

Language Assessment of ELL Students

The current focus for assessment of English language development or proficiency (ELD/P) is on the identification, placement, and reclassification of K–12 students who arrive at school with limited proficiency in English

(Garcia, McKoon, & August, 2006).[1] However, this purview leaves out a sorely needed additional focus on the use of language assessment for instructional purposes. The oral language and literacy skills of ELL students require continual monitoring throughout the school year in order for a teacher to adapt or modify instruction to students' ever-changing needs. Therefore, classroom-level assessments, such as benchmark assessment, formative assessment, and performance assessment, are also added to our discussion of the uses of ELD/P assessment suggested by Garcia and colleagues.

Figure 10.1 illustrates both the purpose and the typical sequence of ELD/P assessments encountered by ELL students in the U.S. schooling system. From this schema we see that the very first "measure" used by school personnel of a student's English language knowledge is the student's exposure to English in the home environment, as reported in a Home Language Survey (HLS). Everything in the ELL language assessment system initially hangs on the parent responses to this survey. Given how critical this piece of the assessment system can be, we return to it in a later section.

Once a determination is made that a new student has been exposed to a language other than English, identification as either a limited English proficient (LEP) or an initial fluent English proficient (I-FEP) student is carried out using a standardized (i.e., norm-referenced) or standards-based (i.e., criterion-referenced) assessment. This assessment may in fact be the same test that is given for placement decision making and annually for monitoring progress. Such usage may result in students being tested

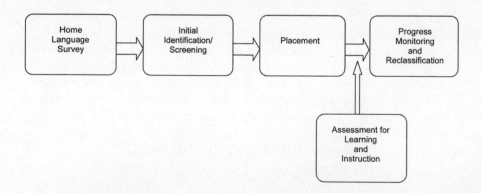

FIGURE 10.1. Language assessments arrayed by purpose and typical sequence encountered by ELL students in the U.S. schooling system.

twice in one school year with the same instrument—once at intake for identification and again during the annual assessment window later in the year. Some ELD/P assessments use different forms only across grade spans, not within them. This can mean repeat use of the same test form with students in their first year of U.S. schooling. Consequently, given just a few months' interval between their first and second administrations of the assessment, students may easily remember items. However, in some states, initial identification may take the form of a shorter screening test, and based on these results a student will be tested further as necessary. For example, the 22 states in the World-Class Instructional Design and Assessment (WIDA) consortium can use the WIDA-ACCESS Placement Test (W-APT) screening test that is the companion to the Assessing Comprehension and Communication in English State-to-State for English Language Learners (ACCESS for ELLs) ELP assessment.[2] This avoids the test–retest biases of using just one test form, as well as cuts down on the time required to establish whether a student has I-FEP status.

The same set of results from the initial identification of a student is also often used for the student's placement in an instructional program. For example, in the case of an older Spanish-speaking student who knows how to read and write in her primary language, but whose ELP assessment results suggest she has yet to become proficient in English literacy, it might be sensible to place her in a transitional bilingual education (TBE) program if available, rather than into a structured English immersion program. In the bilingual instructional setting, she will have the opportunity to transfer her preexisting literacy skills to English. If guided by strategic teaching, she would be able to capitalize on her metalinguistic knowledge in Spanish of such things as the rules for word derivation and Spanish–English cognates (e.g., *observer* [verb]: *observación* [noun], *observation*; *solas* [adjective]: *soledad* [noun], *solitude*).

However, given that most standards-based or standardized assessments are actually a sampling of the different language domains (i.e., measuring a little from a wide array of skills), they are unlikely to yield sufficiently detailed information to usefully make the finer-grained decisions related to classroom instruction. For example, the teacher of the student who is placed in the TBE program on the basis of her initial identification assessment cannot use the information from that assessment to know with any exactitude whether this student has proficiency with any one particular language or literacy skill (including the level of her knowledge of word derivation).

Figure 10.1 therefore makes clear that following the placement of students, there is a critical need to assess English language and literacy development at the classroom level. This process includes benchmark assessments, often provided by districts or accompanying specific ELD curricula; formative assessment, which can be as varied as the use of student self-assessments or teacher observation of student interactions; and performance assessments, wherein students are taught new concepts or a new skill and given a task to complete. Finally, annual progress monitoring is mandated by federal law under Title III of the No Child Left Behind Act (NCLB; 2001). This monitoring must use an assessment that is aligned with state standards for ELD/P; in some states, this will be the same instrument that was used for identification and placement. Many assessments currently used in the area of ELD are not necessarily designed to measure progress in English acquisition—yet, according to Garcia and colleagues (2006), that is often their intended purpose, very likely due to the increased pressure to provide progress information for state and federal accountability. Typically, a student's performance on this assessment can be used alone or with other criteria for determining reclassification, or what is also commonly referred to as *redesignation to fluent English proficient* (R-FEP) status. Other criteria might include a desired threshold on student performance for concurrent content-area assessments (e.g., English language arts), teacher reports, and parent consultation (see Wolf et al., 2008, for details of current state policies).

What is apparent from this description of assessment purposes is the frequent use of just one assessment to cover all purposes. No single assessment can be expected to measure ELD/P just as well in each of the different circumstances. At the very least, empirical evidence is still needed to establish whether test interpretations can be equally meaningful (i.e., valid) when the same test is used for the purposes of identification, placement, and progress monitoring. In particular, there are consequences for failing to develop a test that is suited to the high-stakes decision of reclassification. R-FEP status signals exit from ELL programming, but students may not be ready to participate fully in their classrooms if they are found proficient on a test that does not measure the right kinds of English: that is, all the language demands they encounter in school.

The Home Language Survey: Weakest Link in the ELL Assessment System?

Most often states use an HLS that commonly asks parents to state which language(s) a child speaks and whether the family speaks English in the home (e.g., Kindler, 2002). Wolf and colleagues (2008) report that currently 47 of the U.S. states and the District of Columbia use an HLS.

On the basis of such a brief survey, states often make the very first high-stakes decision in a young child's school career—the decision whether to assess the child's ELP with the state ELD/P identification assessment. In some states the HLS is itself the identification instrument. (For example, the Pennsylvania Department of Education uses an HLS to establish primary or home language other than English [PHLOTE] status of students by asking parents to report the student's first language, any languages the student speaks other than English, languages spoken in the home, and whether the student has spent any prior 3-year period in a U.S. school.)

There is great potential for over- and underidentifying new students' need for either ELD services (in some states) or further assessment (in other states) based upon current survey responses. Anecdotal information from individual schools and state personnel indicates that the quality of the data may be suspect on these short surveys, as parents may misinterpret questions about language use in the home (e.g., some parents report all foreign languages they and their child know, rather than the language spoken at home to the child), or report proficiency only in the parent's primary language, possibly due to sense of cultural pride. Yet others may report that their child is exposed only to English, when, in fact, the family uses another language in the home, for fear of receiving the low-quality schooling frequently associated with ELL status. Moreover, such a survey would appear wholly inadequate in providing teachers with information about the extent and nature of a child's exposure to the kinds of English needed in school.

The exposure children get to both conceptual content and the formal language associated with school during the preschool years has been found critical for later academic success (e.g., Hart & Risley, 1995; National Institute of Child and Human Development, 2000). Attempts by parents or other caregivers to promote language exposure can help build key linguistic abilities necessary for classroom participation and learning. For example, parents may solicit personal oral narratives or storybook recall from their children in either the dominant language or English. If parents are not themselves speakers of English, they may find English-speaking playmates for their children or they may also enroll their children in English-based recreational activities and programs with the deliberate intention of fostering English development before the formal school years.

Information from an enhanced HLS has indeed been used to predict students' later literacy outcomes (Reese & Goldenberg, 2008). Parents of ELL kindergarten students were asked a short series of questions about oral language and reading practices in English and in Spanish with their children. Language-specific questions about both oral language and literacy practices are important; Reese and Goldenberg (2008) found that child literacy outcomes in first grade in Spanish and English were related to parents' reports of reading to their children for both languages. Interestingly, the questions that simply asked generically about reading (i.e., whether they read to their children irrespective of language) did not predict reading outcomes in either language. Furthermore, the enhanced HLS predicted oral language outcomes even more strongly (C. Goldenberg, personal communication, February 24, 2009).

The field of education needs to work with states to create an enhanced HLS that improves the quality of the data collected about students' exposure to English and other languages before the start of formal schooling, or, for older students, during out-of-school contexts. An enhanced survey could, at the very least, contain questions about the types of family activities that research has shown promote oral language and literacy in all the languages to which a child is exposed (see Reese & Goldenberg, Chapter 11, this volume). We may even need instruments that go beyond such a survey; for example, a protocol for home visits or parental interviews may yield more extensive and accurate information or could be used to validate questions on an enhanced survey. Until such efforts are made and empirically validated, the entire system of assessment for gauging the language and literacy abilities of ELL students will be called into question. Such an enhanced HLS may also better enable teachers to make initial placement decisions based on student language exposure and needs, including the need for further diagnostic testing.

English Language and Literacy Development: Implications for Assessment

The acquisition of oral English (i.e., listening comprehension and speaking skills) is an important development in its own right, but oral language also has close ties to print-based skills such as decoding, word recognition, reading comprehension, and writing skills, making it an important precursor and predictor of literacy outcomes for both native English speakers and ELL students alike (see Kohnert & Pham, Chapter 2, and August, Goldenberg, Saunders, & Dressler, Chapter 12, this volume; see also Hiebert & Kamil, 2005, for reviews of research in these areas). However, the English used in content-specific contexts—such as in the oral discourse of math or science classes and in math and science textbooks, for that matter—can be especially challenging for English learners (e.g., Dobb, 2005; Spanos, 1989) because it differs from everyday conversation or social language in that it may contain technical vocabulary and use of less common phrasing and discourse features. This "academic language" that ELL students must also acquire is the focus of the next section of this chapter.

Oral language developments and the links between oral language and literacy give rise to implications for the choice of assessment content. Research suggests that much of the sequence involved in reading development in ELL students is comparable to that of native-speaking students, but that the noticeable exceptions in some skill areas (e.g., syntax) need to be taken into account in test construction. Moreover, not all language skills can be easily assessed in all test formats (e.g., classroom discourse abilities do not lend themselves to large-scale, paper–pencil assessment). To date, there is no ELD/P assessment whose content relies predominantly on empirical research of the development of oral language and literacy skills in ELLs. Without such longitudinal studies of L2 and literacy acquisition, it is difficult to set reasonable learning goals or expectations for test performances, although two of the annual measurable achievement objectives (AMAOs) set by each state for ELL student progress and attainment of proficiency in English and required by NCLB would make this appear otherwise.

Defining Academic Language and Building an Empirical Basis for Assessment

This section deals with the construct of academic language, especially how it has been defined by different educators and researchers, and offers some key characteristics of academic language identified in studies of classroom interactions and curricular materials. Key implications of these characteristics for assessment are then discussed.

Academic English is most typically thought of as a register of the language. A *register* is a variety of the language used in a specific context. Choice of certain words, grammatical features, and the organization of discourse of both oral and print forms become hallmarks of a register. The hallmarks of academic language are those that students will need to acquire, most often in school, for schoolwork and school success.

Academic language has been a key focus in the recent assessment of ELL students[3] and is now thought to be a major gatekeeper of academic achievement. This was not always the case. Until the past decade assessments of the language skills of ELL students had typically not included academic language in their definitions of the test construct, if construct definitions were mentioned at all. The focus was more on the social language register (e.g., the language needed to express relations between individuals). With the shift to holding states accountable for student ELP, as well as for reaching proficiency in the English language arts, math, and science areas, focus has turned to the language demands associated with instruction and learning—that is, the academic language register. In preparing students for college-level study, for example, this has been conceptualized in part as all-purpose academic words that can be found in a corpus of texts representing different academic disciplines (e.g., art, commerce, law, science) (Coxhead, 2000).

Existing ELD assessments were wholly inadequate as indicators of students' language competencies in the academic arena, with ELD assessment scores unrelated to English language arts (ELA) and other achievement outcomes, suggesting a large mismatch between the language tested and the language being used on content tests and in the classroom (Butler, Stevens, & Castellon, 2007). This mismatch has posed a large problem for determining whether (1) students are ready for reclassification to R-FEP status and participation in mainstream content-areas classes, and (2) their scores on content-area assessments are valid indictors of their content knowledge or are stymied by their lack of English language abilities.

Unfortunately, the construct of academic language has become fraught with contention. Can it be adequately defined, specified, and, consequently, measured and taught? Some scholars question whether academic language is even necessary for succeeding in school. Still others have asked whether there is one academic language. Hyland and Tse (2007), for example, have questioned the utility of teaching an all-purpose or general academic vocabulary, because academic language seems to be so content-specific, especially in the higher grades and in college. They question whether there is sufficient language cutting across the content areas to make the notion of general academic language useful.

Academic language appears to mean different things to different people. In the next section, definitions of academic language, offered by practitioners in the field of ELL education, are analyzed to determine the extent of conceptual differences about what academic language represents and to attempt a new, comprehensive synthesis.

Definitions of Academic Language from the Field

Analyses of the definitions of academic language offered by practitioners provide us with even greater insight into the meaning of the construct as it is currently understood by those who typically teach or supervise the teachers of ELL students. During a recent "webinar" on the topic of formative assessment and ELL students, Bailey asked participants whether they were familiar with the term *academic English,* and if so, to reflect on their own definitions of it.[4] Of the webinar respondents, 118 then went on to post definitions of academic English. Using "open coding" of the content of these written definitions, 14 main themes could be identified.[5] Table 10.1 provides a list of the 14 themes with their substantive labels, the number of definitions that included a particular theme, and examples of the themes in the definitions.

The 14 themes can be further categorized thusly:

1. *Degree of specificity.* Academic English can be simply defined as school language; this notion comprised the entire definition for seven of the respondents (theme 1). Fifty-six definitions more specifically tied academic English to instruction and aspects of the school curriculum (i.e., classes, textbooks, tests, and other materials) (theme 2).

2. *Scope of academic English.* Twenty-six definitions narrowed the scope of academic English to just the content-specific uses of language (theme 3). In direct contrast, just four definitions defined academic English from a domain-general perspective as language that cuts across all content areas (theme 4). Related to this theme was a definition by four respondents of academic English as the language used to more broadly communicate or understand directions and procedures in the school setting (theme 5). A further 10 definitions made explicit the distinction between content-specific and domain-general academic English and included both types of language usage in the definition (theme 6).

3. *Language modalities or domains.* Ten of the definitions singled out written language as the modality of academic English (theme 7).

4. *Language skills.* Language skills mentioned in the definitions included vocabulary-only (theme 8), which occurred in 23 definitions. However, 16 definitions included a wider range of language skills (theme 9).

5. *Degree of linguistic formality.* Greater linguistic formality was given as a defining characteristic of academic English in 12 of the definitions (theme 10).

6. *Success in and out of school.* Academic English is explicitly tied to academic success in 14 of the definitions (theme 11). Interestingly, a further 8 definitions expanded the notion of success to include outside/beyond school contexts (theme 12).

TABLE 10.1. Themes Identifiable in Academic Language Definitions

Theme	Number	Examples from the definitions
1. School language	7	"The language of school"; "English used in school"; "The language that is required in the school setting."
2. Language of instruction and curricular materials	56	"Language that is used in an academic setting, including the language of tests, textbooks, and classroom discourse"; "Language that is used for accessing and participating in content instruction in the classroom"; "Academic language is the language of texts and/or the language of instruction."
3. Content-specific uses of language	26	"Academic language allows for the understanding of specific content knowledge of academic subjects"; "The technical language of academic content disciplines"; "Language specific to curricular content areas."
4. Domain-general language	4	"This is the language of school that transcends content areas"; "Academic language is comprised of the words and phrases that are necessary to comprehend the subject and are not necessarily subject specific."
5. Communicate in broader school setting	4	"It is needed to successfully navigate school"; "[for] directions, rules for turning and talking."
6. Combined domain-general and specific	10	"The content words used to correctly describe concepts in content areas and in directions or explanations that teachers give to students when verbalizing lesson objectives."
7. Written language only	10	"English required by student to understand the language used in books"; "Language of written text"; "Words and phrases that are beyond our conversational language and found in higher-level texts."
8. Vocabulary only	23	"Academic language refers to the ability to understand words that are used in academic settings"; "The vocabulary associated with academic school courses"; "Words used in different content areas in school."
9. Array of language skills	16	"Academic English is the vocabulary, grammatical structures, and semantics necessary for academic success in the content areas."
10. Formal language	12	"Academic language refers to content words, process words, and language structures that are used in more formalized registers"; "Formal register—language of content area textbooks."

(continued)

TABLE 10.1. (*continued*)

Theme	Number	Examples from the definitions
11. Tied to academic success	14	"Language students need to be academically successful"; "Language that includes vocabulary and syntax required for academic success."
12. Tied to success outside/beyond school	8	"The language of power," "of professional settings," "of work situations," "of many business and government transactions."
13. Ready-made definitions	6	Academic English is "Cognitive academic language proficiency (CALP; Cummins, J., 1979)"; "Tier 1 is those words that are useful to know across disciplines, e.g., *compare–contrast*. Tier 3 words are those words that are discipline specific, e.g., *equator*."
14. What academic language is not	17	"It is a formal language rather than street language or what is used at home with family"; "It would not be encountered in a setting that is just social"; "Academic language is the language of school, as opposed to BICS [basic interpersonal communicative skills]."

Note. N = 118.

7. *Type of definition.* The form that several definitions took is also noteworthy. Six of the definitions were "ready-made," in that the respondents provided a definition of academic language as cognitive academic language proficiency (CALP), referring explicitly or implicitly to the work of Cummins (1979), or implicitly referring to the work of Beck, McKeown, and Kucan (2002), citing different "tiers" of utility for words: Tier 1 words are those high-frequency words commonly encountered in everyday speech; Tier 2 words are those that occur less frequently and are most often encountered in texts; and Tier 3 words are terms specialized to a specific domain (theme 13). Interestingly, 17 respondents chose to define academic English by what it is not; that is, by giving contrasting characteristics (theme 14). These respondents described academic English as being different from conversational or "everyday" English—the basic interpersonal communicative skills (BICS) contrast with CALP (Cummins, 1979).

Apparent in the wide variety of themes across the 118 definitions is the lack of a dominant definition of academic English. The most widespread theme, included in 47% of definitions, focused on a single situational characteristic of academic language—the language used in an instructional setting and the curricular materials that support instruction. The second most favored theme, included in 22% of the definitions, provided a narrower situational definition of academic language—the content-specific usage of language. This limits the scope of the definition to language that is specialized to a content area such as math or science (e.g., *simultaneous equation, respiration,* X *is greater than* Y), rather than include the language that might be shared across these content areas (e.g., *explain, predict, according to*), or even outside the context of teaching and learning content material but nevertheless occurring within a school setting (e.g., listening to classroom management directions from a teacher, conducting a formal conversation with the principal). One remaining sizable theme, included in 19% of the definitions, limited academic language to word usage only—and yet grammatical structures (e.g., nominalization of verb forms, passive voice) and discourse-level features that are used to organize language beyond the level of the sentence (e.g., expository or narrative genres, discourse connectors such as *however, moreover, first,* and language functions such as explanations, descriptions, comparisons) are linguistic features also characteristic of academic usage.

Different respondents had different pieces of the definition, but few had definitions that included more than two of the defining characteristics identified above. A major goal of the language and education fields should be to bring different pieces of the definition together into a coherent whole. Based on the definitions of these respondents, who are actively engaged in the education of ELL students, the following synthesis is offered as a comprehensive, practice-based definition of academic English:

> Academic English is a formal register of English used in school settings for instructional and procedural/navigational purposes that includes the vocabulary, syntax, and discourse associated with classroom talk, textbooks, tests, and other curricular materials. Academic English includes the language features that may cut across disciplines (e.g., common academic language functions and general academic vocabulary), as well as the language features specific to individual content areas (e.g., technical vocabulary). Academic English encompasses all four modalities of language (i.e., speaking, listening, reading, and writing) and may need explicit instruction, especially when it is less familiar to students whose main exposure to English has been the conversational or social English acquired outside the school setting. Academic language is required for successful academic achievement, and is likely to be as necessary for success outside and/or beyond school in the professional and business worlds students will encounter.

This definition fits well with observations of authentic classroom practices of academic English. In the following, for example, it is possible to match key aspects of the comprehensive definition with observations of science teaching in Mrs. Troy's fourth-grade classroom (Martinez, Bailey, Kerr, Huang, & Beauregard, 2009).[6] Two students of the class of 30 were identified as ELL students, but no separate treatment of these students was observed, and Mrs. Troy reported that she made no distinctions in her teaching practices for ELL and non-ELL students. Her universal use of ELL instructional strategies would perhaps compensate for this lack of distinction (e.g., scaffolding understanding of English by using graphics and providing many opportunities for student–teacher interactions that encouraged elaborated responses).

Mrs. Troy taught the properties of helium, carbon, and hydrogen atoms during one observation and the effects of electrically charged objects during a second. A variety of resources, including science books, worksheets, kits, magazines (e.g., *National Geographic*), computer and video resources, concept posters, and science vocabulary charts, were used or available for use and required skills in listening, speaking, reading, and writing. Classroom activities also required skills across the four language modalities, including teacher-directed instruction, hands-on activities (i.e., making models to represent the atoms), and small-group discussion. The lesson culminated in the completion of individual worksheets. During these science classes, Mrs. Troy emphasized understanding of science concepts, acquisition of basic science facts and background knowledge, conducting inquiries, and developing students' interest in science. She frequently used explicit academic English instructional strategies, particularly scaffolding techniques such as modeling responses to her questions to make her expectations for a formal register and general academic vocabulary explicit (e.g., "My hypothesis is ... and this is why I think so"). During both observations, she emphasized the development of student abilities in listening and reading comprehension skills for science—that is, content-specific uses of language. Across the two observations she stressed the importance of students being able to convey basic facts, as well as to explain and justify scientific ideas using evidence. Indeed, language was frequently needed for higher-order thinking skills such as prediction, inference making, causal reasoning, and hypothesis generation. Not surprisingly, this classroom is found in a school that has far exceeded expectations set for it by the state under NCLB.

It is important to know what teachers are thinking when they conceive of academic language so that we can target curricular materials and professional development correspondingly, but we also need empirical research that can closely describe what is happening in classrooms such as that of Mrs. Troy. This is necessary so that we can more concretely characterize academic English features for creating unambiguous test specifications and ultimately more effective research-based ELD/P assessments.

Operationalizing Academic English

Obviously, much is riding on our ability to operationalize academic language for testing purposes. But academic language is literally a moving target. There is an interaction between a student and the language itself that makes every academic language situation unique. The place and timing of students' first exposure to English, the acquisition context (i.e., in school vs. out of school), the point at which students began their schooling in the United States, whether they are literate in their first language, the modality of the academic language (i.e., oral or print language)—all will be different for different students. For example, the word *blizzard* may constitute everyday language to a student living in the Northeastern United States, but for many other students this will be a term learned and used in an academic context. Circumstance will largely determine whether the context of acquisition is considered academic or not for any given student.

This point was made salient in the work of the Academic English Language Proficiency (AELP) project at the national Center for Research on Evaluation, Standards, and Student Testing (CRESST). My colleagues and I developed tasks of academic language knowledge using texts from mathematics, science, and social studies. Part of the study involved cognitive protocols in which fourth- to fifth-grade students (both ELL and native English speaking) were asked to think aloud as they completed the tasks and then to retrospectively critique the tasks. Different tasks were difficult for different students, and it largely came down to the extent of their prior knowledge of the topic area and their familiarity with the vocabulary in specific texts (Bailey, Huang, Shin, Farnsworth, & Butler, 2006).

This view of academic language puts the construct on a "situational" continuum—a matter of degree for what is considered academic language and what is everyday or social language due to the circumstance or context in which it is used. This is not a simple developmental continuum, however; whereas for some students academic language may build on prior social language knowledge, still others learn academic language before they learn social uses of English—to which some later arriving ELL and college-level ESL students can attest. For test development purposes, we need to operationalize academic language in a way that captures the preponderance of circumstances, not the specifics of any one student's encounter. It is especially important to avoid overreliance on what would constitute early encounters with the basics of the language.

We see how complex a process language development can be for students when taking into account all the features by which academic language can be defined. In prior work, Bailey identified seven defining features that have appeared in much of the literature discussing academic language (see Bailey & Heritage, 2008a). These features include purpose of language usage, degree of formality, context of use, context of acquisition, modality or domain (e.g., listening, speaking, reading, and writing), typical teacher expectations, and typical grade-level expectations. Each can be characterized differently by whether language is being used in a social context or in academic contexts—the instructional context during which curriculum content is being taught and the context of navigating school more broadly, such as student interactions with teachers and peers that are related to classroom management.

Many of the seven features of academic language and the three contexts echo different pieces of the definitions offered by the practitioners above (e.g., formality, modalities). Moreover, it is interesting to examine different ELD/P assessments that are now available to see what aspects of academic language they also include. For instance, the Stanford English Language Proficiency (SELP) test, published by Pearson, has been modified by some states for their own purposes. This assessment does not have any reading and writing modality for social language, so reading and writing are being assessed only in contexts equivalent to the school navigational and instructional language contexts. The English Language Development Assessment (ELDA) developed by the Council for Chief State Schools Officers (CCSSO) consortium does not appear to have social language in their construct definition of ELD/P. The focus, rather, is on the social environment of school, which would be equivalent to the school navigational language context and on the language used during instruction. The ACCESS for ELLS assessment by WIDA has both social and instructional (school navigational) language under a single strand and separate strands for the language associated with each of the content areas (i.e., English language arts, math, science, and social studies) (see Gottlieb, Cranley, & Oliver, 2007, for further details).

With all these factors to be taken into account, this view of academic English is dynamic; that is, it is ever-changing and developing as a student's knowledge of English develops. Unfortunately, this view of academic language does not lend itself in all its facets to being easily assessed using a traditional, static paper-and-pencil test.

For test development purposes we cannot invoke exceptions like the precocious use of *blizzard* as an everyday word for a student in the Northeast. It would be the preponderance of circumstances, if that is knowable. Our speculations can then be more systematically guided by the word lists from linguistic corpora and the linguistic analysis of textbook vocabulary (e.g., Bailey, Butler, Stevens, & Lord, 2007), as well as the state content standards and teacher judgments. A word can be in more than one category based on how it functions in the different contexts. That is, how a word functions in one context is not dependent on how it functions in another context. So ultimately a word may show up on a list of everyday words (e.g., *product* as a natural or manufactured item for retail) as well as on lists of general (e.g., *product* as synonymous with *result*) and specialized academic words (e.g., *product* as a quantity obtained as a result of multiplying).

Implications for Assessment Development

Given that under this view, academic language is context dependent and ever-changing as a student's English language develops, it might be useful to think in terms of differentiated assessment, the way we differentiate instruction. At the classroom level, at least, teachers can individualize and target the kinds of academic language that they need to assess, as the example from a kindergarten science classroom illustrates below. However, there are still important ramifications for test validity. There is a lot of variation in terms of children's opportunity to learn academic language. Students likely receive different amounts of exposure to academic language; how valid can an assessment be when students have not had comparable opportunities to acquire academic English (Martinez et al., 2009)? Moreover, we do not have any information about how social language and academic English develop in native English speakers, but we need to establish these norms so that we do not develop tests that are too challenging even for a native English-speaking student.

BEST PRACTICES

Relating Language Assessment to Instruction

Instructional programs focused solely on reading at the expense of ELD in speaking, listening, and writing have been found to be insufficient to support ELL students' academic success (Callahan, 2006). Thus, the need to support the instruction of both oral language and print-based skills with an array of well-designed and validated measures of the kinds of English ELL students encounter in school is even more pressing. If we can create consensus around the academic English construct and establish longitudinal trajectories of ELD, then learning progressions of ELD/P can be made explicit. This method would allow for some continuity between the different parts of the ELL language assessment system. Specifically, the summative standardized or standards-based assessments used for identification, placement, and progress can be connected to the classroom-based assessments (i.e., formative assessment, benchmark assessments) via underlying learning progressions. Currently, these assessments are developed in isolation. But if we can shift to an underlying well-articulated academic language construct, we might be able to put in place an approach to assessment that is systematic as well as to forge closer ties with instructional practice as well.

A coherent assessment approach will still not be very efficient unless we pay equal attention to the instructional component. In the area of vocabulary, especially, there have been a number of new approaches to academic language instruction that are based on empirical research. For example, Word Generation, a schoolwide program aimed at middle students, and the Vocabulary Improvement Project at the upper-elementary grades offer approaches to enhancing the academic vocabulary of both ELL and native English-speaking students alike.[7] Using the features of written academic language identified by Bailey and colleagues (2007), Wilkinson and Silliman (2008) show how teachers might choose to analyze the linguistic features of both the texts students read and the texts students produce for what these reveal about student learning of academic language features at the word, sentence, and discourse levels. Clearly, these approaches can be only as successful as the level of knowledge of the teachers who implement them. Research on teacher knowledge of academic vocabulary, at least, suggests a critical professional development need in this area, with teachers currently unable to characterize why certain vocabulary might be challenging for their ELL students (Chang, 2009).

Figure 10.2 represents the possibility of a closer integration of ELD/P assessment with ELD and content instruction. The common view of assessment and instruction as two independent endeavors is represented by the opposite-pointing arrows at the top of Figure 10.2. At the most extreme, summative assessments of ELD/P and the content areas are far removed from day-to-day instruction in ELD and the content areas. Now

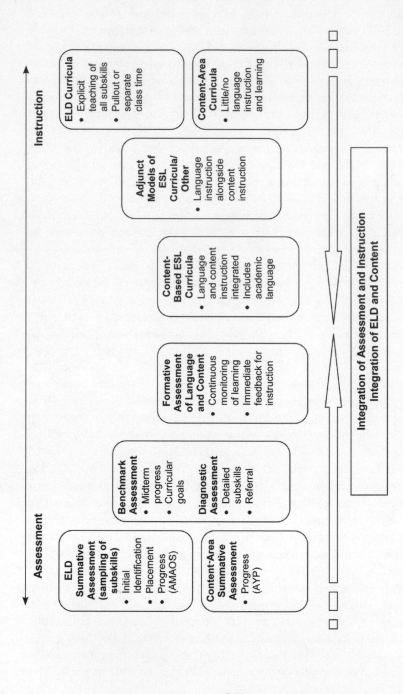

FIGURE 10.2. Linking assessment types to instructional options for ELL students. ELD, English language development; AYP, adequate yearly progress; ESL, English as a second language; AMAOS, annual measurable achievement objectives.

tied to state standards, large-scale summative assessments sample a selection of subskills, so now we often have breadth at the loss of depth of information. Summative assessments are used for calculating progress in ELD/P for AMAOs 1 and 2, and, in the content areas, for reporting adequate yearly progress (AYP). Benchmark and diagnostic assessments bring us closer to the actual instructional materials students encounter, with benchmark assessments measuring midterm progress or the goals of a specific curriculum, and diagnostic assessment giving detailed information on subskills for use in possible referral to special education services.

The closest integration of English assessment with instruction is represented by the converging arrows along the bottom of Figure 10.2, with formative assessment and content-based ESL meeting in the middle. Formative assessment itself is an approach to eliciting evidence about student learning. It provides feedback to teachers and students about the student's language learning. Teachers can then use feedback to adjust their instruction and language learning strategies in real time. Ideally, formative assessment actively involves students in their own language learning by providing them with explicit learning goals and success criteria. The information that formative assessment yields can be documented and collated over time to serve a summative purpose at the classroom level. An extended example of this approach and these principles is provided below.

Content-based ESL curricula stand in contrast to the isolated teaching of content, with content-area teachers providing little or no support for language learning, and with pullout ELD classes, although explicitly teaching the full range of English language skills, taking students away from content class time and the opportunity for authentic academic English exposure. Adjunct models of ESL offer content instruction from a content-area teacher working alongside an ESL instructor. ELD and content areas are integrated most closely when they use specially designed academic instruction in English or content-based ESL approaches that use the authentic context of content-area instruction in math, science, social studies, and English language arts in which to teach English language skills, including general and content-specific academic English.

Example of Formative Assessment of ELD during Science Instruction

The following excerpt was recreated from observational field notes taken at the Para Los Niños Charter Elementary School in downtown Los Angeles as part of a project designed to characterize academic language at the prekindergarten and kindergarten levels. The goal of this work was to help teachers build strategies that would facilitate the transition of young students from one scholastic setting to the next. In this instance, the kindergartners are Spanish primary language students who have been receiving English language exposure and instruction through their math and science classes. This example is taken from a science lesson, but the principles outlined below can easily be generalized to other content areas.

> The kindergarteners have been working on understanding the seasons of the year. On this day the teacher sends children to work in pairs at various activities she has planned to construct trees representing the months of the year. The students immediately get to work. They are eager to make the trees. The children talk among themselves excitedly, primarily in English, planning how they will make their trees and figuring out who will do what. The teacher comes by to check on the students' progress.

This excerpt serves as a starting point to illustrate how instruction and assessment can be seamlessly integrated along with ELD and science instruction—ideas that were laid out in Figure 10.2. The focus is on three key aspects: science concept-building exchanges, language-building exchanges, and formative assessment conducted during each.

1. *Concept-building exchanges.* By pointing out differences between children's work, the teacher can facilitate a dialogue between students and highlight aspects of the science concept that are most important. For example, the teacher could say, "José and Danny, I notice that the trees you made look very different! What season was each of you trying to represent? Why do your trees look so different?" Or, "Alex, I notice that your winter tree looks very different from Lila's. Why is that?"

2. *Language-building exchanges.* By talking with and listening to students, the teacher facilitates the acquisition of language at the vocabulary, grammar, and discourse levels:

Vocabulary. Questions such as "What do we call that season?" give children opportunities to retrieve vocabulary in ways that are more cognitively demanding than questions where the choice of vocabulary is supplied (e.g., "Is this tree in spring or summer?").

Grammar and discourse. Open-ended prompts such as "I'm so curious to hear about your work—tell me about your tree," encourage children to respond with more than just one word. Indeed, open-ended prompts should lead to elaborated responses that can also encourage dialogue between students, not only between student and teacher.

3. *Formative assessment.* By talking with and listening to students, the teacher can make a dual evaluation of their language and science learning using explicit learning goals and success criteria.

Learning goals. By setting up the activity such that children select their own materials, the teacher opens up many opportunities to simultaneously assess and scaffold children's learning by asking questions such as "What season are you representing with this tree? What materials are you planning to use? Why?"

Success criteria. Children should be able to articulate, with little prompting from the teacher, why they have chosen certain materials by explaining the aspects of the season that warrant their selection. They should be able to produce appropriate vocabulary (e.g., *sun, cold, warm, seasons, winter, summer*) and syntax (e.g., *further/ nearer than*) in their explanations.

SUMMARY OF MAIN IDEAS

This chapter focuses on the language and literacy assessment of ELL students. Language assessment is discussed with regard to issues of its purpose, English language and literacy development, and with an emphasis on defining academic language and establishing an empirical basis for assessment development. The chapter covers types of typical assessments, the roles of social and academic language in assessment, and how language assessment relates to language and content instruction.

IMPLICATIONS FOR RESEARCH, PRACTICE, AND POLICY

We are a long way from having achieved our goal of a valid assessment of academic English. There are at least five areas where efforts must be continued: (1) Teachers need to continually monitor the progress of their ELL students' language and literacy development, but they should not feel they need to do this alone. Educational administrators need to provide the necessary supports and opportunities for professional development for teachers to learn how to design and effectively use the information yielded by their own classroom assessments. (2) Relatedly, educational practitioners, such as teachers, ESL specialists, and clinicians, can most profitably work together to increase the use and usefulness of classroom assessment of English acquisition. (3) The profession may have a better sense of what academic English is, but we still need to know how it develops over time. We need longitudinal studies to do this well, of course, but in the meantime we can conduct cross-sectional studies of academic uses of language across the K–12 spectrum so that we can assess progress and ultimate attainment. (4) There will be a fine line between measuring academic language and unintentionally crossing over into measuring science or math knowledge, for example. While the results of studying academic uses of language suggest that the different content areas may differ in the use of word, sentence, and discourse features sufficiently to warrant an approach that separates academic language by content area (e.g., an approach already adopted by WIDA for ACCESS for ELLs), we also need to vigilantly avoid creating language assessments that inadvertently measure content-area knowledge by requiring math or science abilities in order to respond accurately to language test items. (5) Finally, we should not devise assessments of academic language separate from how we teach academic language in the content areas. We need a coherent and integrated approach to instruction and assessment; a greater emphasis on formative assessment that can also be collated into summative evidence of learning is offered as one such way to reach this goal.

All these efforts can go toward ensuring the validity of new language assessments. The *valid* test measures what it claims to measure and is meaningful and useful—useful to teachers teaching students, useful to a district reporting to parents and the state, and useful to a state reporting to its citizens and the federal government.

ACKNOWLEDGMENTS

I would like to thank Louise Wilkinson, Frances Butler, and Frank Ziolkowski for their comments and suggestions, and Julie Duffield at WestEd for permission to use the SchoolsMovingUp webinar data, as well as participants who kindly posted responses. I also wish to acknowledge Yiching Huang for valuable research assistance and the UCLA Center for Community Partnerships for generous funding of the UCLA/Para Los Niños Project: Closing the Academic Language Gap for English Language Learners Transitioning from Pre-Kindergarten to Kindergarten.

NOTES

1. In recent years there has been a shift from use of the term *ELD* to *ELP*. The ELP construct might be viewed as a level of proficiency analogous to the

NCLB goal of being "proficient" in content areas such as math or science, and the ELD construct as development that occurs on route to proficiency.
2. WIDA is one of the state consortia responding to the U.S. Department of Education Title III requirement for all states to develop ELP assessments linked to state ELP standards.
3. Academic English is an explicit component of the new frameworks created for states to use in order to gauge the quality of their ELD/P standards and aligned assessments (e.g., National Clearinghouse for English Language Acquisition, 2009).
4. The terms *academic English* and *academic language* are used interchangeably in this context, but one might view *academic language* as the broader construct that can encompass academic uses of a student's primary language, such as Spanish or Mandarin.
5. Of a possible 166 participants who had interactive access to the webinar (Bailey & Heritage, 2008b), 120 posted responses indicating that they were familiar with the term *academic English*, and 118 of these posted definitions of academic English. In an iterative process, once a theme was identified in a definition, all other definitions were reread to determine if the emerging theme was also present. In order to contain the number of different themes, for reporting purposes a theme needed to be mentioned in four or more definitions; thus several were unique to just one or two definitions (e.g., language characterized by its unfamiliar and less frequent words and phrases, by words that are multisyllabic, by the need to be age/grade appropriate, and by the need for explicit teaching). The 14 main themes are not mutually exclusive; a respondent's definition could include one or more themes. Consequently, the total frequency of occurrences for the themes (215) sums to more than the number of individuals posting definitions. Specifically, 50 definitions had just one identifiable theme, a further 43 contained two identifiable themes, 20 definitions had three identifiable themes, four definitions contained four identifiable themes, and the remaining definition contained five themes.
6. *Mrs. Troy* is a pseudonym.
7. Word Generation: A Middle School Academic Language Program. Strategic Education Research Partnership (*www.wordgeneration.org*) and the Vocabulary Improvement Program for English Language Learners and Their Classmates (*ies.ed.gov/ncee/wwc/reports/english_lang/vip*).

REFERENCES

Bailey, A. L., Butler, F. A., Stevens, R., & Lord, C. (2007). Further specifying the language demands of school. In A. L. Bailey (Ed.), *The language demands of school: Putting academic English to the test* (pp. 103–156). New Haven, CT: Yale University Press.
Bailey, A. L., & Heritage, M. (2008a). *Formative assessment for literacy, grades K–6: Building reading and academic language skills across the curriculum.* Thousand Oaks, CA: Corwin/Sage.
Bailey, A. L., & Heritage, M. (2008b, October 8). English learner literacy devel-

opment through formative assessment of oral language [webinar]. Available at *www.schoolsmovingup.net/cs/smu/view/e/3352.*

Bailey, A. L., Huang, B., Shin, H. W., Farnsworth, T., & Butler, F. A. (2006). *Developing academic English language proficiency prototypes for 5th grade reading: Psychometric and linguistic profiles of tasks.* Final deliverable (December) to IES Contract No. R305B960002 (Tech. Report No. 727). Los Angeles: University of California, National Center for Research on Evaluation, Standards, and Student Testing (CRESST).

Beck, I. L., McKeown, M. G., & Kucan, L. (2002). *Bringing words to life: Robust vocabulary instruction.* New York: Guilford Press.

Butler, F. A., Stevens, R., & Castellon, M. (2007). ELLS and standardized assessments: The interaction between language proficiency and performance on standardized tests. In A. L. Bailey (Ed.), *The language demands of school: Putting academic English to the test* (pp. 27–49). New Haven, CT: Yale University Press.

Callahan, R. M. (2006). The intersection of accountability and language: Can reading intervention replace English language development? *Bilingual Research Journal, 30*(1), 1–21.

Chang, S. (2009). *Teacher rationales for selection of instructional vocabulary: Views from five teachers of English language learners.* Unpublished master's thesis, University of California at Los Angeles.

Coxhead, A. (2000). A new academic word list. *TESOL Quarterly, 34*(2), 213–238.

Cummins, J. (1979). Linguistic interdependence and the educational development of bilingual children. *Review of Educational Research, 49,* 222–25l.

Dobb, F. (2005). Inquiry-based instruction for English language learners: Ten essential elements. In R. H. Audet & L. K. Jordan (Eds.), *Integrating inquiry across the curriculum* (pp. 202–226). Thousand Oaks, CA: Corwin Press.

Garcia, G., McKoon, G., & August, D. (2006). Language and literacy assessment of language-minority students. In D. August & T. Shanahan (Eds.), *Developing literacy in second-language learners* (pp. 597–624). Mahwah, NJ: Erlbaum.

Gottlieb, M., Cranley, M. E., & Oliver, A. R. (2007). *WIDA English language proficiency standards and resource guide: Pre-kindergarten through grade 12.* Madison: University of Wisconsin–Madison, WIDA Consortium.

Hart, B., & Risley, T. (1995). *Meaningful differences in the everyday experiences of young American children.* Baltimore: Brookes.

Hiebert, E. H., & Kamil, M. L. (2005). *Teaching and learning vocabulary: Bringing research to practice.* Mahwah, NJ: Erlbaum.

Hyland, K., & Tse, P. (2007). Is there an academic language? *TESOL Quarterly, 41*(2), 235–253.

Kindler, A. (2002). *Survey of the states' limited English proficient students and available educational programs and services: 2000–2001 Summary report.* Washington, DC: National Clearinghouse for English Language Acquisition.

Martinez, J.-F., Bailey, A. L., Kerr D., Huang B. H.-H., & Beauregard S. (2009). *Measuring opportunity to learn and academic language exposure for English language learners in elementary science classrooms.* Final deliverable

(June) to IES PR/Award Number R305A050004. Los Angeles: University of California, National Center for Research on Evaluation, Standards, and Student Testing (CRESST).

National Clearinghouse for English Language Acquisition. (2009). *A brief on supporting high-quality English language proficiency standards and assessments.* Washington, DC: Author.

National Institute of Child Health and Human Development. (2000). *Report of the National Reading Panel. Teaching children to read: An evidence-based assessment of the scientific research literature on reading and its implications for reading instruction* (NIH Publication No. 00-4769). Washington, DC: U.S. Government Printing Office.

No Child Left Behind. (2001, December 13). Title III: Language instruction for limited English proficient and immigrant students. 107th Congress, First Session.

Pennsylvania Department of Education. (2005). *Home Language Survey.* Retrieved March 23, 2009, from *www.able.state.pa.us/esl/lib/esl/UPDATED_HOME_LANGUAGE_SURVEY_form_10–05.doc.*

Reese, L., & Goldenberg, C. (2008). Community literacy resources and home literacy practices among immigrant Latino families. *Marriage and Family Review, 43,* 109–139.

Spanos, G. (1989). On the integration of language and content instruction. *Annual Review of Applied Linguistics, 10,* 227–240.

Wilkinson, E. R., & Silliman, E. R. (2008). Academic language proficiency and literacy instruction in urban settings. In L. C. Wilkinson, L. M. Morrow, & V. Chou (Eds.), *Improving literacy achievement in urban schools: Critical elements in teacher preparation* (pp. 121–142). Newark, DE: International Reading Association.

Wolf, M. K., Kao, J., Griffin, N., Herman, J. L., Bachman, P. L., Chang, S. M., et al. (2008). *Issues in assessing English language learners: English language proficiency measures and accommodation uses—practice review* (CSE Tech. Report No. 732). Los Angeles: University of California, National Center for Research on Evaluation, Standards, and Student Testing (CRESST).

11

Extended Implications
for Practice
Families as Allies

Leslie Reese
Claude Goldenberg

FOCUS POINTS

- Parents of English language learners are interested in and able to support their children's school achievement. They highly value school and want their children to be successful.

- Educators often assume that parents of English language learners are unwilling or unable to help support their children's academic achievement; however, parents are important potential allies in efforts to promote higher levels of school achievement for English language learners.

- Although we do not know precisely what types of parent involvement have the most impact on student outcomes, increasing learning opportunities at home is likely to be the most directly related to improving student school success.

- There is conflicting evidence on language use in the home and academic outcomes in English; experiments with young learners point to the benefits of encouraging home language literacy, whereas correlational studies across a range of ages suggest that more English in the home is associated with higher achievement in English.

- There are many possible differences between the customs, norms, and behaviors in language-minority families and those expected at school. One promi-

248

nent hypothesis in this area of research is that by bridging these "discontinuities," schools could improve students' school success.

• Whatever differences exist between English language learners' homes and
  schools, there are also areas of similarity, or continuity, which could provide a
  foundation for successful home–school collaboration.

CHAPTER PURPOSE

The purpose of this chapter is to review research evidence on the involvement of parents of English language learners (ELLs) in their children's education, particularly with respect to literacy activities in the home, and the
relationship between these home activities and child outcomes. Themes of
particular interest to educators are addressed: the role of home learning
activities in the primary language (L1), the role of activities in the second
language (L2; in this case, English), and the role of families as sources of
cultural knowledge and experiences. We describe examples of promising
practices that effectively promote and sustain the participation of parents
of ELLs in their children's education in school settings and at home. We
conclude with key recommendations for schools and teachers.

The role of parents and families in children's academic achievement has been a topic of inquiry for more than 40 years, and research
consistently cites parent involvement as a contributor to student success
(Jeynes, 2003). Perhaps the most common suggestion that teachers make
to parents of children in the early school years is to read to their children
at home—a practice found to be associated with gains in literacy development (Snow, Burns, & Griffin, 1998). Studies have shown positive relationships between vocabulary knowledge and home literacy practices,
particularly shared reading (Purcell-Gates, 2000), language in the home,
and children's language development (Hart & Risley, 1995). Texts shared
orally with young children are characterized by a range of features that
is rarely employed in conversational language with children, including
subordinate clauses, passive constructions, unfamiliar expressions, col-
loquialisms, and idioms (Bus, 2001).

In general, these findings hold true for children for whom English
is not the home language; however, several questions arise that are not
issues in monolingual home settings, for example:

• Should use of L2 at home by parents and children be encouraged,
  or are home activities best carried out in the language that parents
  and children speak and understand best?

- Is reading to the child in L1, L2, or both of equal value in supporting literacy development?
- Does L1 reading at home contribute to literacy development in L2 generally, and particularly when the child's instructional program at school is in English only?
- Are findings related to the efficacy of home literacy activities in L1 equally applicable across language and cultural groups?
- Is the primary issue that of language—whether it is more advantageous to use L1 or L2 for activities with children at home—or are there cultural experiences or differences that also play a role in home literacy and learning activities?
- With respect to the role of teachers and schools, what are "best practices" with regard to enhancing the involvement of parents of ELLs in their children's learning at school and at home?

REVIEW OF RESEARCH AND THEORY

Literacy and Learning Activities in ELL Homes

Teachers often perceive immigrant and low-income families as providing few literacy or academic learning opportunities to children, and school personnel might assume that there is little that language-minority parents can do, or want to do, to support their children's learning at home (Brooker, 2002; Goldenberg, 2004; Valencia, 1997). However, many studies carried out in the homes of low-income immigrant families do not support these common assumptions. Families of ELLs do engage in a variety of literacy activities at home often, but not exclusively in the family's primary language (Paratore, Melzi, & Krol-Sinclair, 2003; Xu, 1999). For example, primary language literacy use for religious purposes has been documented across cultures and religions (Farr, 2005: Gregory, 1994; Huss, 1995). Children have the opportunity to observe and participate with family members in tasks involving reading and writing for multiple purposes, including shopping, entertainment, work, and legal and medical engagements. Although home literacy activities are often are carried out in the family's L1—the language that many immigrant parents speak, read, and write best—different languages may be employed in different domains (Farr, 1994). In immigrant homes children are often called upon to serve as translators for their parents in interactions with the school and other service institutions (Orellana, Reynolds, Dorner, & Meza, 2003).

More home literacy experiences and opportunities are generally associated with superior literacy outcomes, according to a review of the research on parent involvement and its effects on ELLs' literacy achievement (Goldenberg, Rueda, & August, 2006). However, findings are not consistent. Measures of parent and family literacy often predict children's literacy attainment, but two studies found that parents' reading behavior was unrelated to children's literacy outcomes (Aarts & Verhoeven, 1999; Pucci & Ulanoff, 1998). Family influences on academic outcomes are not limited to literacy opportunities. Working from a sociocultural perspective, Rueda and colleagues have found that features of family life (e.g., domestic workload, religious activities) seem to influence the value children place on reading and their self-concepts as readers (Rueda, MacGillivray, Monzó, & Arzubiaga, 2001).

In addition to intrinsic family influences on child outcomes, immigrant parents are also responsive to the academic demands of their children's school. One study reported that children's school entry increases their home literacy experiences, either in the home language or in English, particularly when teachers make it a point to send home reading and other academic materials such as homework or books to read (Goldenberg, Reese, & Galllimore, 1992). Parents also express the desire to help and support their children's success in school, and they report more satisfaction with the school (and teacher) when they feel they are invited and encouraged to do so (Goldenberg, 2004). Parent involvement in schooling and homework, moreover, increases when children are enrolled in L1 instructional programs (Ramírez, 1992). Parents provide encouragement and advice for students even when their own language proficiency in L2 does not permit more instrumental help with homework in English. Support for homework, as well as for opportunities for English use, are often provided by siblings and other family members (De la Piedra & Romo, 2003; Gregory, 1998).

Despite the fact that parents of ELLs express willingness and often have the ability to help their children succeed academically, schools underestimate and do not take full advantage of parents' interest, motivation, and potential contributions (Goldenberg et al., 2006). Although views about literacy and literacy practices may differ between home and school, literacy activities are not absent in home settings, and parents consistently express the desire to support their children's academic success (Carter & Chatfield, 1986; Shannon, 1995). In sum, research suggests that teachers seeking to forge partnerships with immigrant parents are likely to find that parents are interested in promoting their children's academic progress and are responsive to school demands. Parents are often unsure about whether they can continue to speak to children, help them with homework, and read to them at home in their native language, or if native language use will be confusing or detrimental to children who are in the process of learning English. This is why it is imperative that teachers and school establish close and productive communication with parents.

Role of L1 in Home Literacy and Learning Activities

Cummins (1986, 2001) posits that a "common underlying proficiency" provides the foundation for linguistic competence in one or more languages. According to this view, language competence comprises two distinct clusters of knowledge and skills: First are the aspects of language that are most apparent and comprise what we think of as language proficiency—for example, vocabulary, syntax, pronunciation, and fluency. But second is a deeper underlying structure of concepts and understandings that are accessed through whatever language, or languages, an individual learns to speak. For example, discussing democracy, decoding (reading) words, and writing a five-paragraph theme require (1) the linguistic competence to do these things but also (2) the underlying conceptual understanding of what these things *are*. This underlying conceptual understanding is what Cummins refers to as "common underlying proficiency." To the extent that we learn through the use of language, this underlying proficiency is achieved through language (as well as through nonlinguistic means), but it is not language-specific. That is, once an individual knows a concept such as democracy, decoding, or the five-paragraph theme, he or she can apply this understanding in whatever language he or she can speak and understand.

There are several important corollaries of the "common underlying proficiency" hypothesis. One is that greater academic language development in a person's L1 will form the basis for similarly higher levels of development in the L2. Another is that there will be cognitive advantages associated with *additive bilingualism,* that is, when an individual develops both languages rather than sacrificing one for the sake of another, known as *subtractive bilingualism*. The reason is that experiences in either language can promote language development in both by contributing to the common underlying proficiency, which then contributes to further competence in both languages.

Studies in school settings support this perspective by indicating that L1 reading instruction is associated with greater success in *both* L1 literacy and English literacy. Five quantitative syntheses (Francis, Lesaux, & August, 2006; Greene, 1997; Rolstad, Mahoney, & Glass, 2005; Slavin & Cheung, 2005; Willig, 1985) over the past 25 years have concluded that instruction in a student's L1 makes a positive contribution to literacy achievement in the student's L2 when compared to students being instructed exclusively in the L2. Researchers have found evidence of cross-language transfer, such that knowledge and skills learned in a student's L1 (e.g., phonological awareness, decoding and comprehension skills) facilitate acquisition of those skills in the L2 (August & Shanahan, 2006; Genesee, Lindholm-Leary, Saunders, & Christian, 2006).

Although childhood bilingualism has been studied for many years (e.g., Homel, Palij, & Aronson, 1987), we know much less about L1 and L2 use at home and its relationship to children's achievement than we do about L1 and L2 use at school and its effects on achievement (particularly with respect to acquisition of reading skills). The home research is less extensive and includes a much more mixed group of studies, some of which support the notion of a common underlying proficiency across languages and others that point to language-specific effects (i.e., experiences in one language are associated with learning in that language but not in a second language).

Dolson's (1985) study of fifth- and sixth-grade Hispanic students in the United States supports the proposition that continued use of L1 at home confers an advantage in both L1 and L2 achievement and in school functioning more generally. Dolson found that on five of ten academic measures—mathematics achievement, Spanish reading vocabulary, academic and effort grades, and grade retention—students from additive bilingual homes (where Spanish was maintained as the primary language) outperformed students from subtractive homes (where Spanish gave way to English). Additive bilingual students had more positive profiles on other measures as well—English reading, oral English skills, limited English proficiency (LEP) status, attendance, and disciplinary referrals—but none was statistically significant.

Roberts's (2008) studies with Hmong-speaking and Spanish-speaking preschool students also support the proposition that learning experiences in L1 have a positive effect on knowledge and skill development in L2. Roberts conducted two studies; each time she randomly assigned children to groups that were read to at home for 6 weeks in either their home language or English. In her first study the children who took home books in the primary language showed an advantage in their vocabulary development; in the second study there was no difference between the groups. Roberts also showed that children who were read to in their L1 identified significantly more vocabulary from the storybooks in English than did children read to in English (L2) but only after classroom reading of the story in English. While the findings show that both L1 and L2 reading served to promote L2 vocabulary, parents who received the L1 materials reported significantly more reading to their children than did the families who received the L2 materials. When caregivers were given a choice of reading material, they overwhelmingly selected L1 materials to read with their children. In a similar experimental study, Hancock (2002) also reported finding that sending home Spanish books and promoting Spanish reading in the home improved kindergarten children's preliteracy skills (measured in English), in comparison to sending home English language books.

Consistent with this group of studies, Tabors and Snow (2001) cautioned that for skills to transfer from children's L1 to L2, they must first be developed in L1. The authors recommend continued L1 use at home, particularly for literacy activities. This suggests that parents who can read to and converse with their children at home in their native language should not be discouraged from doing so. Concepts introduced and discussed in the children's L1 form part of the common underlying proficiency in linguistic concepts that will assist with their L2 development. Later, in "Best Practices," strategies are discussed to help parents maximize the effectiveness of their L1 use and the academic support they provide for their children at home.

Role of L2 in Home Literacy and Learning Activities

While the studies described above support the notion of continued use of the primary language for home learning activities, another group points in a different direction. For example, Oller and Eilers's (2002) ambitious study of nearly 1,000 bilingual (Spanish–English) and monolingual (English-only) elementary-age students in South Florida found positive cross-language correlations on most parallel language and literacy measures (thus supporting the common underlying proficiency perspective discussed above). However, they also found that for the bilingual students, more English use in the home was associated with higher achievement in English, particularly for the oral language measures. Conversely, more Spanish in the home was associated with higher achievement in Spanish, again, particularly for the oral language measures. These findings complement those of Herman (as cited in Bialystok, 2001). Herman's study of bilingual French–English preschoolers found a significant relation between children's ability to use the literacy register in English and the amount of exposure to English storybooks that they had received at home. Bialystok (2001) concluded that reading to bilingual children fosters both general literacy understandings as well as language-specific competence in the language of the stories.

In a study involving over 1,400 first-grade Spanish-dominant English learners, we (Reese & Goldenberg, 2008) found moderate correlations between literacy practices in English or Spanish and reading outcomes in that language. Greater frequency of reading to the child at home in English predicted higher student achievement in English reading (but not Spanish), and greater frequency of reading to the child in Spanish predicted higher achievement in Spanish. We concluded that the *language* in which literacy activities occur is a key dimension connecting community influences, family influences, and child outcomes.

Several other studies have found language-specific effects of home language use and children's literacy achievement. These studies report negative cross-language correlations, suggesting that greater use of L1 at home is associated with lower achievement in L2. Hansen (1989), for example, found that more Spanish in the home predicted lower English reading comprehension and English oral vocabulary growth in an Hispanic ELL population. Connor (1983) reported that students in grades 2–12 from families of diverse language backgrounds scored slightly lower on the Metropolitan Achievement Test when a language other than English was used 100% of the time in their homes compared to students whose native language was used no more than 50% of the time.

More recently, Duursma and colleagues (2007) found a pattern of positive within-language and negative across-language correlations: Greater exposure to Spanish in the home led to higher vocabulary scores in Spanish but lower in English; more exposure to English led to higher vocabulary in English but lower in Spanish. Duursma et al. found complex interactions with students' language of instruction (some students were in primary language, or bilingual, programs; others were in all-English), but the overall pattern suggested language-specific effects of home language experiences and student vocabulary development.

Taken together, these studies suggest a contrasting set of conclusions from those reviewed in the previous section: Greater exposure to one language at home has positive effects on outcomes in that language and negative effects on outcomes in a second language, particularly when looking at oral language measures. One problem is that these are correlational studies, so we do not know what is cause and what is effect with any confidence. It might well be that parents and other family members tend to talk more English with students who are acquiring English more rapidly or are more motivated to speak English, or more Spanish with students who are developing less rapidly in their English or showing less

interest in English. These scenarios would explain the pattern of correlations observed but not necessarily point to the amount of English or
Spanish spoken in the home as directly contributing to higher or lower
levels of achievement in either language.

As discussed previously, the few experiments that have been conducted on this issue support findings from school-based research indicating that promoting use of L1 at home makes a positive contribution
to achievement in English. These few studies are themselves limited
because they involve only young children and a limited range of outcomes. Clearly, this is an area in need of additional research, particularly
experimental interventions that test the effects of different types of home
interventions in different languages. Findings from other studies, however, suggest that more exposure to English is associated with positive
outcomes for children and should be encouraged at home. This is not to
say that more exposure to English needs to take place to the exclusion of
the child's native language. Rather, it possible that both languages contribute to children's overall linguistic development and that both should
be encouraged.

Role of Home Cultural Experiences
in Children's Learning

Language-minority families often have customs, behaviors, and beliefs
that, to one degree or another, differ from those of "mainstream" U.S.
culture. The number of possible "cultural" differences is enormous—for
example, regarding gender roles, child discipline and socialization, norms
for interpersonal communication, standards of etiquette, beliefs about
education, and the role of the individual in family and society. Perhaps
due to the many ways in which social groups differ and the fact that many
children and youth from "nonmainstream" groups do more poorly in
school, educators and researchers have speculated that if schools bridged
these differences by using educational practices more closely aligned with
children's home cultures, children's achievement would improve (Jacob
& Jordan, 1987).

This "cultural discontinuities" model has been one of the guiding
paradigms in research on ELLs. And indeed there is evidence of discontinuities between language-minority children's homes and the schools they
attend, for example, with respect to cultural models of literacy (Reese &
Gallimore, 2000; Volk & de Acosta, 2001), participation structures (Au,
1980), and emphasis on isolated skill practice rather than more meaningful and situated literacy experiences (Xu, 1999). But there is limited

evidence for the proposition that bridging home and school in terms of cultural practices will help improve ELL students' achievement (Goldenberg et al., 2006). Although it makes intuitive sense that educators should be aware of these sorts of differences and how they might influence the educational process, it is also the case that an exclusive focus on differences between the homes and cultures of immigrant families may have the unintended consequence of serving to undermine the potential for partnerships between teachers and parents.

While there are often differences between home and school, it is also important to note that there are similarities as well. These similarities—or complementarities—are often unrecognized by teachers. For example, immigrant parents value formal schooling and want their children to succeed; high aspirations for children's achievement in American schools have been documented across immigrant groups. Parents believe—as do their children's teachers—that school success is important and increases the likelihood of social and economic success. Parents might define school success in different ways; some emphasize behavior (comportment) more than others, for example. But by and large, all parents want their children to be successful in school. Parents also value being informed of their children's progress in school and invited to participate in supporting it. Different parents are able to provide different levels of support, but they still value school attempts to elicit their participation. Parents also value effort and motivation as important for school success (Goldenberg, 2004; Goldenberg, Gallimore, Reese, & Garnier, 2001; Huss-Keeler, 1997; Smith-Hefner, 1993; Suarez-Orozco & Suarez-Orozco, 2001). In addition, "mainstream practices" such as storybook reading to children are not exclusive to mainstream homes and may also be present in language-minority families (Del Valle, 2005).

One approach to understanding, documenting, and utilizing the lived, cultural experiences of language-minority children and families is based on the concept of *funds of knowledge* (González, Moll, & Amanti, 2005). This term refers to "historically accumulated and culturally developed bodies of knowledge and skills essential for household or individual functioning and well-being" (Moll, Amanti, Neff, & Gonzalez, 2005, p. 72). Funds of knowledge—which may include such bodies of knowledge as ranching and farming, construction, herbal and folk medicine, and appliance repair—are discovered by teachers through home visits and are incorporated into classroom lessons through work on collaborative teacher study teams. Teachers attribute changes in instructional practice, including increased communication and rapport with families as well as greater reflection on their teaching assumptions and practices, with participation in funds of knowledge projects (Messing, 2005). However, Garcia (2000) points out that researchers have not examined whether providing these types of literacy activities affect their children's literacy development.

Another way, similar to the "funds of knowledge" approach, in which culture might have an impact on achievement involves the use of culturally familiar materials. To the extent that parents can play a role in helping identify or provide such materials, this can be a possible venue for parent-school collaboration. A 3-year case study by Kenner (1999, 2000) provides a useful illustration. Kenner examined the biliteracy development of a Gujarati (from northwest India) child who attended a London multilingual/multicultural preschool. Parents and children in the multilingual preschool were invited to bring literacy materials from home in the home language. These materials were placed in a "home corner" and a "writing area." Parents and children were invited to write in the classroom in different languages and genres-cards, letters to relatives, posters, and travel brochures. Children drew on their knowledge and experience, made accessible in their home languages, to explore and produce different genres of writing, such as letters, lists, greeting cards, and recipes. Kenner reports that letter-writing at home, together with letter-writing opportunities in preschool, probably contributed to his focal child's knowledge about this writing genre and to her knowledge of written conventions in both English and Gujarati.

It is important to point out that the examples Kenner provides show that home-based interests and experiences are not necessarily rooted in natal culture. Rather, the connections children made were with their lived experiences rather than elements of their natal culture per se. Nonetheless, and regardless of the "cultural" origin of texts and activities, children drew on familiar resources, in both English and their native language, to engage in numerous literacy activities and develop literacy skills in their first and second languages. Kenner's (1999, 2000) work suggests that enlisting parents to help build upon children's out-of-school experiences and using familiar materials and content in the classroom might help promote learning among English learners. Future studies should of course attempt to test this hypothesis experimentally.

BEST PRACTICES

In the sections above, we have described the desires and expectations that parents have for their children's success and the literacy use and activities that are part of the home life of immigrant families. At the same time, there are very real challenges for schools and teachers who wish to build upon these family values and experiences to forge stronger and more effective partnerships with parents. Language itself can present challenges—parents' limited familiarity with English, and schools' limited access to bilingual materials and personnel to work with parents. Access to literacy materials for home use and in languages that the parents can understand and use present other challenges. In this section we describe successful efforts on the part of teachers and schools to enhance children's language and literacy development through strengthened family involvement.

One example of a successful effort to strengthen home–school connections is the Book Loan Program (Yaden, Madrigal, & Tam, 2005). Implemented at a comprehensive child care center in downtown Los Angeles, this is an example of a university-sponsored program that successfully fostered home reading by low-income Hispanic families to 3- and 4-year-old children. This program was organized around three research-based guiding principles: providing easy access to books, respecting cultural variations and beliefs, and encouraging parent choice. The project addressed the need to enhance the number of books available in the homes of participating families by first assessing the constraints in the families' daily routines. This led to establishing a lending "library" in the hallway outside the children's classrooms, and to keep the library open in the hours when parents dropped children off or picked them up from school. Children and parents were allowed to choose the book topics as well as the language (English or Spanish) in which they wished to read. Many of the books in the library were in the families' native language, as well as addressing culturally relevant themes. The checkout and selection process was facilitated by bilingual members of the university research team. Parent suggestions and preferences were solicited through both written and oral surveys, informal contacts, and short questionnaires. The workshops conducted twice a year with parents consciously built upon these findings and parents' primary language, literacy, and storytelling knowledge.

Findings from the Book Loan Program study indicated an increase in the rate of book checkouts and in the number of children participating in the program over the 3-year period of implementation. Qualitative data collected by the team documented the strategies that non-English-speaking parents employed to make story reading available to their children in English, such as using a tape recorder provided by the older sibling's school library to listen to stories in English, or enrolling in adult English classes. Teachers also observed greater participation in classroom reading activities and greater enjoyment of reading among children participating in the book loan program. This program demonstrated that simply facilitating access by families to appropriate children's books in the language with which parents were more comfortable was a key factor in increasing reading aloud to young ELLs. Teachers can make similar successful accommodations in their own classrooms by providing L1 books in the classroom library that can be checked out by children and parents for reading at home. Teachers, realizing that low-income homes may lack books for children, can also send home books and other reading materials each time home reading is required. One study found that teachers' systematically sending home reading materials with children probably contributed to improvements in Spanish reading achievement over a 2- to 3-year period (Goldenberg & Gallimore, 1991).

Whereas the Book Loan Program was designed to address the need for greater access to books and children's literacy materials in the home, Project FLAME (Family Literacy: Aprendiendo, Mejorando, Educando) addressed the need for improving parents' language and literacy skills, including areas identified as important by participants themselves. Initiated in 1989, this project was designed to support parents of ELL preschoolers and primary-grade students by sharing knowledge about ways to provide a home environment rich in literacy learning opportunities for their children (Rodríguez-Brown, 2009). Based on a sociocultural framework, the FLAME program activities arise from four essential, research-based dimensions of home support for literacy learning: literacy and access to literacy materials and practices, modeling of literacy use by family members, interaction between family members and children in both formal and informal literacy activities, and connections between home and school. The program includes two modules: parents as teachers, and parents as learners. The parents-as-teachers module consists of bimonthly meetings in which parents discuss and practice activities and strategies for increasing home literacy opportunities and interactions. These sessions cover such topics as community literacy, including ways in which parents can share literacy uses with their children while in community locales outside of the home, and book selection, including criteria for selecting quality books to read and share with children. The parents-as-learners module includes instruction in ESL basic skills, or for the general equivalency diploma (GED), based on the needs of the participants.

In her book *Home–School Connection: Lessons Learned in a Culturally and Linguistically Diverse Community,* Rodríguez-Brown (2009) shares findings on the effectiveness of Project FLAME over the years. A quasi-experimental study carried out in 1991–1992, comparing 4-year-olds in a public preschool program with 4-year-olds not enrolled in preschool whose parents were participating in FLAME, found that although the FLAME children started out significantly lower than the non-FLAME preschool children on the measures listed above, by the end of the year the FLAME children had caught up, and there were no significant differences between the two groups. This growth occurred despite the fact that the children were not enrolled in a school program during the year of their parents' participation in FLAME activities. These findings underscore the potential impact of home activities when parents understand how to work with their children in ways that will enhance children's literacy development and academic performance at school. Classroom teachers who provide parent workshops in which they share materials and model their use, and teachers who invite parents into the classroom to observe how read-alouds or other activities are carried out, are engaging in the kinds of home–school connections suggested by Project FLAME. Other successful teachers employ mini-workshops lasting no longer than 15–20 minutes to provide parents with the targeted skills that they need to assist their children.

Although assisting parents to hone their skills in literacy and homework help is an obvious way to enhance home–school partnerships, there are other activities that are less direct but nonetheless powerful in creating relationships of understanding and trust that build on families' home languages and cultural experiences. The Hmong Literacy Project (Kang, Kuehn, & Herrell, 1996) is one such example. This project was developed and implemented by members of the Hmong community in Fresno, California, in response to immigrant parents' concerns that their children were losing the Hmong language, were not developing Hmong literacy skills, did not understand the Hmong heritage, and would not be able to pass on this heritage to their own children. Because the Hmong language has existed in written form for only about 30 years, many of the parents were not literate in their home language. Parents also wanted to be able to support their children's schooling in English. Thus, the Hmong Literacy Project aimed at helping adults develop skills in reading and writing in their native language as a precursor to the study of English language and literacy. The curriculum was developed in response to parent needs and interests, and included activities such as production of the Hmong Parents' Newsletter and incorporation of computer literacy into classes.

Results indicated increased opportunities for children to be exposed to literacy activities in the home after parent participation in the Hmong Literacy Project. Observational data of class participation indicated that parents began bringing their children with them to Hmong literacy classes and that children often participated with parents in class. Observers found that children, already literate in English, were sometimes quicker to develop reading and writing skills in Hmong than their parents; children assisted their parents with reading, while parents taught children unknown words in Hmong and corrected their children's oral skills. Teachers reported that the parents attending the Hmong classes were more likely to attend parent conferences and other school events than were parents who did not attend classes (Kang et al., 1996). Teachers who design homework activities that require parent participation and sharing of home language and culture with their children and their child's class are utilizing strategies found to be successful in the Hmong Literacy Project. These teachers recognize that successful partnerships with families of ELLs acknowledge and respect the cultural and linguistic resources that families bring to the collaboration.

All of the projects described above were carried out with immigrant parents with low incomes, little proficiency in English, and lower levels of education than the U.S. population at large. This constellation of parent characteristics often proves daunting for schools and teachers as they attempt to involve parents in their children's schooling and enhance home learning opportunities. Although they varied in specific program components and participating populations, the projects illustrated some of the key elements of parental involvement in ELL children's education (Goldenberg, 2006):

- Programs recognize and build upon the fact that parents care deeply about their children's school success and they want to support the school's efforts to promote student achievement.
- Parents are welcomed at school and given information about school events, programs, and resources in a language that they understand.
- Activities are carried out in the parents' native language, and parents understand that their participation is valued.
- Young children are welcome at the parent activities.

In addition, the projects' successes also point to the impact on home activities of parents as students and learners. As parents improved their own native language reading and writing skills, they reported feeling more confident in working with their children on homework.

A final element that the exemplary programs had in common was a grounding in, and responsiveness to, the cultural histories and experiences of the families. Each project did more than simply provide training and translations in the native language of the immigrant families. The projects provided ways for parents to share cultural traditions with their second-generation children being raised in the United States. Cultural values and experiences were shared through group discussions, through choice of multicultural books for shared reading, and through joint writing of folktales, stories, and histories from the parents' homelands. Parents valued the enhanced intergenerational communication that occurred as an outcome of their participation in literacy trainings and felt that it contributed to their children's identity development, positive self-concept, and ability to withstand the lure of gang involvement and delinquency.

SUMMARY OF MAIN IDEAS

The home experiences of ELLs influence their school achievement. Contrary to what many educators assume, children are exposed to literacy and other learning opportunities, although these opportunities are not necessarily as plentiful as they are in mainstream and middle-class families. Perhaps as important, parents care deeply about their children's school success and are responsive to efforts by schools and teachers to become involved in their children's schooling and to support their academic success. A major problem, however, is that school personnel often conclude that parents are uninterested, assuming that either they do not value formal schooling or that they are too economically stressed to accord it a priority. All too often parents of ELLs want to collaborate with educators to promote their children's school success and, moreover, express greater satisfaction with the school program when teachers actively enlist their support. A challenge for educators and researchers is to determine what forms of parent involvement are most likely to have the greatest benefit for children's school success.

A major question about which we have insufficient data for clear guidelines is whether schools should try to promote home literacy and other learning opportunities in the home language or in English. The few experiments indicate that promoting L1 use has positive effects on

English outcomes. However, a number of correlational studies suggest that more English in the home is associated with better outcomes in English, whereas more L1 (and less English) use is associated with poorer outcomes in English. It is likely that the use of some combination of both languages in learning activities at home is beneficial for academic progress of children growing up bilingually in the United States. It is also plausible that what matters for children's language and literacy development is not the language, per se, whether it is Spanish or English, for example, but rather the quality and amount of language to which children are exposed that really matters (Hart & Risley, 1995; Hoff, 2003). We presently have no research to help resolve this very important issue.

Aside from the home language use, many educators and researchers have suggested that the home culture should play a role in helping create successful school programs for ELLs. That is, schools should build on the knowledge and experience that children bring from home in order to bridge differences between school and home that might interfere with children's academic success. One approach that has gained a great deal of interest is "funds of knowledge," a phrase that refers to knowledge, skills, experiences, and competencies that exist in children's homes and that teachers could use to develop classroom learning activities that help children achieve academic learning goals.

Despite differences, or discontinuities, between home and school, there are also similarities, or continuities, that are often unrecognized by educators. For example, home (parents) and school (teachers) both value formal schooling, want children to succeed, and see formal schooling as a means of social and economic upward mobility. Literacy and literate behavior are valued in both settings. These home–school compatibilities should help provide a basis for active collaboration between parents and teachers who share a common goal of promoting children's school success.

IMPLICATIONS FOR RESEARCH, PRACTICE, AND POLICY

Engage Parents in Students' Academic Learning

The most important conclusion we draw from the studies reviewed here is that schools should look for ways to engage the parents of ELLs in their children's academic development. There is ample evidence that language-minority parents are motivated and, in many cases, capable of actions that would lead to improved student outcomes. Moreover, studies of apparently successful school contexts suggest that parent–home–community involvement helps to explain school success. Advocates of parent involvement argue that schools should actively seek ways to collaborate with parents for children's academic benefit (e.g., Epstein, 1992; Goldenberg, 1993).

An obvious question is, what are the most beneficial types of parent involvement? In order to address this question, studies must empirically connect specific types of parent involvement with measured student outcomes. The few studies that have done this with ELLs find that promoting direct experience with reading and other academic experiences at home is most likely to enhance student learning and school achievement. However, there might be other forms of parent involvement that can help promote learning, achievement, and student motivation. Practitioners and researchers must work to seek these out and evaluate their impact on students.

Encourage L1 or L2 Use?

A related question is whether parents should be encouraged to speak or use the home language or English. The few experimental studies available point to the benefits of promoting L1 use at home to enhance children's early reading achievement in L2. But the studies are not only few; they are limited in scope as well. A larger pool of correlational studies suggest that less English at home is associated with lower levels of English achievement, and more English at home predicts higher English levels, particularly with respect to measures of oral language vocabulary. We must be cautious about interpreting correlational studies, however. Correlation is not causation, and more English use at home might be the result—not the cause—of greater English proficiency among students. It is possible that what matters most is not whether L1 or L2 is used at home, but rather the quantity and quality of language children hear and have a chance to use. This finding is well established for monolingual populations (Hart & Risley, 1995; Hoff, 2003); we hope future research will shed light on this question for language minorities. Moreover, it is also plausible that both L1 and L2 at home have a role to play—rather than parents' having to choose one or the other. But here, again, specific guidelines must await more detailed study.

One issue that probably cannot be resolved empirically is the benefit of maintaining the home language, regardless of its impact on English language development. It is not unreasonable to argue that because of the benefits of bilingualism and biliteracy, home language maintenance is itself desirable, even if at some expense to English proficiency. Whether such a tradeoff exists, and if so, how to evaluate it are, again, important topics future research should address.

Educators should be aware of cultural differences but also build on home–school continuities. Language-minority families have customs, behaviors, and beliefs that can differ from those of "mainstream" U.S. culture and, more specifically, from those of the schools children attend. Although there is limited evidence that bridging cultural differences has an impact on student achievement, it makes intuitive sense that educators should be aware of these sorts of differences and how they might influence the educational process.

But educators must also be aware that there are numerous continuities between families and schools. Building on these is important to the efforts of promoting school success for ELLs. The most important of these continuities is that parents value formal schooling and want their children to do well in school. Parents also value being informed of their children's school progress and invited to contribute to children's school success. A critical problem seems to be that educators are often not aware of parents' interest or of how best to take advantage of that interest to help promote ELLs' achievement. One hypothesis that could help explain this lack of awareness is that educators focus more on the differences between schools and families than on what they have in common.

Schools in general and teachers in particular need to develop parent-friendly ways of communicating to parents what they can do to help their children be successful in school. There is little question that the parents of ELLs want very much—some might say, desperately—for their children to succeed in school and become productive, responsible members of the society. With teachers' support and collaboration, parents can play an important role in bridging the gap between home and school so that school learning and success become truly accessible for all children.

REFERENCES

Aarts, R., & Verhoeven, L. (1999). Literacy attainment in a second language submersion context. *Applied Psycholinguistics, 20,* 377–393.

Au, K. H. (1980). Participation structures in a reading lesson with Hawaiian children: Analysis of a culturally appropriate instructional event. *Anthropology and Education Quarterly, 11,* 91–115.

August, D., & Shanahan, T. (Eds.). (2006). *Developing literacy in second-lan-*

guage learners: Report of the National Literacy Panel on language-minority children and youth. Mahwah, NJ: Erlbaum.

Bialystok, E. (2001). *Bilingualism in development: Language, literacy, and cognition.* Cambridge, UK: Cambridge University Press.

Brooker, L. (2002). "Five on the first of December!": What can we learn from case studies of early childhood literacy? *Journal of Early Childhood Literacy, 2,* 292–313.

Bus, A. (2001). Joint caregiver–child storybook reading: A route to literacy development. In S. B. Neuman & D. K. Dickinson (Eds.), *Handbook of early literacy research* (Vol. 1, pp. 179–191). New York: Guilford Press.

Carter, T., & Chatfield, M. (1986). Effective bilingual schools: Implications for policy and practice. *American Journal of Education, 95,* 200–232.

Connor, U. (1983). Predictors of second-language reading performance. *Journal of Multilingual and Multicultural Development, 4*(4), 271–288.

Cummins, J. (1986). Empowering minority students: A framework for intervention. *Harvard Educational Review, 56,* 18–36.

Cummins, J. (2001) *Negotiating identities: Education for empowerment in a diverse society* (2nd ed.). Los Angeles: California Association for Bilingual Education.

De la Piedra, M., & Romo, H. (2003). Collaborative literacy in a Mexican immigrant household: The role of sibling mediators in the socialization of preschool learners. In R. Bayley & S. Schecter (Eds.), *Language socialization in bilingual and multilingual societies* (pp. 44–61). Clevedon, UK: Multilingual Matters.

Del Valle, T. (2005) "Successful" and "unsuccessful" literacies of two Puerto Rican families in Chicago. In M. Farr (Ed.), *Latino language and literacy in ethnolinguistic Chicago* (pp. 97–131). Mahwah, NJ: Erlbaum.

Dolson, D. (1985). The effects of Spanish home language use on the scholastic performance of Hispanic pupils. *Journal of Multilingual and Multicultural Development, 6,* 135–155.

Duursma, E., Romero-Contreras, S., Szuber, A., Snow, C., August, D., & Calderón, M. (2007). The role of home literacy and language environment on bilinguals' English and Spanish vocabulary development. *Applied Psycholinguistics, 28,* 171–190.

Epstein, J. (1992). School and family partnerships. In M. Alkin (Ed.), *Encyclopedia of educational research* (6th ed., pp. 1139–1152). New York: Macmillan.

Farr, M. (1994). *En los dos idiomas*: Literacy practices among Chicago Mexicanos. In B. Moss (Ed.), *Literacy across communities* (pp. 9–47). Cresskill, NJ: Hampton Press.

Farr, M. (2005). Literacy and religion: Reading, writing, and gender among Mexican women in Chicago. In M. Farr (Ed.), *Latino language and literacy in ethnolinguistic Chicago* (pp.305–321). Mahwah, NJ: Erlbaum.

Francis, D., Lesaux, N., & August, A. (2006). Language of instruction. In D. August & T. Shanahan (Eds.), *Developing literacy in second-language learners: Report of the National Literacy Panel on language-minority children and youth* (pp. 365–414). Mahwah, NJ: Erlbaum.

Garcia, G. (2000). Bilingual children's reading. In M. Kamil, P. Mosenthal, P. D. Pearson, & R. Barr (Eds.), *Handbook of reading research* (Vol. III, pp. 813–834). Mahwah, NJ: Erlbaum.

Genesee, F., Lindholm-Leary, K., Saunders, W., & Christian, D. (2006). *Educating English language learners.* New York: Cambridge University Press.

Goldenberg, C. (1993). The home–school connection in bilingual education. In B. Arias & U. Casanova (Eds.), *Ninety-second yearbook of the National Society for the Study of Education. Bilingual education: Politics, research, and practice* (pp. 225–250). Chicago: University of Chicago Press.

Goldenberg, C. (2004). *Successful school change: Creating settings to improve teaching and learning.* New York: Teachers College Press.

Goldenberg, C. (2006). Involving parents of English learners in their children's schooling. *Instructional Leader, 29*(3), 1–2, 11–12.

Goldenberg, C., & Gallimore, R. (1991). Local knowledge, research knowledge, and educational change: A case study of first-grade Spanish reading improvement. *Educational Researcher, 20*(8), 2–14.

Goldenberg, C., Gallimore, R., Reese, L., & Garnier, H. (2001). Cause or effect?: A longitudinal study of immigrant Latino parents' aspirations and expectations and their children's school performance. *American Educational Research Journal, 38,* 547–582.

Goldenberg, C., Reese, L., & Gallimore, R. (1992). Effects of school literacy materials on Latino children's home experiences and early reading achievement. *American Journal of Education, 100,* 497–536.

Goldenberg, C., Rueda, R., & August, D. (2006). Social and cultural influences on the literacy attainment of language-minority children and youth. In D. August & T. Shanahan (Eds.), *Developing literacy in second-language learners: Report of the National Literacy Panel on language-minority children and youth* (pp. 269–318). Mahwah, NJ: Erlbaum.

González, N., Moll, L., & Amanti, C. (Eds.). (2005). *Funds of knowledge: Theorizing practices in households, communities, and classrooms.* Mahwah, NJ: Erlbaum.

Greene, J. (1997). A meta-analysis of the Rossell and Baker review of bilingual education research. *Bilingual Research Journal, 21,* 103–122.

Gregory, E. (1994). Cultural assumptions and early years' pedagogy: The effect of the home culture on minority children's interpretation of reading in school. *Language Culture and Curriculum, 7*(2), 111–124.

Gregory, E. (1998). Siblings as mediators of literacy in linguistic minority communities. *Language and Education, 1,* 33–55.

Hancock, D. R. (2002). The effects of native language books on the pre-literacy skill development of language minority kindergartners. *Journal of Research in Childhood Education, 17,* 62–68.

Hansen, D. A. (1989). Locating learning: Second language gains and language use in family, peer and classroom contexts. *NABE: The Journal of the National Association for Bilingual Education, 13*(2), 161–180.

Hart, B., & Risley, T. R. (1995). *Meaningful differences in everyday experiences of young American children*. Baltimore: Brookes.

Hoff, E. (2003). The specificity of environmental influence: Socioeconomic status affects early vocabulary development via maternal speech. *Child Development, 74*, 1368–1378.

Homel, P., Palij, M., & Aronson, D. (Eds.). (1987). *Childhood bilingualism: Aspects of linguistic, cognitive, and social development*. Hillsdale, NJ: Erlbaum.

Huss, R. L. (1995). Young children becoming literate in English as a second language. *TESOL Quarterly, 29*(4), 767–774.

Huss-Keeler, R. L. (1997). Teacher perception of ethnic and linguistic minority parental involvement and its relationships to children's language and literacy learning: A case study. *Teaching and Teacher Education, 13*(2), 171–182.

Jacob, E., & Jordan, C. (Eds.). (1987). Explaining the school performance of minority students [Theme issue]. *Anthropology and Education Quarterly, 18*(4).

Jeynes, W. (2003). A meta-analysis: The effects of parental involvement on minority children's academic achievement. *Education and Urban Society, 35*, 202–218.

Kang, H., Kuehn, P., & Herrell, A. (1996). The Hmong literacy project: Parents working to preserve the past and ensure the future. *Journal of Educational Issues of Language Minority Students, 16*. Retrieved October 25, 2008, from *www.ncela.gwu.edu*.

Kenner, C. (1999). Children's understandings of text in a multilingual nursery. *Language and Education, 13*(1), 1–16.

Kenner, C. (2000). Biliteracy in a monolingual school system?: English and Gujarati in South London. *Language Culture and Curriculum, 13*(1), 13–30.

Messing, J. (2005). Social reconstructions of schooling: Teacher evaluations of what they learned from participation in the Funds of Knowledge Project. In N. González, L. Moll, & C. Amanti (Eds.), *Funds of knowledge: Theorizing practices in households, communities, and classrooms* (pp. 183–198). Mahwah, NJ: Erlbaum.

Moll, L., Amanti, C., Neff, D., & González, N. (2005). Funds of knowledge for teaching: Using a qualitative approach to connect homes and classrooms. In N. González, L. Moll, & C. Amanti (Eds.), *Funds of knowledge: Theorizing practices in households, communities, and classrooms* (pp. 71–88). Mahwah, NJ: Erlbaum.

Oller, D. K., & Eilers, R. (Eds.). (2002). *Language and literacy in bilingual children*. Clevedon, UK: Multilingual Matters.

Orellana, M., Reynolds, J., Dorner, L., & Meza, M. (2003). In other words: Translating or "para-phrasing" as a family literacy practice in immigrant households. *Reading Research Quarterly, 38*, 12–34.

Paratore, J., Melzi, G., & Krol-Sinclair, B. (2003). Learning about the literate lives of Latino families. In D. M. Barone & L. M. Morrow (Eds.), *Literacy and young children: Research-based practices* (pp. 101–118). New York: Guilford Press.

Pucci, S. L., & Ulanoff, S. H. (1998). What predicts second language reading success?: A study of home and school variables. *International Review of Applied Linguistics, 121–122,* 1–18.

Purcell-Gates, V. (2000). Family literacy. In M. Kamil, P. Mosenthal, P. D. Pearson, & R. Barr (Eds.), *Handbook of reading research* (Vol. III, pp. 853–870). Mahwah, NJ: Erlbaum.

Ramirez, D. (1992). Executive summary. *Bilingual Research Journal, 16,* 1–62.

Reese, L., & Gallimore, R. (2000). Immigrant Latinos' cultural model of literacy development: An evolving perspective on home–school discontinuities. *American Journal of Education, 108,* 103–134.

Reese, L., Garnier, H., Gallimore, R., & Goldenberg, C. (2000). A longitudinal analysis of the ecocultural antecedents of emergent Spanish literacy and subsequent English reading achievement of Spanish-speaking students. *American Educational Research Journal, 37,* 633–662.

Reese, L., & Goldenberg, C. (2008). Community literacy resources and home literacy practices among immigrant Latino families. *Marriage and Family Review, 43,* 109–139.

Roberts, T. (2008). Home storybook reading in primary or second language with preschool children: Evidence of equal effectiveness for second-language vocabulary acquisition. *Reading Research Quarterly, 43,* 103–130.

Rodriguez-Brown, F. (2009). *The home–school connection: Lessons learned in a culturally and linguistically diverse community.* New York: Routledge.

Rolstad, K. Mahoney, K., & Glass, G. (2005). The big picture: A meta-analysis of program effectiveness research on English language learners. *Educational Policy, 19,* 572–594.

Rueda, R., MacGillivray, L., Monzó, L., & Arzubiaga, A. (2001). Engaged reading: A multi-level approach to considering socio-cultural features with diverse learners. In D. McInerny & S. Van Etten (Eds.), *Research on sociocultural influences on motivation and learning* (pp. 233–264). Greenwich, CT: Information Age.

Shannon, S. M. (1995). The hegemony of English: A case study of one bilingual classroom as a site of resistance. *Linguistics and Education, 7,* 175–200.

Slavin, R., & Cheung, A. (2005). A synthesis of research on language of reading instruction for English language learners. *Review of Educational Research, 75,* 247–284.

Smith-Hefner, N. J. (1993). Education, gender, and generational conflict among Khmer refugees. *Anthropology and Education Quarterly, 24,* 135–158.

Snow, C., Burns, M., & Griffin, P. (1998). *Preventing reading difficulties in young children.* Washington, DC: National Academy Press.

Suarez-Orozco, C., & Suarez-Orozco, M. (2001). *Children of immigration.* Cambridge, MA: Harvard University Press.

Tabors, P., & Snow, C. (2001). Young bilingual children and early literacy development. In S. B. Neuman & D. K. Dickinson (Eds.), *Handbook of early literacy research* (Vol. 1, pp. 159–178). New York: Guilford Press.

Valencia, R. (1997). *The evolution of deficit thinking.* Bristol, PA: Falmer Press.

Volk, D., & de Acosta, M. (2001). "Many differing ladders, many ways to climb ... ": Literacy events in the bilingual classroom, homes, and community of three Puerto Rican kindergartners. *Journal of Early Childhood Literacy, 1*, 193–224.

Xu, H. (1999). Reexamining continuities and discontinuities: Language-minority children's home and school literacy experiences. *Yearbook of the National Reading Conference, 48*, 224–237.

Yaden, D., Madrigal, P., & Tam, A. (2005). Access to books and beyond: Creating and learning from a book lending program for Latino families in the inner city. In G. García (Ed.), *English learners: Reaching the highest level of English literacy* (pp. 357–386). Upper Saddle River, NJ: Pearson/Merrill Prentice Hall.

Recent Research on English Language and Literacy Instruction

What We Have Learned to Guide Practice for English Language Learners in the 21st Century

Diane August
Claude Goldenberg
William M. Saunders
Cheryl Dressler

FOCUS POINTS

- This chapter synthesizes the research on English language development and literacy instruction for English language learners and provides recommendations for classroom practice.

- Although there is much work to be done to develop an empirical research base from which to build effective English language development and literacy programs, it is important to use the existing research to guide practice.

- In developing English language proficiency, English language learners need curriculum and instruction that combine explicit instruction in language forms with opportunities for meaningful and communicative use of the language.

- In developing literacy in English language learners it is important to build on effective research-based practices used with monolingual English speakers, but make adjustments that take into account the unique strengths as well as needs of English language learners.

CHAPTER PURPOSE

The purpose of this chapter is to synthesize what we have learned about English language development and literacy instruction of English language learners (ELLs) in order to help inform instructional practices in the 21st century. The review of English language development (ELD) instruction draws on several recent analyses, whereas the review of literacy instruction draws on experimental and quasi-experimental research conducted between 1990 and 2008.

The importance of implementing instructional practice consistent with the evolving knowledge base is underscored by the increasing numbers of ELLs in our schools and their generally poor educational outcomes. There were approximately 5 million ELLs enrolled in public schools in the United States in the 2003–2004 school year, an increase of 65% since 1994 (Batalova, 2006). This number represents about 10.1% of the total school enrollment. In 1999, among 18- to 24-year-olds not enrolled in a secondary school, 31% of language-minority students (defined as students from homes where a language other than English is spoken) had not completed high school, compared with 10% of students who spoke English at home. Within this group, those with lower levels of English proficiency had a lower probability of completing high school; about 51% of those who spoke English with difficulty had not completed high school, compared with about 18% of those who spoke English very well.

The following section first describes methods used to conduct the review and then turns to research syntheses related to developing language and literacy in ELLs.

REVIEW OF RESEARCH AND THEORY

Methods: ELD Instruction

Several recent syntheses and meta-analyses provide the basis for trying to derive some research-based principles of effective ELD instruction (Ellis, 2005; Genesee, Lindholm-Leary, Saunders, & Christian, 2006; Keck, Iberri-Shea, Tracy-Ventura, & Wa-Mbaleka, 2006; Lyster, 2007; Norris & Ortega, 2000; Russell & Spada, 2006). We suggest guidelines relevant to ELD instruction from this research and from educational research more broadly. The guidelines have varying degrees of research supporting them, as noted below, so in general most are suggestive rather than definitive.[1]

English Literacy Instruction

This review of literacy instruction draws on the work of the National Literacy Panel on Language-Minority Children and Youth (August & Shanahan, 2006),[2] updated with studies conducted between 2003 and 2008. The methods used to conduct the review are consistent with those used by the National Literacy Panel and include (1) establishing criteria for the identification and selection of all relevant studies, (2) locating relevant studies, and (3) synthesizing the information using qualitative techniques. The review focuses on language-minority students (defined as students from homes where a language other than English is spoken) 3–18 years old learning to read in English. Further details of the search procedures for studies can be found in August and Shanahan (2006).

Research on ELD Instruction[3]

This section synthesizes existing research that provides direction for ELD instruction. It focuses specifically on instruction delivered within some portion of the school day that is separate from literacy and other content-area (e.g., math, social studies) instruction. ELD instruction should not be confused with "sheltered instruction" (e.g., Echevarría, Vogt, & Short, 2008), the primary goal of which is to provide comprehensible content instruction in English. The primary goal of ELD instruction is learning and acquiring English. A secondary goal of ELD instruction can be learning content, such as social studies or mathematics, but the primary focus is on learning the English language.

There is surprisingly little research that focuses specifically on improving K–12 ELD outcomes for the population of U.S. students that concerns us in this chapter. The scarcity of research directly based on the population of interest leads to some interesting questions, such as whether it is better to use research based on different types of students (e.g., adults learning a second language) or to say that there is no research on a particular issue (e.g., whether it is effective to teach specific grammatical forms). In the absence of a comprehensive body of research, the field of ELD instruction has been driven forward largely by theory. The result is a large body of accepted practice based on theory that has yet to be fully supported by empirical research. Thus, in this section we draw on the widest possible range of research but are mindful of the limitations of research not conducted with the population of interest.

Recommendations for ELD Instruction

Here we offer 13 recommendations[4] for practice on the basis of existing research. Teachers might observe that much of the practice they have come to accept as standard—or even exemplary—is not represented. This does not necessarily mean that teachers are engaged in "wrong" practices but, rather, that the standard wisdom of the field needs to be examined further through the lens of research. Readers should keep in mind that there are considerable controversies and disagreements in the field of second-language (L2) acquisition, particularly when it applies to ELD instruction for ELLs. The following represents our best appraisal of the current state of knowledge.

1. ELD instruction is better than no ELD instruction. There is ample evidence that providing ELD instruction, in some form, is more beneficial than not providing it. It is perhaps difficult for contemporary audiences to conceive, but 25 years ago "Does second language instruction make a difference?" (Long, 1983) was a viable question. A dominant view was Krashen's (1982) "monitor" hypothesis, which proposed that formal instruction is of limited utility for L2 acquisition; instead, Krashen argued, large amounts of exposure to comprehensible input in authentic communicative contexts is critical. However, in his review of available studies comparing L2 instruction to L2 exposure, Long (1983) concluded that indeed instruction aided L2 learning. This was true for young as well as older learners and at intermediate and advanced as well as beginning levels. There are certainly benefits to exposure—that is, living, working, and going to school with speakers of a target language—and to sheltered instruction that seeks to make academic subjects comprehensible. But L2 instruction clearly has added benefits (Genesee et al., 2006; Lyster, 2007).

2. A daily dedicated block of time should be devoted to ELD instruction. Saunders, Foorman, and Carlson (2006) found small positive, but significant, effects on oral language proficiency among Spanish-speaking kindergartners who received ELD instruction during a dedicated block of time, in comparison to kindergartners whose teachers integrated ELD instruction within their larger language arts block. Kindergartners from ELD block classrooms made greater gains on end-of-year measures of English oral language proficiency (and on word identification as well). Students were in different types of language programs, including both bilingual and English immersion. Even in the English immersion classrooms, where instruction was delivered almost exclusively in English,

ELLs provided with a dedicated ELD instructional block outperformed ELLs whose teachers tried to integrate ELD within the language arts block.

The size of the benefit of a separate ELD instructional block might have more to do with what teachers actually do within that dedicated ELD time than with the block format, per se. O'Brien (2007) found that first-grade students (age range, 5–7) who received a dedicated ELD block and used an ELD program that involved attention to grammar (e.g., using prepositions), function (e.g., asking and responding to questions), and vocabulary (e.g., geography terms, such as *map, ocean, continent, world*) scored significantly higher than students in conditions that either did not provide a separate ELD block or, if they did, did not provide explicit systematic teaching of language forms and vocabulary. These results support the proposition that more attention to developmentally appropriate explicit language teaching (e.g., grammar, function, and vocabulary) will make dedicated time for ELD instruction even more productive in terms of improved oral language development.

3. ELD instruction should teach elements of English (e.g., vocabulary, grammar, syntax, conventions). Exposure to an L2 in meaning-based school programs designed to promote L2 learning (e.g., content-based L2 instruction) can lead to the development of comprehension skills, oral fluency, self-confidence, and communicative abilities in an L2. However, L2 learners can still experience difficulties with pronunciation and morphological, syntactic, and pragmatic features (Spada & Lightbown, 2008). Spada and Lighbown conclude that explicit instructional attention to these features (referred to as *forms* in the L2 literature) is likely to facilitate students' L2 learning in a way that solely relying on meaning- and communication-oriented instruction alone will not. Norris and Ortega (2000) also make the case for explicit instruction of language forms, meaning, instruction that explicitly focuses students' attention on the targeted language element, or form.

The research supporting this conclusion does have limitations for our purposes, since it was conducted primarily with older populations. In addition, most of the studies were of short duration, conducted under more laboratory-type conditions, and/or quite narrow in scope (i.e., teaching a specific feature of language, such as verb tense, adverb placement, relative pronouns, or *wh-* questions). Nonetheless, the O'Brien (2007) study cited above provides evidence for the value of teaching elements of English, such as vocabulary or syntax, even to young children.

4. The ELD block can incorporate reading and writing but should emphasize listening and speaking. Assuming ELLs are in a comprehensive instructional program where they receive English literacy instruction, it seems most beneficial to emphasize speaking and listening during ELD instruction. We would hope that speaking and listening are emphasized in other parts of the instructional day, but the textual demands of literacy and content-area instruction need to be given priority during those other instructional times. The time allotted for ELD is the one opportunity to prioritize speaking and listening.

It is certainly possible that students' oral language could benefit from reinforcement through literacy instruction. That is, speaking and listening might be more productively taught in the context of written text that acts as a springboard for much more sophisticated language—for example, focused instruction on revision and word choice, or focused instruction on the meaning of figurative language in literary works. The two studies that address this issue—although both are with young children, thereby limiting generalizability to older learners—suggest that devoting more instructional time to listening and speaking yields higher levels of oral language proficiency. Saunders and colleagues (2006), as discussed above, found that a separate ELD block was associated with kindergarten ELLs' modestly higher oral language scores, in comparison to students in classrooms where teachers integrated ELD into other language arts instruction. When Saunders et al. looked at what teachers in the ELD block were actually doing, they found that teachers were devoting 57% of their ELD time to activities that focused exclusively on oral language (without text) and 32–39% on instructional activities that involved some form of reading or writing.

O'Brien's (2007) study presents more direct evidence. Teachers in Condition 1 implemented a specific program designed to emphasize speaking, listening, and specific language objectives. Instruction focused at least half the time on grammar and language functions, which were completely absent from instruction in Condition 2. (Condition 3 contained no separate ELD instructional block.) Teachers in Condition 1 carried out this focus on grammar and language functions almost exclusively through listening and speaking tasks: 96% of the ELD block was devoted to listening and speaking, as opposed to tasks that involved some form of reading or writing or some other type of activity. Teachers in Condition 2 devoted only 55% of the ELD block to listening and speaking, with the remaining time devoted to tasks involving reading, writing, or something else. Students in Condition 1 scored significantly higher than students in Conditions 2 and 3 on English listening and speaking subtests of the California English Language Development Test (CELDT) at the beginning of second grade.

5. ELD instruction should integrate meaning and communication to support explicit teaching of language. Meaning obviously plays a central role in language use. We use language to engage in meaningful communication with others and to help build understandings for ourselves. Meaning also plays a central role in language learning insofar as being able to express and comprehend meaningful communication in the language being learned probably motivates and compels language learning. Although there is little controversy about the role of meaning and communication in language development and use, their role in language instruction is more complicated. Should authentic, meaningful communication drive instruction—that is, should it be assigned top priority in L2 instruction? Or, alternatively, should explicit teaching of language forms drive instruction? Research on L2 learning and acquisition has advanced over the last two decades in coming to understand that instructed language learning must involve meaning and communication, but it also must direct students' attention to elements and functions of the language being learned. No doubt the interplay between meaning making and conscious attention to language vary for different aspects of language, levels of L2 proficiency, the age of the learner, the learner's first language (L1), and other factors (Lighbown & Spada, 2008). Unfortunately, we do not have sufficient empirical evidence to understand this dynamic interplay fully, although Lightbown and Spada (2008) offer a number of useful hypotheses for L2 educators.

6. ELD instruction should emphasize academic language as well as conversational language. It is widely believed that successful performance in school requires proficiency in academic language and that a major objective of education for both majority and minority language students is teaching the academic language skills they need to master the diverse subjects that comprise the curriculum. For example, Snow, Cancino, De Temple, and Schley (1991) found that performance on highly decontextualized tasks, such as providing a formal definition of words, predicted academic performance, whereas performance on highly contextualized tasks, such as face-to-face communication, did not. Within L2 literature, the concept of academic language was first proposed by Cummins (1984) in his distinction between "basic interpersonal communicative skills" and "cognitive academic language proficiency." Since that time, a number of writers has proposed definitions of academic language (e.g., Bailey, Chapter 10, this volume; Bailey, 2007; Scarcella, 2003). In the simplest

terms, *academic language* is the language that is needed in academic situations such as those students encounter during classroom instruction.

7. ELD instruction should provide students with corrective feedback on form. Providing ELLs with feedback on form is probably not a matter of *whether* but of *how best* to do it. During ELD instruction wherein the primary objective is studying and learning language, corrective feedback can be beneficial. Russell and Spada (2006) conducted a meta-analysis on 15 experimental and quasi-experimental studies that examined the effects of corrective feedback specifically on grammar. The studies include a mixture of foreign-language, L2, and English as a second language (ESL) contexts, some of which were conducted in classrooms and some under laboratory conditions. Unfortunately, Russell and Spada do not report the age or grade of the students involved in the studies, which makes it difficult to gauge the relevance of their findings to K–12 ELD contexts. Despite this limitation, all 15 studies found that providing students with corrective feedback led to better language learning than not providing the feedback. Lyster (2007) also reports how feedback provided through more and less explicit forms might function differentially depending on teachers' relative emphasis on form versus meaning.

Once again, because of limited research we are not sure how applicable this principle is to younger learners.

8. Use of English during ELD instruction should be maximized; L1 should be used strategically. Although many studies have shown the advantages of teaching students to read in their primary language and then bootstraping English literacy development on to L1 literacy, we do not know with certainty the impact of L1 use during ELD instruction. In general, the evidence suggests that ELLs' language choices tend to align with the dominant language of instruction (e.g., Chesterfield, Chesterfield, Hayes-Latimer, & Chávez, 1983). Among grade 2 ELLs in Spanish bilingual programs where at least a majority of instruction was delivered in Spanish, both Milk (1982) and Malave (1989) found that ELLs were more likely to use Spanish during peer interactions; in fact, Malave found students using Spanish over English by a ratio of 6 to 1. Based on these studies and assuming that a practical goal of ELD instruction is increased use of English during ELD instruction, we would conclude that this goal is probably better served by delivering instruction and carrying out tasks primarily in English. Note that the relationship between students' L1 oral language development and their ELD might be different from their L1 literacy development and their English literacy development (see below). Correlations for literacy skills measured in students' L1 and L2 tend to

be quite robust. In contrast, correlations between L1 and L2 oral language skills less directly related to literacy are more variable or in some cases have not even been investigated (Genesee, Geva, Dressler, & Kamil, 2006). Although hardly definitive, this pattern does suggest that L1–L2 relationships are different for literacy skills than for oral language skills. Nonetheless, L1 can play a limited but strategic role during ELD instruction to ensure that students understand task directions, draw students' attention to cognates, and teach language learning and metacognitive strategies.

9. Teachers should incorporate communication and language learning strategies into ELD instruction. Genesee, Geva, and colleagues (2006) found that more proficient ELLs demonstrate a wider repertoire of language-learning strategies than less proficient ELLs. These strategies appear to emerge in the same order—from less to more sophisticated—and to be correlated with levels of language proficiency. L2 learners first use and rely most heavily on fairly simple receptive strategies, such as repetition and memorization, as they learn words and phrases. As they progress to the middle levels of language development, ELLs begin to use more interactive strategies, such as verbal attention getters and elaboration to engage in and sustain interactions with others. At more advanced levels ELLs use language- and communication-monitoring strategies, such as requesting clarification and appealing for assistance, in order to maintain and, as needed, repair communication with others.

It is unclear to what extent these increasingly sophisticated strategies can actually be taught—as opposed to their being a by-product of increased language competence. But some studies do suggest the benefit of explicit instruction for ELLs on how to use communication strategies effectively. For example, O'Malley, Chamot, Stewner-Manzanares, Russo, and Kupper (1985) tested the effects of an 8-day (50 minutes per day) intervention designed to train high school ELLs to use metacognitive and cognitive strategies in the context of integrative tasks—listening to lectures and making oral presentations. The training produced significant effects for speaking but not for listening. In a weaker study that did not include a control group, Carrier (2003) found that seven intermediate-level ESL high school students who received ten 20- to 30-minute listening strategy instruction sessions (e.g., listening to the rhythm and sounds of English, how to listen for specific information, how to take notes) significantly improved their performance on discrete listening tasks and video listening and note-taking tasks. Teachers might need to use students' L1 (when they can) to teach strategies for students who are at lower levels of L2 proficiency (Macaro, as cited in Chamot, 2005).

10. ELD instruction should be planned and delivered with specific language objectives in mind. The use of instructional objectives is often considered important for effective instruction. Theoretically, good instructional objectives—sometimes called *behavioral objectives*—function as starting points and rudders to help keep lessons and activities focused and heading toward productive ends (Gage & Berliner, 1975; Slavin, 2000). The evidence for instructional objectives is generally positive, although it *is* mixed (White & Tisher, 1986). But we do not know empirically the degree to which what seems to be generally true for other academic subjects also holds true for ELD instruction. However, indirect evidence is provided by Norris and Ortega's (2000) meta-analysis, which found strong effects for explicit instruction of targeted language forms. A subset of the studies analyzed by Norris and Ortega included direct contrasts between treatments that specifically focused students' attention on the targeted language form and comparison conditions that involved simple exposure to, or experience with, the same language form. Such comparisons showed that instruction focusing student attention on the targeted language form substantially increased the success of such lessons. It is likely that formulating clear language objectives would support teachers' efforts to direct students' attention to the targeted language form. Thus, our hypothesis is that instructional objectives will be useful for ELD instruction, as they are for other types of academic instruction.

11. ELD instruction should continue at least until students reach level 4 (early advanced) and possibly through level 5 (advanced).[5] This guideline is consistent with federal law that requires that ELLs receive ELD instruction until they are redesignated as fluent in English. From a research standpoint, this guideline emerges from evidence that many ELLs develop intermediate English proficiency fairly rapidly (approximately 2–3 years), but then slow down or even "plateau" (Saunders & O'Brien, as cited in Genesee, Lindholm-Leary, et al., 2006). It might be that more advanced levels of English proficiency—both oral language proficiency and literacy—develop over 5 or more years (August & Shanahan, 2006; Collier, 1987). Our hypothesis is that if ELLs continue to receive explicit ELD instruction once they reach middle levels of English proficiency and as they move into early-advanced and advanced levels, they might attain native-like levels of oral proficiency more rapidly. As we discussed in Guideline 8, language instruction for ELLs at higher levels of proficiency probably requires considerable attention to academic

language. However, we do not have models of ELD instruction shown to be effective in promoting ELLs' academic language proficiency.

12. ELLs should be carefully grouped for ELD instruction, not in classrooms segregated by language proficiency but by language proficiency during specific ELD instruction. We know of no research that directly addresses grouping for ELD instruction. However, as is the case for instructional objectives, many studies have examined the pros and cons of different types of grouping arrangements in other content areas, primarily, reading and mathematics. This research, which was synthesized by Slavin (1987, 1989), suggests that (1) keeping students of different achievement/ability levels in entirely separate ("homogeneous") classes for the entire school day (and throughout the school year) leads to depressed achievement among lower-achieving students, with little to no benefit for average and higher-achieving students; (2) students in mixed ("heterogeneous") classrooms can be productively grouped by achievement level for instruction in specific subjects (e.g., math or reading). Grouping can be done with students in the same classroom or students in different classrooms. Based on this research, we expect that grouping students by English language proficiency levels for ELD instruction would result in enhanced language learning provided that (1) instruction is well tailored to students' proficiency level; and (2) students are frequently assessed and regrouped, as needed, to maintain optimal matching with their language needs—that is, students are taught what they need to know to make continuous progress; and (3) students are given ample opportunities to interact with proficient speakers of the language they are acquiring.

13. Interactive activities among students can be productive, but they must be carefully planned and carried out. Creating opportunities for student interaction and producing actual gains in proficiency involve more than simply pairing ELLs with native English speakers or more proficient ELLs (Saunders & O'Brien, as cited in Genesee, Lindholm-Leary, et al., 2006). Young-adult L2 learners focus more on "supportive and friendly discourse," than on negotiation of meaning or efforts to elicit "comprehensible input" (Foster & Ohta, 2005). In such cases, one can ask whether any language proficiency gains are likely to occur. If interactive activities are to benefit ELLs, careful consideration must be given to the design of the tasks in which students engage; the training of the more proficient English speakers who interact with ELLs; and the language proficiency of the ELLs themselves (August, 1987; Johnson, 1983; Peck, 1987). If careful attention is not paid to these factors, interactive activi-

ties in oral language learning and literacy tend *not* to yield any language learning opportunities (Cathcart-Strong, 1986; Jacob, Rottenberg, Patrick, & Wheeler, 1996).

This guideline is supported by research on older L2 learners. Keck and colleagues (2006) conducted a meta-analysis of 14 studies with high school and adult L2 learners. The pivotal feature in their analysis was the nature of the interactive tasks. Experimental groups received treatments explicitly and intentionally designed to elicit from students the targeted language form (e.g., past tense, reflexive pronoun, particular vocabulary word). Comparison groups received a treatment either without the interactive task and/or without features designed explicitly to prompt learners to use the targeted language form as part of their interaction. Keck and colleagues found that interactive tasks designed to require learners to use the targeted language led to better performance on assessments of the targeted language up to a month later, in comparison to interactive tasks where the targeted language was not essential.

Summary of ELD Instruction

Clearly there is much work to be done to develop an empirical research base from which to build effective ELD instructional programs. Important efforts are underway to develop effective ELD programs for both elementary and secondary school students. Such programs have the potential to increase academic language proficiency. It is imperative to complement these efforts and interest with careful research and evaluation. Particularly important is research on effective methods, with care given to the interaction between methods and students' backgrounds, especially age and levels of L1 and L2 proficiency. From our experience, strong opinion too often trumps careful weighing of evidence.

Research on English Literacy Instruction

This section synthesizes existing research that provides direction for English literacy instruction. We define literacy skills as including prereading skills such as concepts of print and alphabetic knowledge; word-level skills, including decoding, word reading, pseudo-word reading, and spelling; and text-level skills, including fluency, reading comprehension, and writing skills (August & Shanahan, 2006). There is considerable overlap in the skills and knowledge related to literacy and language proficiency (or language development). While both entail reading and writing,

English proficiency also includes oral language skills involving phonology, vocabulary, morphology, grammar, and discourse domains; and it encompasses skills in both comprehension and expression.

Research on developing literacy in ELLs builds on L1 research. The National Reading Panel issued a report that provided an analysis of research on the teaching of reading to native speakers of English (National Institute of Child Health and Human Development, 2000). That report indicated that it is helpful to explicitly teach young children (1) to hear the individual English sounds or phonemes within words (phonemic awareness); (2) to use the letters and spelling patterns within words to decode the word's pronunciations (phonics); (3) to read text aloud with appropriate speed, accuracy, and expression (oral reading fluency); (4) to know the meanings of words and affixes (vocabulary); and (5) to think in particular ways during reading (reading comprehension). A subsequent review of the research on teaching literacy to ELLs (August & Shanahan, 2006) uncovered far fewer experimental studies focused on developing these literacy components than the National Reading Panel uncovered for native English speakers. However, the general pattern found with native English speakers seemed to hold: Explicit instruction focused on developing key aspects of literacy learning provides clear learning benefits for ELLs (August & Shanahan, 2008). However, the interventions generally had a greater impact on decoding and fluency than on reading comprehension. Instruction and support in ELD were evident in some studies, but not in others, and this difference may help explain the inconsistency in success with reading comprehension or the smaller effect sizes for these procedures with L2 students.

Recommendations for English Literacy Instruction

In the next section we provide recommendations for effective literacy instruction for ELLs. In doing so, we focus on key component skills—phonological awareness and phonics, fluency, vocabulary, and comprehension—and describe how the experimental studies built these literacy skills in L2 learners while attending to their ELD. (See Appendix 12.1 for a list of studies in each domain.)

  1. Provide explicit instruction in components of literacy. The studies of phonological awareness and phonics conducted with language-minority students all revealed that explicit instruction in these areas benefited students' literacy development in various areas, including phonological awareness, word reading and word-attack skills, fluency, and even com-

prehension. Five of the studies of phonological awareness and phonics explicitly taught fluency. These interventions significantly and positively impacted students' oral reading fluency, as compared to students who did not receive intervention instruction.

Many of the studies of vocabulary included the explicit teaching of word meanings and word-learning strategies as one component (e.g., Biemiller & Boote, 2006; Carlo et al, 2004; Silverman, 2007). In studies with comprehension as an outcome, there was also explicit instruction of word meanings (Ehri, Dreyer, Flugman, & Gross, 2007; Koskinen et al., 2000; Liang, Peterson, & Graves, 2005) and comprehension strategies (Ehri et al., 2007; Saunders, 1999) such as predicting, summarizing, and questioning text. In most cases strategy instruction (e.g., focusing on helping students decode words or understand text) was only one component of the reading comprehension programs. Concurrently, teachers worked to make the text comprehensible to students through some form of interactive reading. For example, in work with younger children (Ehri et al., 2007), tutors prompted the application of reading skills and strategies (e.g., decoding words; confirming the identity of words through crosschecking with meaning and pictures) in the context of talking through the books, page by page, with students to ensure that they comprehended what they were reading.

2. Build on programs that are effective with monolingual English speakers. The reason that common instructional procedures would be effective with ELLs is probably due to the fact that students are very similar in perceptual skills, memory capacity, ability to learn, etc., no matter what their language background, so the roles of modeling, explanation, and practice in instruction probably do not differ very much from one group to another. Many of the methods used in studies of phonics and fluency were published instructional programs or strategies that had been found to be effective in previous research with monolingual English speakers. Phonics programs included Success for All, Reading Mastery, Early Interventions in Reading, Read Naturally, Corrective Reading, Jolly Phonics, and Fast ForWord Language. Strategies that had been previously found effective included the use of a scope and sequence for phonics instruction developed by Torgesen and Bryant (1994), the Auditory Depth and Discrimination Program developed by Lindamood and Lindamood (1975), orthographic rules developed by Lindamood and Lindamood (1975) and Simms (1974), and peer-assisted learning strategies (PALS) developed and adapted by Fuchs, Fuchs, Mathes, and Simmons (1997).

Likewise, the vocabulary methods used in studies with ELLs built on effective vocabulary instruction for monolingual English speakers: direct teaching of vocabulary, teaching word-learning strategies, building word consciousness, and providing enriched language environments (Graves, 2006; Nagy & Stahl, 2006). As with phonics, fluency, and vocabulary, the research on comprehension used methods borrowed from the L1 literacy research: explicitly teaching comprehension strategies (Saunders, 1999), explicitly teaching vocabulary (e.g., Koskinen et al., 2000; Liang et al., 2005), and using interactive shared reading (e.g., Saunders & Goldenberg, 1999).

3. Ensure that students have the knowledge required to successfully engage in the literacy activity. Although there are important similarities between the kinds of teaching that best support L1 and L2 learners in their literacy development, there are also important differences. Given that the role of background experience and prior knowledge in comprehension and learning have been well documented, the differences that exist in the language and background experiences of ELLs should be reflected in the instruction designed for them. Some adjustments to methods used with monolingual English speakers that provided ELLs with the knowledge to successfully engage in literacy tasks included modeling; using visual aids, realia, and gesture; making content more comprehensible through interaction around text; and building on students' L1 proficiency and knowledge.

Modeling was used to provide students with the knowledge they needed to successfully engage in a task on their own. For example, in the PALS intervention used by Calhoon, Al Otaiba, Cihak, King, and Avalos (2007), strategies were first modeled by the teacher and then students were given opportunities for reinforcement by practicing these strategies in pairs. Visual aids, realia, and gesture were used to help students understand instruction in an L2, for example, by reinforcing word meaning (Roberts & Neal, 2004; Silverman, 2007). These techniques have been found to be effective in instruction in other subject areas as well, such as math, where use of gestures made a significant difference in students' math knowledge (Church, Ayman-Nolley, & Mahootian, 2004), and in teaching English as a foreign language, where images were used for teaching words with multiple meanings (Morimoto & Loewen, 2007). Making content more comprehensible through shared interactive reading was a third method used to help ELLs successfully participate in literacy tasks. During shared interactive reading, techniques such as identifying and clarifying difficult words and passages and consolidating text knowledge through carefully orchestrated discussion (called *instructional conversations*) were used (Koskinen et al., 2000; Liang et al., 2005; Saunders, 1999; Saunders & Goldenberg, 1999).

Finally, many studies built on students' L1 content knowledge and literacy skills to develop vocabulary and literacy in English. For example, in a study by Carlo and colleagues (2004) translation equivalents of English target words were provided, the text was previewed in the students' L1 (Spanish), and students were taught to recognize Spanish–English cognates. Although using students' L1 has been effective, it is important to consider how the L1 is used and for what purpose. For example, Ulanoff and Pucci (1999) found that previewing and reviewing the story in the primary language resulted in greater vocabulary learning for ELLs than the use of concurrent translation (the simultaneous use of the primary language and English). Specifically, they found that in the concurrent translation condition, students were not exposed to comprehensible input in English, and further that they tuned out the English, knowing that Spanish would be spoken.

Even with these techniques, some ELLs with lower levels of proficiency will not benefit; for these students additional scaffolding should be considered. For example, in one study that explored the use of captioned television with a science focus for eighth-grade students (Neuman & Koskinen, 1992), the authors found that higher levels of vocabulary growth were associated with higher levels of initial oral English proficiency. Students below a certain level of proficiency did not benefit from the intervention, whereas students with higher levels of proficiency did. While this study suggests that significant learning of vocabulary may take place incidentally when "comprehensible input"—in this case, in the form of captioned television—is present, it also suggests the importance of taking into account students' levels of English proficiency.

4. Use literacy instruction as an opportunity to develop language proficiency. The most salient characteristic that distinguishes ELLs from their monolingual peers is that ELLs are acquiring English proficiency at the same time that they are developing L2 literacy (August & Shanahan, 2006). Many of the studies developed language proficiency in the context of developing students' literacy.

One prominent method of developing language proficiency was to build vocabulary knowledge, an area of particular and widespread weakness for ELLs, in contrast to other important but "smaller-problem-space" determinants of reading comprehension, such as word reading accuracy and fluency (August & Shanahan, 2006; García, 1991; Verhoeven, 1990). Across the studies other methods that were used to build oral language proficiency included grouping ELLs with fluent English speakers in peer response and conferencing groups to provide rich opportunities for students to interact with native English speakers (Calhoon et al., 2007; Carlo et al., 2004) and providing additional time after school to read books in English with adult support, as needed (Tudor & Hafiz, 1989).

5. Align instruction with student skill levels (and other needs). ELLs are a diverse group with regard to levels of L1 proficiency and literacy, content knowledge, and L2 proficiency and literacy, and they benefit from instruction that is geared to their levels of development. One method of aligning instruction with students' levels of proficiency or literacy is to provide instruction in small groups wherein students are all at about the same level. This practice was widely used, especially in studies focused on developing word-level skills. For example, in 9 of the 12 studies of phonics, instruction was provided to small groups of students, either in a pullout setting or within regular classrooms (Giambo & McKinney, 2004; Gunn, Biglan, Smolkowski, & Ary, 2000; Gunn, Smolkowski, Biglan, & Black, 2002; Gunn, Smolkowski, Biglan, Black, & Blair, 2005; Kamps et al., 2007; Swanson, Hodson, & Schommer-Aikins, 2005; Troia, 2004). A 10th study (Ehri et al., 2007) used the Reading Rescue tutoring intervention model, in which at-risk first-grade students receive individualized tutoring from trained adult tutors. In four of the studies, the small-group instruction was focused on children with reading difficulties (Gunn et al., 2000, 2002, 2005; Swanson et al., 2005); in three of these studies (Gunn, 2000, 2002, 2005; Swanson et al., 2005) students were older (third to fourth grade in the Gunn studies and seventh to eighth grade in the Swanson study), as compared to the other studies, which involved students in grades K–2. In one of the studies focused in part on developing students' comprehension (Koskinen et al., 2000), one difference between the treatment and control groups was that the intervention—shared reading in a book-rich environment—was delivered in small groups rather than in a whole group. The groups were formed to be able to address the needs of particular children; thus it was possible to give students books at their instructional level and to provide more reading options for children who were emergent readers. As mentioned in the section on ELD instruction, grouping can be also done with students from different classrooms (sometimes referred to as

"Joplin plans") by regrouping students by ability level for certain blocks of time (Slavin & Madden, 1999).

Summary of English Literacy Instruction

In summary, research that examined literacy instruction for ELLs provided explicit instruction in the components of literacy that the National Literacy Panel (National Institute of Child Health and Human Development, 2000) found were important to address—phonological awareness and phonics, fluency, vocabulary, and comprehension. Much of the instruction borrowed effective practices from the research on monolingual English speakers. However, in many cases there were alterations to these methods and materials to ensure that ELLs had the knowledge to successfully engage in the literacy tasks. Alterations included additional modeling; using visual aids, realia, and gesture; making content more comprehensible through interaction around text; and building on students' L1 literacy and knowledge required in an L1 text in order to promote their English literacy development. Moreover, in most cases the literacy learning was used as a springboard for developing language proficiency. Finally, practices that were effective were aligned with students' level of second-language proficiency and literacy (See Newman, Chapter 5, in this volume.)

IMPLICATIONS FOR RESEARCH, PRACTICE, AND POLICY

With regard to developing both listening and reading comprehension, real leverage may be in the continual, systematic, everyday ways that we engage children in learning new knowledge and information across the content areas, starting in the early years (Glaser, 1984; Hirsch, 2003; Neuman, 2001). This is because students who have to learn only the English labels for L1 concepts are much more likely to make greater gains in English language and literacy development than students who must learn both the English label and the concept. Many of the techniques described in this chapter to scaffold instruction can also be applied to instruction in the content areas. When these techniques are used in the content areas (that includes language arts), they are referred to as *sheltered instruction* or specially designed academic instruction in English (SDAIE). The dual purpose of these techniques is to teach knowledge and skills in the content areas, as well as to support ongoing acquisition and learning of English as it relates to these content areas.

A second point is that the likelihood of establishing and/or sustaining effective ELD and literacy instructional programs increases when schools and districts make it a priority.[6] A sizeable literature suggests that a sustained and coherent focus on academic goals in schools and districts is associated with higher levels of student achievement. Due to the dearth of experimental research and detailed case studies in this area, it is very difficult to draw firm conclusions about cause and effect. However, numerous dimensions of school and district functioning—leadership, common goals and curricula, professional development, ongoing support and supervision, collaboration among teachers, regular assessments that inform instruction—are levers that can be used by school and district administrators to help shape the academic experiences of students (e.g., Fullan, 2007; Goldenberg, 2004; McDougall, Saunders, & Goldenberg, 2007).

Third, although this chapter focused exclusively on the development of English language and literacy skills for ELLs, it is important to remember that overall, bilingual approaches have been more effective than English-only approaches in this area. Five quantitative syntheses show that compared to immersing children in English, teaching them to read in their native language as well as in English produces superior results in English reading achievement (Francis, Lesaux, & August, 2006; Greene, 1997; Rolstad, Mahoney, & Glass, 2005; Slavin & Cheung, 2004; Willig, 1985).

Finally, as is abundantly clear from the reviews, there is a need for more research on ELD and literacy instruction. Most of the research on ELD has been conducted with older learners and learners acquiring English as a foreign language. In the area of literacy, whereas the National Reading Panel found over 450 studies focused on developing the components of literacy in monolingual English speakers, our review of studies conducted between 1990 and 2008 located approximately 30 experimental and quasi-experimental studies focused on school-based instructional practices for developing English literacy. Besides the importance of confirming the general findings accrued from a small body of research, research is needed that examines the effects of interventions over time, the effects for students with different levels of L1 and L2 proficiency, and the effects of different L1 backgrounds. Moreover, most research has targeted one or two components of literacy; more comprehensive interventions are needed, as are studies of how to accommodate the language learning and literacy of students with diverse skills and capacities within the same classroom.

APPENDIX 12.1. Studies in Key Literacy Domains

Phonological Awareness and Phonics: Calhoon, Otaiba, Cihak, King, and Avalos (2007); Ehri, Dreyer, Flugman, and Gross (2007); Giambo and McKinney (2004); Gunn, Biglan, Smolkowski, and Ary (2000); Gunn, Smolkowski, Biglan, and Black (2002); Gunn, Smolkowski, Biglan, Black, and Blair (2005); Kamps et al. (2007); Roberts and Neal (2004); Slavin and Madden (1999); Stuart (1999); Swanson, Hodson, and Schommer-Aikins (2005); Troia (2004).[7]

Fluency: Calhoon et al. (2007); Gunn et al. (2000, 2002, 2005); Kamps et al. (2007).

Vocabulary: Biemiller and Boote (2006); Carlo et al. (2004); Giambo and McKinney (2004); Neuman and Koskinen (1992); Roberts and Neal (2004); Silverman (2007); Uchikoshi (2005); Ulanoff and Pucci (1999).

Comprehension: Carlo et al. (2004); Ehri, Dreyer, Flugman, and Gross (2007); Elley (1991); Liang, Peterson, and Graves (2005); Koskinen et al. (2000); Saunders (1999); Solari and Gerber (2008).

ACKNOWLEDGMENT

This chapter builds on our previous work, *Developing Literacy in Second-Language Learners*. For more information, see August and Shanahan (2006).

NOTES

1. See Saunders and Goldenberg (in press) for more details on guidelines and the research base supporting them. We are grateful to Elise Trumbull for her many contributions to that chapter.
2. The work is adapred from Part IV, "Educating Language Minority Students: Instructional Approaches and Professional Development," of the report *Developing Literacy in Second-Language Learners*, edited by Diane August and Timothy Shanahan, Copyright 2006. It appears by permission of Taylor and Francis Group, LLC, a division of Informa plc. Whereas the panel report reviewed studies conducted between 1980 and 2002, this chapter draws on more recent research, published between 1990 and 2008.
3. Condensed and adapted (with permission) from Saunders and Goldenberg (in press).
4. The recommendations are presented in a different order here from what is presented in Saunders and Goldenberg (in press). Recommendation 14 is presented below, "Implications for Research, Practice, and Policy."
5. Students at an early-advanced English proficiency level can use English in complex ways and in cognitively demanding situations across the curriculum but would likely benefit from learning advanced vocabulary (receptive and

productive) and how to use oral and written English for more more complex purposes such as debating, discussing social issues, and analyzing challenging texts. Advanced speakers of English are nearing native-like proficiency; indeed it is often very difficult to distinguish advanced speakers from native speakers at comparable academic levels. There is scant research on this topic, but it is again likely that advanced speakers could benefit from learning about subtleties and nuances of the language (e.g., vocabulary, syntax, discourse conventions) so that they gain skill in using English in highly sophisticated ways for a wide range of purposes.

6. Excerpted from Guideline 14 in Saunders and Goldenberg (in press).
7. It is important to note that in the study by Troia (2004), the only students who showed significant gains in letter–word identification and word attack, compared with a no-treatment control, were those students who were below the 25th percentile on an assessment of oral language proficiency.

REFERENCES

August, D. (1987). Effects of peer tutoring on the second language acquisition of Mexican-American children in elementary school. *TESOL Quarterly, 21*(4), 717–736.

August, D., & Shanahan, T. (2006*). Developing literacy in second-language learners: Report of the National Literacy Panel on language-minority children and youth.* Mahwah, NJ: Erlbaum.

August, D., & Shanahan, T. (Eds.). (2008). *Developing reading and writing in second-language learners: Lessons from the Report of the National Literacy Panel on language-minority children and youth.* Mahwah, NJ: Erlbaum.

Bailey, A. L. (2007). *The language demands of school: Putting academic English to the test.* New Haven, CT: Yale University Press.

Batalova, J. (2006). *Spotlight on limited English proficient students in the United States.* Washington, DC: Migration Policy Institute.

Biemiller, A., & Boote, C. (2006). An effective method for building vocabulary in primary grades. *Journal of Educational Psychology, 98*(1), 44–62.

Calhoon, M. B., Al Otaiba, S., Cihak, D., King, A., & Avalos, A. (2007). Effects of a peer-mediated program on reading skill acquisition for two-way bilingual first-grade classrooms. *Learning Disability Quarterly, 30*(3), 169–184.

Cathcart-Strong, R. L. (1986). Input generation by young second language learners. *TESOL Quarterly, 20*(3), 515–529.

Carlo, M. S., August, D., McLaughlin, B., Snow, C. E., Dressler, C., Lippman, D., et al. (2004). Closing the gap: Addressing the vocabulary needs of English language learners in bilingual and mainstream classrooms. *Reading Research Quarterly, 39*(2), 188–215.

Carrier, K. A. (2003). Improving high school English language learners' second language listening through strategy instruction. *Bilingual Research Journal, 27*(3), 383–408.

Chamot, A. U. (2005). Language learning strategy instruction: Current issues and research. *Annual Review of Applied Linguistics, 25*, 112–130.

Chesterfield, R. A., Chesterfield, K. B., Hayes-Latimer, K., & Chávez, R. (1983). The influence of teachers and peers on second language acquisition in bilingual preschool programs. *TESOL Quarterly, 17*, 401–419.

Church, R. B., Ayman-Nolley, S., & Mahootian, S. (2004). The role of gesture in bilingual education: Does gesture enhance learning? *Bilingual Education and Bilingualism, 7*(4), 303–319.

Collier, V. P. (1987). Age and rate of acquisition of second language for academic purposes. *TESOL Quarterly, 21*(4), 617–641.

Cummins, J. (1984). Wanted: A theoretical framework for relating language proficiency to academic achievement among bilingual students. In C. Rivera (Ed.), *Language proficiency and academic achievement* (pp. 2–19). Clevedon, UK: Multilingual Matters.

Echevarría, J., Vogt, M. E., & Short, D. (2008). *Making content comprehensible for English language learners: The SIOP model* (3rd ed.). Upper Saddle River, NJ: Pearson.

Ehri, L. C., Dreyer, L., Flugman, B., & Gross, A. (2007). Reading rescue: An effective tutoring intervention model for language-minority students who are struggling readers in first grade. *American Educational Research Journal, 44*(2), 414–448.

Elley, W. B. (1991). Acquiring literacy in a second language: The effect of book-based programs. *Language Learning, 41*(3), 375–411.

Ellis, R. (2005). *Instructed second language acquisition*. Wellington, New Zealand: Research Division, Ministry of Education.

Foster, P., & Ohta, A. S. (2005). Negotiation for meaning and peer assistance in second language classrooms. *Applied Linguistics, 26*(3), 402–430.

Francis, D. J., Lesaux, N. K., & August, D. (2006). Language of instruction. In D. L. August & T. Shanahan (Eds.), *Developing literacy in a second language: Report of the National Literacy Panel* (pp. 365–410). Mahwah, NJ: Erlbaum.

Fuchs, D., Fuchs, L. S., Mathes, P. G., & Simmons, D. C. (1997). Peer-assisted learning strategies: Making classrooms more responsive to diversity. *American Educational Research Journal, 34*, 174–206.

Fullan, M. (2007). *The new meaning of educational change* (4th ed.). New York: Teachers College Press.

Gage, N., & Berliner, D. (1975). *Educational psychology*. Chicago: Rand-McNally.

García, G. E. (1991). Factors influencing the English reading test performance of Spanish-speaking Hispanic children. *Reading Research Quarterly, 26*(4), 371–392.

Genesee, F., Geva, E., Dressler, C., & Kamil, M. (2006). Synthesis: Cross-linguistic relationships. In D. August & T. Shanahan (Eds.), *Developing literacy in second-language learners: Report of the National Literacy Panel on language-minority children and youth* (pp. 153–174). Mahwah, NJ: Erlbaum.

Genesee, F., Lindholm-Leary, K., Saunders, W., & Christian, D. (2006). *Educat-*

ing English language learners: A synthesis of research evidence. New York: Cambridge University Press.

Giambo. D. A., & McKinney, J. D. (2004). The effects of a phonological awareness intervention on the oral English proficiency of Spanish-speaking kindergarten children. *TESOL Quarterly, 38*(1), 95–117.

Glaser, R., (1984). Education and thinking: The role of knowledge. *American Psychologist, 39*(2), 93–104.

Goldenberg, C. (2004). *Successful school change: Creating settings to improve teaching and learning.* New York: Teachers College Press.

Graves, M. F. (2006). *The vocabulary book.* New York: Teacher's College Press.

Greene, J. P. (1997). A meta-analysis of the Rossell and Baker review of bilingual education research. *Bilingual Research Journal, 21*(2/3), 1–22.

Gunn, B., Biglan, A., Smolkowski, K., & Ary, D. (2000). The efficacy of supplemental instruction in decoding skills for Hispanic and non-Hispanic students in early elementary school. *Journal of Special Education, 34*(2), 90–103.

Gunn, B., Smolkowski, K., Biglan, A., & Black, C. (2002). Supplemental instruction in decoding skills for Hispanic and non-Hispanic students in early elementary school: A follow-up. *Journal of Special Education, 36*(2), 69–79.

Gunn, B., Smolkowski, K., Biglan, A., Black, C., & Blair, J. (2005). Fostering the development of reading skill through supplemental instruction: Results for Hispanic and non-Hispanic students. *Journal of Special Education, 39,* 66–85.

Hirsch, E. D. (2003, Spring). Reading comprehension requires knowledge—of words and the world. *American Educator,* pp. 10–29.

Jacob, E., Rottenberg, L., Patrick, S., & Wheeler, E. (1996). Cooperative learning: Context and opportunities for acquiring academic English. *TESOL Quarterly, 30*(2), 253–280.

Johnson, D. M. (1983). Natural language learning by design: A classroom experiment in social interaction and second language acquisition. *TESOL Quarterly, 17*(1), 55–68.

Kamps, D., Abbott, M., Greenwood, C., Arreaga-Mayer, C., Wills, H., Longstaff, J., et al. (2007). Use of evidence based, small-group reading instruction for English language learners in elementary grades: Secondary-tier interventions. *Learning Disability Quarterly: Journal of the Council of Learning Disabilities, 30*(3), 153–168.

Keck, C. M., Iberra-Shea, G., Tracy-Ventura, N., & Wa-Mbaleka, S. (2006). Investigating the empirical link between task-based interaction and acquisition: A meta-analysis. In J. M. Norris & L. Ortega (Eds.), *Synthesizing research on language learning and teaching* (pp. 91–131). Philadelphia: Benjamins.

Koskinen, P. S., Blum, I. H., Bisson, S. A., Phillips, S. M., Creamer, T. S., & Baker, T. K. (2000). Book access, shared reading, and audio models: The effects of supporting the literacy learning of linguistically diverse students in school and at home. *Journal of Educational Psychology, 92,* 23–36.

Krashen, S. (1982). *Principles and practice in second language acquisition.* Oxford, UK: Pergamon.

Liang, L. A., Peterson, C., & Graves, M. F. (2005). Investigating two approaches to fostering children's comprehension of literature. *Reading Psychology, 26,* 387–400.

Lindamood. C. H., & Lindamood P. (1975). *Auditory discrimination in depth.* Allen, TX: DLM/Teaching Resources.

Long, M. (1983). Does second language instruction make a difference?: A review of research. *TESOL Quarterly, 17*(3), 359–382.

Lyster, R. (2007). *Learning and teaching languages through content: A counterbalanced approach.* Philadelphia: Benjamins.

Malave, L. (1989). Contextual elements in a bilingual cooperative setting: The experiences of early childhood LEP learners. *NABE Journal, 13,* 96–122.

McDougall, D., Saunders, W., & Goldenberg, C. (2007). Inside the black box of school reform: Explaining the how and why of change at Getting Results schools. *International Journal of Disability, Development, and Education, 54,* 51–89.

Milk, R. D. (1982). Language use in bilingual classrooms: Two case studies. In M. Hines & W. Rutherford (Eds.), *On TESOL '81* (pp. 181–191). Washington, DC: TESOL.

Morimoto, S., & Loewen, S. (2007). A comparison of the effects of image-schema-based instruction and translation-based instruction on the acquisition of L2 polysemous words. *Language Teaching Research, 11*(3), 347–372.

Nagy, W. E., & Stahl, S. A. (2006). *Teaching word meanings.* Mahwah, NJ: Erlbaum.

National Institute of Child Health and Human Development. (2000). *Report of the National Reading Panel. Teaching children to read: An evidence-based assessment of the scientific research literature on reading and its implications for reading instruction* (NIH Publication No. 00-4769). Washington, DC: U.S. Department of Health and Human Services.

Neuman, S. B. (2001). The role of knowledge in early literacy. *Reading Research Quarterly, 36*(4), 468–475.

Neuman, S. B., & Koskinen, P. (1992). Captioned television as comprehensible input: Effects of incidental word learning from context for language minority students. *Reading Research Quarterly, 27*(1), 94–106.

Norris, J. M., & Ortega, L. (2000). Effectiveness of L2 instruction: A research synthesis and quantitative meta-analysis. *Language Learning, 50*(3), 417–528.

O'Brien, G. (2007). *The instructional features across three different approaches to oral English language development instruction.* Unpublished doctoral dissertation, University of Southern California.

O'Malley, J. M., Chamot, A. U., Stewner-Manzanares, G., Russo, R., & Kupper, L. (1985). Learning strategy applications with students of English as a second language. *TESOL Quarterly, 19*(3), 557–584.

Peck, S. (1987). Signs of learning: Child nonnative speakers in tutoring sessions with a child native speaker. *Language Learning, 37*(4), 545–571.

Roberts, T., & Neal, H. (2004). Relationships among preschool English learners oral proficiency in English, instructional experience and literacy development. *Contemporary Educational Psychology, 29,* 283–311.

Rolstad, K., Mahoney, K., & Glass, G. (2005). The big picture: A meta-analysis of program effectiveness research on English language learners. *Educational Policy, 19*(4), 572–594.

Russell, J., & Spada, N. (2006). The effectiveness of corrective feedback for the acquisition of L2 grammar. In J. M. Norris & L. Ortega (Eds.), *Synthesizing research on language learning and teaching* (pp. 133–164). Philadelphia: Benjamins.

Saunders, W. M. (1999). Improving literacy achievement for English learners in transitional bilingual programs. *Educational Research and Evaluation, 5*(4), 345–381.

Saunders, W. M., Foorman, B., & Carlson, C. (2006). Is a separate block of time for oral English language development in programs of English-learners needed? *Elementary School Journal, 107*(2), 181–198

Saunders, W. M., & Goldenberg, C. (1999). Effects of instructional conversations and literature logs on limited- and fluent-English proficient students' story comprehension and thematic understanding. *Elementary School Journal, 99*(4), 277–301.

Saunders, W. M., & Goldenberg, C. (in press). Research to guide English language development instruction. In D. Dolson & L. Burnham-Massey (Eds.), *Improving education for English language learners: Research-based approaches*. Sacramento, CA: CDE Press.

Scarcella, R. C. (2003). *Accelerating academic English: A focus on the English learner*. Oakland: Regents of the University of California.

Silverman, R. (2007). Vocabulary development of English-language and English-only learners in kindergarten. *Elementary School Journal, 107*(4), 365–383.

Simms, (1974). *Worktext for spelling: Patterns of sounds*. New York: McGraw Hill.

Slavin, R. (1987). Ability grouping and student achievement in elementary schools: A best-evidence synthesis. *Review of Educational Research, 57*, 293–336.

Slavin, R. (Ed.). (1989). *School and classroom organization*. Hillsdale, NJ: Erlbaum.

Slavin, R. E. (2000). *Educational psychology*. Boston: Allyn & Bacon.

Slavin, R. E., & Madden, N. A. (1999). Effects of bilingual and English as second language adaptations of Success for All on the reading achievement of students acquiring English. *Journal of Education for Students Placed At Risk, 4*(4), 393–416.

Slavin, R. E., & Cheung, A. (2004). *A synthesis of research on language of reading instruction for English language learners*. Baltimore: Johns Hopkins University.

Snow, C. E., Cancino, H., De Temple, J., & Schley, S. (1991). Giving formal definition: A linguistic or metalinguistic skill? In E. Bialystok (Ed.), *Language processing in bilingual children* (pp. 90–113). New York: Cambridge University Press.

Solari, E., & Gerber, M. (2008). Early comprehension instruction for Spanish-speaking English-language learners: teaching text-level reading skills while maintaining effects of word-level skills. *Learning Disabilities Research,* *23*(4), 155–168.

Spada, N., & Lightbown, P. M. (2008). Form-focused instruction: Isolated or integrated? *TESOL Quarterly, 42*(2), 181–207.

Swanson, T., Hodson, B., & Schommer-Aikins, M. (2005). An examination of phonological awareness treatment outcomes for 7th grade poor readers from a bilingual community. *Language, Speech, and Hearing Services in Schools, 36,* 336–345.

Torgesen, J. K., & Bryant, B. R. (1994). *Phonological awareness training for reading.* Austin, TX: PRO-ED.

Troia, G. A. (2004). Migrant students with limited English proficiency: Can Fast ForWord Language make a difference in their language skills and academic achievement? *Remedial and Special Education, 25,* 353–366.

Tudor, I., & Hafiz, F. (1989). Extensive reading as a means of input to L2 learning. *Journal of Research in Reading, 12*(2), 164–178.

Uchikoshi, Y. (2005). Narrative development in bilingual kindergarteners: Can Arthur help? *Developmental Psychology, 41*(3), 464–478.

Ulanoff, S. H., & Pucci, S. L. (1999). Learning words from books: The effects of read-aloud on second language vocabulary acquisition. *Bilingual Research Journal, 23*(4), 409–422.

Verhoeven, L. T. (1990). Acquisition of reading in a second language. *Reading Research Quarterly, 25*(2), 90–114.

White, R., & Tisher, R. (1986). Research on natural sciences. In M. Wittrock (Ed.), *The handbook of research on teaching* (3rd ed., pp. 874–905). New York: Macmillan.

Willig, A. (1985). A meta-analysis of selected studies on the effectiveness of bilingual education. *Review of Educational Research, 55*(3), 269–317.

Index